Hidden History

※※※

Lost
Civilizations,
Secret
Knowledge,
AND
Ancient
Mysteries

Brian Haughton

New Page Books
A division of The Career Press, Inc.
Franklin Lakes, NJ

935,196/930 1

Copyright © 2007 by Brian Haughton

HIDDEN HISTORY
EDITED BY ASTRID deRIDDER
TYPESET BY EILEEN DOW MUNSON
Cover design by Dutton and Sherman
Printed in the U.S.A. by Book-mart Press

To order this title, please call toll-free 1-800-CAREER-1 (NJ and Canada: 201-848-0310) to order using VISA or MasterCard, or for further information on books from Career Press.

The Career Press, Inc., 3 Tice Road, PO Box 687,
Franklin Lakes, NJ 07417
www.careerpress.com
www.newpagebooks.com

Library of Congress Cataloging-in-Publication Data

Haughton, Brian, 1964-
    Hidden history : lost civilizations, secret knowledge, and ancient mysteries / by Brian Haughton.
        p. cm.
    Includes bibliographical references and index.
    ISBN-13: 978-1-56414-897-1
    ISBN-10: 1-56414-897-1
    1. Civilization, Ancient—Miscellanea. 2. Curiosities and wonders—Miscellanea. 3. Antiquities—Miscellanea. I. Title.

CB311.H34 2007
930.1--dc22
                                                                2006016822

For my mum and dad

 Acknowledgments

For help with photographs, I would like to thank Dr. Erich Brenner of the University of Innsbruck, David Hatcher Childress, Carlos A. Gomez-Gallo, Julie Gardiner of Wessex Archaeology, Martin Gray of Sacred Sites, John Griffiths, Paul Haughton, Thanassis Vembos, and Rien van de Weygaert. Many thanks also to Frank Joseph for providing a wonderfully erudite Foreword while going through the traumatizing experience of moving house. Special thanks go to Michael Pye at New Page, and my ever helpful agent Lisa Hagen of Paraview. Finally, I would not have been able to write this book without the encouragement and support of my wife, Dr. A. Siokou, who also read the manuscript.

Contents

Foreword
By Frank Joseph

In response to popular dissatisfaction with mainstream scholars' often inadequate explanations of the world we live in, publishers are fielding a growing number of books posing alternative considerations to prevailing orthodoxy. In confronting official paradigms, their unconventional authors are typically provocative, but usually more imaginative than credible. Brian Haughton differs from his colleagues, because he strives for an accord between evidence accumulated by university-trained scientists and fresh theories postulated by avocational investigators. The result is *Hidden History: Lost Civilizations, Secret Knowledge, and Ancient Mysteries*. It is a balance of fact and theory written with the old integrity of Roman writers, such as Livy and Cicero, who clearly set out the facts and provided leading interpretations, but invited us to come to our own conclusions. Haughton's readers will find themselves engaged in the same kind of participation that challenges their imagination by expanding it. The cause is self-evident: His is a truly encyclopedic work, dealing with 49 historical enigmas from around the globe. His work spans the deep antiquity of Britain's Stonehenge and Egypt's Great Pyramid to current discoveries about the Shroud of Turin and the Dead Sea Scrolls. As such, *Hidden History* is at once a superb introduction to these mysteries for anyone unacquainted with them, as well as a sourcebook eclectic investigators will find indispensable.

Haughton begins with Atlantis, widely considered the greatest enigma of all (and among the most controversial). Merely presenting thumbnail sketches of all the theories used to describe it would require a full-length book in itself. But Haughton deftly sorts out the leading arguments for and against the existence and location of Plato's "lost continent," leaving us less bewildered by the plethora of contending opinions than intrigued by the possibilities for a 21st century discovery. *Hidden History* does not neglect Atlantis's Pacific counterpart, especially in view of recent discoveries made around the Japanese islands. Under the clear waters of Yonaguni, scuba divers recently found a pyramidal structure sitting nearly a hundred feet below the surface. Could this artificial-looking formation of massive stone be the result of a natural process? Or is it the remains of the lost civilization of Lemuria, also known as Mu, mentioned in the Hindu monastery records of Burma and India?

The inhabitants of both Atlantis and Lemuria were said to have possessed a technology far ahead of the times in which they lived, and Haughton presents physical evidence suggesting the former existence of scientific advances at odds with the period of their invention and use. A foremost specimen includes the so-called Baghdad Battery powered by citrus juices to electro-plate statuettes with gold. Although a simple device, it nonetheless suggests that at least the fundamentals of electricity were understood and applied more than 2,000 years before Thomas Edison switched on the first electric light bulb. Haughton's comparison of the Mayan Calendar with Germany's Nebra Disc and the Antikythera Mechanism (dredged up from the bottom of the Aegean Sea), proves that the ancients were computer literate. The Mayan Calendar is well-known for its ominous prediction of global change (scheduled to occur on the winter solstice of 2012), and Haughton explains in clear language the incredibly high-level mathematics that went into the creation of this unquestionably great scientific achievement. While such sophisticated devices have been known in the West since the Spanish Conquest, 500 years ago, another pre-Industrial Age computer was found just two years ago in northern Germany. Dated to the Late Bronze Age (circa 1500 B.C.), the Nebra Disc is an astronomical clock of sophisticated capabilities and workmanship, far in advance of anything from the same time and place. Its mere existence implies that a higher level of material society flourished in a region far beyond the cultural orbit of the Greco-Roman World than previously imagined. It predates—by more than 14 centuries—a comparable instrument hauled up in a fisherman's net around the turn of the 20th century off the Greek island of Antikythera. The device is a complex intermeshing of intricate gears that historians formerly believed would not have been possible until the European Renaissance. Apparently, the Classical World had its own Leonardo da Vinci, who fashioned an efficient astronomical computer small enough to be carried aboard ships for purposes of celestial navigation.

Earlier still, another disc has been found in the Cretan city of Phaestos, and is 200 years older than the Nebra device. While not as complicated as the German, Greek, or Mayan versions, the Minoan plate of baked clay was impressed with tiny images made by movable type, almost 30 centuries before Johannes Gutenberg's press was up and running. Haughton shows that our ancestors' technology was far more elevated that mainstream scholars would have us believe. *Hidden History*'s description of these anomalous finds is succinct and lucid, and readers will search in vain for another book in which these examples of unexpectedly high technology are brought together in the same volume. Its inquiry ranges far beyond typical scientific accomplishments to visit "Mysterious Places"—including Easter Island, with its gaunt colossi; a pre-Columbian city in the Grand Canyon; and the oldest building on Earth, the enormous, quartz-fronted burial mound of Ireland's Newgrange, 30 miles north of Dublin.

The "Mysterious People" visited are King Arthur, keeper of the Holy Grail; the Amazons, who carried women's liberation on the edge of their swords; Indonesia's race of extinct, quick-witted dwarves; and the historical facts behind the fabled figures of Robin Hood, the Queen of Sheba, and Pharaoh Tutankhamun. The fate of ancient Egypt's most famous monarch is particularly up-to-date, as Brian Haughton cites the latest CAT scan of the royal mummy. Did King Tut die of an accident that allowed his aged successor, a commoner, to usurp the throne? Or was covert assassination the cause? Nowhere else has such a broad collection of diverse information about ancient wonders been assembled. Haughton's obvious preference for credibility over theory combines with his powers of clear, concise presentation to make *Hidden History* not merely a rehash of already familiar material, but a freshly comprehensive encyclopedia of the strange and the intriguing, which will be sought out by anyone fascinated with the remote past for many years to come.

Introduction

One of the numerous legacies of our ancient past is a bewildering variety of mysteries. Some are genuinely puzzling, while others are more easily solved with a little research. Mysterious places, such as Stonehenge and the Great Pyramid, may be famous throughout the world, but how much do we really know about their construction, purpose, and the people who built them? Strange artifacts, sometimes of unknown origin and purpose, or of inexplicably advanced manufacture can provide us with a fascinating glimpse into the often amazingly sophisticated cultures of the ancient world. And then there are the people themselves. Modern techniques such as DNA studies and Oxygen Isotope Analysis (performed on tooth enamel to locate a person's origins) are shedding fascinating new light on the enigmatic peoples of ancient history. Intriguingly, while solving one puzzle, modern scientific techniques have sometimes created others. For example, chemical analysis of the aristocrat buried close to Stonehenge 4,200 years ago shows that he was probably born in Switzerland. Which poses the question: What was he doing so far from home?

A person's interpretation of the past often depends on what he or she wants from history. If the study of ancient mysteries is approached with an agenda in mind, or a belief to be proved, the odds are that some kind of evidence to fit the theory will be found. On rare occasions, such as the 19th century excavations by Heinrich Schliemann at the supposed site of Troy, this approach can yield spectacular—if not entirely accurate—results.

Unfortunately, evidence for a pet theory is usually obtained by ignoring conflicting data, or taking an individual artifact, person, or even place out of its original context. Let's imagine a situation where, for example, you wanted to prove that Ireland had been invaded by the Romans, even though the vast majority of archaeologists and historians are convinced it never was. There are a fair amount of Roman finds in the country, some from sealed archaeological contexts, which you could use to support your case. But if these Roman objects are looked at in greater detail and their original contexts examined, then it becomes apparent that the artifacts are of the portable variety: pottery, coins, and jewelry. Roman objects in Ireland are usually found at religious sites, such as the huge burial mound at Newgrange, north of Dublin, which were already thousands of years old by the Roman period. This would indicate that, rather than signifying a

Roman invasion, the objects were the result of religious offerings by pilgrims, probably visiting from Britain. A cursory glance at the artifacts in isolation could never have arrived at this conclusion.

Of course, one must always be careful to distinguish between genuine and spurious mysteries, and for this reason a few puzzles of the spurious category have been included in this book. It is surprising how many apparently inexplicable mysteries (especially those relating to unusual objects) prove on closer examination to have prosaic explanations. With the proliferation of Websites dedicated to ancient mysteries, secret societies, and out-of-place artifacts, stories are fabricated entirely on the Internet, without any supporting evidence or research, and are reproduced uncritically as fact. One of the best examples of these "Internet truths" is the supposedly ancient Coso Artifact, a short chapter on which is included in this book. A major problem with many of the speculations that surround unexplained ancient artifacts is that the objects are taken out of their original context in order to provide evidence for a favorite theory. Just because the peoples of prehistoric Britain and ancient Peru carved figures into the landscape doesn't mean there was any contact between the two places. What it does signify is a basic human need to express oneself using the landscape, of which the people perhaps believed themselves to be a part. The lives of many of the cultures of antiquity were full of magic and mystery, but to acquire even a partial understanding of this often entails cutting oneself off from present-day preoccupations and desires. If this is

not done, then we are in danger of clothing the ancient peoples of the world in modern, ill-fitting garments, and transforming them into 21st century ancients who would not have been recognized in their original cultures.

On the other hand, to deny the mysteries of the past completely, to believe that modern archaeology and science have the answers to every ancient enigma, is equally ill-advised. (It also makes dull reading.) Alternative theorists, such as Graham Hancock, Robert Bauval, and Christopher Knight may sometimes be too uncritical when dealing with the evidence for lost civilizations and ancient technology, but they are better writers than most archaeologists. Academics are never going to convey the fascination of their subject to the general public if their commercial publications read like technical reports, or notes written for a lecture to a group of Ph.D. students. There are, of course, exceptions: Mike Pitts's *Hengeworld*, Francis Pryor's *Britain BC*, and Barry Cunliffe's *Facing the Ocean: The Atlantic and Its Peoples, 8000 BC to AD 1500*, should be read by everyone with an interest in ancient history.

In *Hidden History*, ancient mysteries are divided into three categories: Mysterious Places, Strange Artifacts, and Enigmatic People. The choice of subjects included in the book was a personal one, made to bring together the most interesting of ancient mysteries, and to cover a wide range of cultures, time periods, and types of mystery. The book has no hidden agenda; I hope my readers will use the evidence presented to make up their own minds about these riddles of our enigmatic past.

PART I

❧

Mysterious
Places

The Lost Land of Atlantis

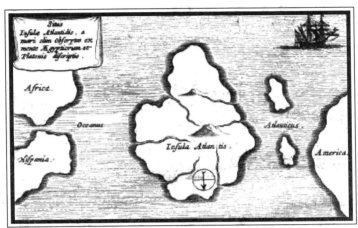

Athanasius Kircher's map of Atlantis's possible location. From Mundus Subterraneus *(1669).*

The magical lost land of Atlantis has captured the imagination of poets, scholars, archaeologists, geologists, occultists, and travelers for more than 2,000 years. The notion of a highly advanced island civilization (that flourished in remote antiquity only to be destroyed overnight by a huge natural catastrophe) has inspired believers in the historical truth of the Atlantis tale to search practically every corner of the Earth for remnants of this once great civilization. Most archaeologists are of the opinion that the Atlantis story is just that, a story, an allegorical tale with no historical value whatsoever. And then there are the occultists, many of whom have approached the story of Atlantis from the standpoint that it represents either a lost spiritual homeland (such as Mu/Lemuria), or a different plain of existence entirely. What is it about Atlantis that has inspired such diverse interpretations? Could there be any truth behind the story?

The original source from which all information about Atlantis ultimately derives is the Greek philosopher Plato, in his two short dialogues *Timaeus* and *Critias*, written somewhere between 359 and 347 B.C. Plato's supposed source for the story of Atlantis was a distant relative of his, a famous Athenian lawmaker and Lyric poet named Solon. Solon had, in turn, heard the story while visiting the court of Amasis, king of ancient Egypt from 569 to 525 B.C., in the city of Sais, on the western edge of the Nile Delta. While at the court of Amasis, Solon visited the Temple of Neith and fell into conversation with a priest who related the story of Atlantis to him. The priest described a great island, larger than Libya and Asia combined, that had existed 9,000 years before their time, beyond the Pillars of Hercules (the Strait of Gibraltar) in the Atlantic Ocean. Atlantis was rule over by an alliance of kings descended from Poseidon, god of the sea and earthquakes, whose eldest son, Atlas, gave his name to the island and the surrounding ocean.

The Atlanteans possessed an empire that stretched from the Atlantic into the Mediterranean as far as Egypt in the south and Italy in the north. During an attempt to extend their empire further into the Mediterranean, the Atlanteans came up against the combined powers of Europe, led by the city-state of Athens. In this remote time, Athens was already a great city and a society ruled by a warrior-elite class who disdained riches and lived a spartan lifestyle. The armies of Atlantis were eventually defeated by the Athenians alone, after their allies deserted them. However, soon after the victory there was a devastating earthquake followed by huge floods, and the continent of Atlantis sank beneath the Ocean "in a single dreadful day and night," in the words of Plato.

The destruction of Atlantis and its location beyond the Strait of Gibraltar takes up only a few lines in Plato's *Dialogues*, in contrast to his much more detailed description of the island's physical and political organization. Initially Atlantis had been an idyllic place, endowed with a wealth of natural resources; there were forests, fruits, wild animals (including elephants), and abundant metal ores. Each king on the island possessed his own royal city over which he was complete master. However, the capital city, ruled by the descendents of Atlas, was by far the most spectacular. This ancient metropolis was surrounded by three concentric rings of water, separated by strips of land on which defensive walls were constructed. Each of these walls was encased in different metals, the outer wall in bronze, the next in tin, and the inner wall "flashed with the red light of orichalcum," an unknown metal. The Atlanteans dug a huge subterranean channel through the circular moats, which connected the central palace with the sea. They also carved a harbor from the rock walls of the outer moat. The main Temple of Poseidon, on the central citadel, was three times larger than the Parthenon in Athens, and was covered entirely in silver (with the exception of the pinnacles, which were coated in gold). Inside the temple, the roof was covered with ivory and decorated with gold, silver, and orichalcum; this strange metal also covered the walls, pillars, and floor of the temple. The temple interior also contained numerous gold statues, including one of Poseidon in a chariot driving six winged horses, which was of such a colossal size that the god's head touched the roof of the 381 foot high ceiling.

All other ancient sources for the lost continent of Atlantis are subsequent to Plato, and at best provide tantalizing glimpses of what the people antiquity really believed about Atlantis. In the fourth century B.C. the Greek Philosopher and student of Aristotle, Theophrastus of Lesbos, mentioned colonies of Atlantis, but unfortunately the bulk of his work has been lost. In his commentaries on Plato's dialogues, Proclus, writing in the fifth century A.D., commented on the reality of Atlantis, stating that the Atlanteans "for many ages had reigned over all islands in the Atlantic sea." Proclus also tells us that Crantor, the first commentator on the works of Plato in the fourth century B.C., had visited Sais in Egypt and had seen a golden pillar with hieroglyphs recording the history of Atlantis. Claudius Aelianus, a second century A.D. Roman writer, mentions Atlantis in his work *On the Nature of Animals,* describing a huge island out in the Atlantic Ocean, which was known in the traditions of the Phoenicians (and sebsequently the Carthaginians of Cádiz), as an ancient city on the coast of southwest Spain.

For the most part, the legend of Atlantis lay dormant for many centuries before its revival in the 19th century. The modern quest for the fabled island began in ernest in 1882, with the publication of *Atlantis: the Antediluvian World* by Ignatius Donnelly, an American congressman and writer. Donnelly took Plato's account of Atlantis literally, and attempted to establish that all known ancient civilizations were descended from the lost continent. Around the same time, Madame Helena Blavatsky (the co-founder of the Theosophical Society, and a leader in the growing occult movement) began to take an interest in the idea of lost continents such as Atlantis and Lemuria. Blavatsky mentions Atlantis numerous times in her first work *Isis Unveiled*, written in 1877. Madame Blavatsky's massive opus *The Secret Doctine* (1888), was apparently based on a mystical work called *The Book of Dzyan*, allegedly written in Atlantis. In it she gives a detailed description of Atlantis and its inhabitants, which includes advanced technology, ancient flying machines, giants, and supernormal powers. Some of these wilder aspects of Blavatsky's descriptions were to have a significant influence on a number of Atlantis theorists, though her lost continent seems to exist on another, more spiritual, level—altogether different from the physical continent proposed by Donelly.

In the early 20th century, world-renowned psychic Edgar Cayce gave many readings that involved Atlantis. He believed that Atlantis was a highly evolved civilization that possessed ships and aircraft (which echoes Blavatsky) and were powered by a mysterious energy crystal. Cayce predicted that part of Atlantis would be discovered in 1968 or 1969 in the region of Bimini, near the Bahamas.

American congressman and author Ignatius Donnelly.

In September of 1968, a half-mile stretch of precisely aligned limestone blocks, now known as the Bimini Road, was discovered off the coast of North Bimini, suggesting to many that this was the remains of lost Atlantis.

However, in 1980, Eugene Shinn of the U.S. Geological Survey published the conclusions of his examination of the underwater stones at Bimini. The results of his tests indicated that the blocks must have been laid there by natural means. The radiocarbon dates obtained from the shells embedded in the stones gave dates in the range of 1200 B.C. to 300 B.C., for the laying down of the so-called road. This is generally a lot later than the proposed dates for Atlantis.

Taking the ancient writers at their word, many researchers have searched for Atlantis in the mid-Atlantic, identifying the Mid-Atlantic Ridge—a long chain of undersea volcanoes running along the center of the ocean, as the remains of the lost continent. With the modern understanding of continental drift (which is due to the action of plate tectonics) geologists have ruled out the possibility of a sizeable continent existing in the Atlantic. However, plate tectonics is still only a theory, so until it is proven as fact, believers in a lost continent in the Atlantic will continue their search. If the island is in the mid-Atlantic, researchers reason (echoing Ignatius Donnelly back in the 1880s) that the Azores, a cluster of nine islands amid a chain of underwater mountains, may be its remnants. Others add Madeira, the Canary Islands, and Cape Verde to its remains, though as yet not a shred of proof exists in these areas for a vanished ancient civilization.

Almost every year, without fail, the headline "Atlantis Found!" screams out from the newspapers. In fact, the range of hypothetical locations for Atlantis is staggering. The Minoan civilization of Late Bronze Age Crete, supposedly destroyed by a colossal earthquake on the neighboring island of Thera (modern day Santorini), was long thought to have been an indirect influence on Plato's Atlantis. However, research into Late Bronze Age Crete has shown that the Minoan civilization continued to flourish long after the Theran quake. Other suggested locations within Europe and the Mediterranean include Ireland, England, Finland, the island of Heligoland off the northwest German coast, Andalucia in southern Spain, the island of Spartel in the Strait of Gibraltar, Sardinia, Malta, the city of Helike on mainland Greece, an area in the Mediterranean between Cyprus and Syria, Israel, Troy in northwest Turkey, and Tantalis. Elsewhere in the world the Black Sea, India, Sri Lanka, Indonesia, Bolivia, French Polynesia, the Caribbean, and Antarctica have all been suggested as locations of the lost city.

This vast array of wildly different theories has contributed to the scepticism of many researchers, who believe that Plato's Atlantis was merely a political allegory designed to glorify Athens as the perfect state fighting against a decadent and greedy Atlantean Empire. For them the story begins and ends with Plato. Solon never visited Egypt or heard the story from the priest at Sais. They reason that Plato located Atlantis in the Atlantic, beyond the Pillars of Hercules, because in his time this vast ocean represented the limit of the known world. Nevertheless, although there are no references to Atlantis in ancient literature prior to Plato, we do have a reference in *The Histories* by the Greek historian Herodotus (484 B.C.–425 B.C.), which states that Solon borrowed certain laws from Amasis of Sais in Egypt. This indicates that Solon was in Egypt during the time stated by Plato in his dialogues. It is obvious from Plato's writings that he was aiming in part to glorify Athens, and convey his political and philosophical ideas regarding the inability of wealth and power to overcome a perfectly formed and well-governed society. In order to color his account, Plato may well have added details from actual events involving a catastrophic destruction. For this, the philosopher would not have had to look far.

In the summer of 426 B.C. one of the most disastrous earthquakes in ancient history hit Greece just north of Athens. The tsunami from this colossal quake caused havoc along the coast north of Athens, destroying part of an island called *Atalante*. In 373 B.C. (only around 15 years before Plato wrote his *Dialogues*) a catastrophic earthquake and tsunami destroyed and submerged the wealthy ancient Greek city of Helike, on the southern shore of the Gulf of Corinth, on mainland Greece. Helike was known as the City of Poseidon, and contained a sacred grove of the terrible god of earthquakes and the sea, which was second only to that at Delphi. There are certainly parallels between these earthquakes and the destruction of Plato's Atlantis, which indicate the philosopher was drawing on his own country's recent history for much of his narrative. However, if Plato was

simply using recent disasters in Greece to make his point, why did he attribute his story to Egyptian priests? Surely his contemporaries would have recognized a description of a catastrophic earthquake in the area of Athens or Corinth, especially one that had occurred only a decade or two before. There still seems to be an element missing from Plato's sources for his story.

The most recent theory for the location of Atlantis was put forward in 2004 by Dr. Rainer Kuehne of Wuppertal University in Germany. Using satellite photographs, Kuehne identified an area of southwestern Spain that reveal features apparently matching Plato's description of Atlantis. The photographs, of a salt marsh region called Marisma de Hinojos, near the city of Cadiz, show two rectangular structures and parts of concentric rings that may once have surrounded them. Dr. Kuehne thinks that the rectangular features may be the remains of a silver temple devoted to Poseidon and a golden temple devoted to Cleito and Poseidon, as described by Plato in his *Dialogues*. He also believes that the area was possibly destroyed by a flood between 800 B.C. and 500 B.C. He supports this mainland—rather than island—location for Atlantis by suggesting that Greek sources may have confused an Egyptian word for *coastline* with one meaning *island* during translation of the story. Dr. Kuehne hopes to organize excavations at the site in the near future to test his theories. Will these excavations, in an area just beyond the Pillars of Hercules, finally solve the mystery of Atlantis?

America's Stonehenge: The Puzzle of Mystery Hill

© *Stan Shebs (GNU Free Documentation License)*
View of part of America's Stonehenge.

Mystery Hill, or America's Stonehenge, as it has become known, is situated in North Salem, New Hampshire, about 40 miles north of Boston. This enigmatic megalithic complex is scattered over roughly 30 acres and consists of a disordered mix of standing stones, stone walls, and underground chambers. Mystery Hill is not an isolated site, but one of hundreds of areas of unusual stone arrangements and underground chambers in North America, many of which are in New England. Examples from Massachusetts include the Upton Chamber, stone-lined tunnels in Goshen, and a beehive-style stone chamber in Petersham. There are also stone chambers and walls at Gungywamp in Groton, Connecticut, and a large stone chamber in South Woodstock, Vermont. The exact functions of some of these unusual buildings are unknown, but many people have speculated that they were built by prehistoric European settlers for ceremonial meetings and astronomical events.

The recent history of Mystery Hill began with Jonathan Pattee, a farmer who lived on the site from 1826 to 1848.

There are various accounts of Pattee, including suggestions that he ran an illicit alcoholic still on the site. A more supportable story is that he and his son Seth were abolitionists, who operated a way station on the underground railroad that helped slaves escape from the South. In fact, there is some evidence for this in the form of shackles discovered on the site, which are now displayed in the America's Stonehenge Visitor's Center. During the next 50 years, quarrymen bought and removed a large portion of the stone structures at Mystery Hill. It is thought that most of the stones were taken to the town of Lawrence, Massachusetts, to be used in the construction of the Lawrence Dam and for street curbing. In 1937, William Goodwin, an insurance agent, bought the Mystery Hill site, and during his excavations made many structural changes to reinforce his theory that Irish monks had once lived there. Consequently, the site's history is now extremely confused. In 1950, Mystery Hill was leased by Robert Stone, who purchased the property in 1956. He began restoration, study, and preservation of the area around Mystery Hill, and in 1958 built a visitors center and opened the site to the public. Christened America's Stonehenge, it is now a major tourist attraction.

One of the most enigmatic features of Mystery Hill is a large, 4.5 ton flat stone slab, approximately 9 feet long and 6 feet wide, resting on four stone legs, similar to an enormous table. There is a deep groove running around the edge of this structure, leading to a spout, which has persuaded some to label it the Sacrificial Stone. According to one popular theory, the groove around the edge of the stone allowed the draining of blood from the sacrificed victims into libation bowls. Unfortunately, this Sacrificial Stone shows marked similarities to another large stone in the Farmer's Museum in western Massachusetts. But rather than being connected with any lurid sacrificial rites, this object was used in the process of soap making, and is in fact known as a lye-leaching stone. It is a relatively common find around New England colonial farm sites.

Another feature of the Mystery Hill complex is the many inscribed stones that have been found on the site over the years. The late Dr. Barry Fell, a professor of biology at Harvard University, did extensive work on the inscriptions at Mystery Hill, and many other sites in North America, many of which he claimed (in his 1976 book *America B.C.*), were Ogham (ancient Irish), Phoenician, and Iberian Punic scripts. The inscriptions, the astronomical alignments, and the megalithic style of architecture have led many to believe that Mystery Hill functioned as a prehistoric ceremonial center built by European immigrants. They conjecture that Phoenicians (a seafaring culture from modern day Syria and Lebanon, at their height c. 1200-800 B.C.) were in America at least 2,500 years ago, trading with the Celtic (western European tribes prevalent from the eighth to the first centures B.C.) community already living at Mystery Hill. These are indeed extraordinary claims; the question is whether there is any extraordinary evidence to back them up. In the first place, Fell's book has been widely discredited by archaeologists and linguists. The photos in *America B.C.* of the Ogham and Punic inscriptions are particularly unconvincing. The majority of the lines and scratches, identified by Fell as ancient scripts, appear to be completely random, and more believable explanations would be haphazard scrapes left by a plough; relatively modern graffiti; the results of farmers' quarrying methods; or merely the natural lines, fissures, and cracks found on most rocks. A reexamination of these stones by archaeologists and epigraphers would be needed to test the claims of Fell more fully. Unfortunately, as some of the inscribed stones from Mystery Hill have been taken from the site and "put away for safe keeping" their original context is now lost, making the task of accurate identification and dating even more difficult.

If one takes a closer look at archaeological evidence from Mystery Hill, it becomes clear that it does not support the theory that the site was an ancient temple complex, occupied by the Celts and visited by the Phoenicians. The lack of dateable pre-colonial artifacts found in context at the site is a major problem for its prehistoric European origins. Excavations conducted by Gary S. Vescelius in 1955 recovered 8,000 artifacts, all of which suggested late-18th century occupation of the site. An important fact noted by Vescelius was that many of these 18th century artifacts were found in situ underneath and inside stone walls in the Y-cavern, proving that this structure must postdate the objects. In fact, to date, there has not been a single Phoenician or Celtic object found in an archaeological context anywhere in North America. These Celts and Phoenicians

who were supposedly in America carving inscriptions did not leave any other trace of their presence, not even a single pottery shard to prove their existence.

Much of the seemingly unexplained stone work at Mystery Hill and elsewhere in New England can be attributed to the work of 18th and 19th century farmers in the form of walled field boundaries, walled building foundations, and stone storage structures. Some of the remaining structures may have an origin with the local Native American population, as noted by Edwin C. Ballard in his research into the U-shaped stone structures of the area. It is also a distinct possibility that parts of the Mystery Hill complex were given over to the production of potash and pearlash. Potash is made by extracting all the water from a lye solution obtained from the leaching of wood ashes. The potash is then baked in a kiln until all the carbon impurities are burned off, resulting in a fine, white powder, which is the pearlash. There are various references that show the importance of potash and pearlash to the economy of the country in the 18th century. In 1765, the Governor of Massachusetts is recorded to have stated that the production of potash and hemp and the transporting of lumber to England were the best business enterprises for the colonies.

Potash was made on farms and homesteads and sold to peddlers, who would then sell it on to manufacturers, who converted it to pearlash at their factories, known as ashies. As well as the kiln for converting the potash to pearlash, these factories would contain a small stone structure, called an ashery, in which they burned large quantities of wood. These buildings included a roof with a hole in it and two openings, one in the middle of one side for adding the wood to the fire, and the other at the bottom for removing the ashes. Taking into consideration the lye-leeching stone and the various stone structures at the site, it is highly likely that this sort of activity went on at Mystery Hill. The structures that were once part of these pearlash factories have never been identified as such, perhaps because such a prosaic explanation for the site does not fit the theories of those promoting more fantastic functions for Mystery Hill.

However, there are radiocarbon dates, obtained from charcoal found alongside a stone pick and a hammer stone, which do prove human occupation at Mystery Hill going back to the second millennium B.C. But this is much more likely to indicate a Native American presence than that of Bronze or Iron Age Europeans. Some researchers have claimed that many of the stones at Mystery Hill are aligned to obvious astronomical points, and that the site can still be used today as an accurate astronomical calendar, utilizing the stones to determine specific solar and lunar events in the year. However, the so-called celestial alignments at the site (if they are not entirely accidental) can be ascribed to American Indians, whose interest in sun and moon alignments can be seen from other Native American Indian sites such as the pyramids of Kahokia, near St. Louis.

So what, then, is the explanation for Mystery Hill? It is probable that the origin of the site lies in a Native American hunting camp, probably established some time during the second millennium B.C. As for the structures on the site, the vast majority of them can be explained in terms of postcolonial farming and industrial activity from the late 18th century onwards, though one or two remain enigmatic. The confused state of the Mystery Hill complex itself leads easily to misunderstanding, and it is clear that even with a concise series of excavations, the site's mystery may never be solved. People are of course free to claim a prehistoric European origin for America's Stonehenge, even if the available evidence points in a completely different direction. In the end, these beliefs tell us more about the believers than about the real origins and functions of Mystery Hill.

Petra: The Mysterious City of Rock

Hewn out of the solid rock, the ancient ruined city of Petra (the word *petra* means *stone* or *rock* in Greek) lies within a ring of forbidding sandstone mountains in the desert southwest of modern Amman, 50 miles south of the Dead Sea in Jordan. Such is the site's protected position that even today this spectacular complex of temples, tombs, and houses can only be accessed on foot or on horseback. Entrance to Petra is via a dark winding crevice in the

© *Thanassis Vembos.*
The Siq, the narrow entrance to Petra.

rock, known as the *siq* (*cleft* in Arabic), which is in places as little as a few feet wide. This great mystery of the desert contains nearly 1,000 monuments, and once possessed fountains, gardens, and a permanent water supply. But why was it carved out of the sandstone in such a secluded, arid location? Who built this majestic city and what happened to its inhabitants?

The earliest known population of Petra was a Semitic-speaking tribe known as the Edomites, mentioned in the Bible as descendents of Esau. But it was a culture called the Nabateans who were responsible for most of the incredible architecture at Petra. The Nabateans were of nomadic Arabic origin, but by the fourth century B.C. had begun to settle down in various parts of Palestine and southern Jordan, and around this time they made Petra their capital city. The naturally fortified position of the site on a trade route between Arabian, Assyrian, Egyptian, Greek, and Roman cultures allowed the strength of the Nabateans to grow. Gaining control of the caravan route between Arabia and Syria, the Nabateans soon developed a commercial empire that extended as far north as Syria, and the city of Petra became the center for the spice trade.

The wealth accumulated by the Nabateans at Petra (through their commercial enterprise) allowed them to build and carve in a style that combined native traditions with Hellenistic (Greek) influence. One of the Nabateans' most oustanding achievements at Petra sprang from necessity. Their city lay on the edge of the parched desert, so a water supply was of prime concern. Consequently, they developed highly sophisticated dams, as well as water conservation and irrigation systems. But the wealth of the Nabateans brought the envy of their neighbors and they were forced to repel several attacks against their capital during the late fourth century B.C., by the Seleucid king Antigonus. The Seleucid Empire was founded in 312 B.C. by Seleucus I, one of Alexander the Great's generals, and included much of the eastern part of Alexander's Empire. In 64–63 B.C., the Nabateans were conquered by the Roman general Pompey, and in A.D. 107, under the Emporer Trajan, the area became part of the Roman province of Arabia Petraea. Despite the conquest, Petra continued to thrive during the Roman period, and various structures, including a vast theater, a colonnaded street, and a Triumphal Arch across the *siq*, were added to the city. It has been estimated that the population of Petra may have been as great as 20,000 to 30,000 at its height. However, as the importance of the city of Palmyra, in central Syria, grew on a trade route linking Persia, India, China, and the Roman Empire, Petra's commercial activity began to decline.

In the fourth century, Petra became part of the Christian Byzantine Empire, but in A.D. 363 the free-standing parts of the city were destroyed in a devastating earthquake, and it is around this time that the Nabateans seem to have left the city. No one is sure exactly why they abandoned the site, but it seems unlikely they deserted their capital because of the earthquake, as very few valuable finds have been unearthed at the site, indicating that their departure was not a sudden one. A further catastrophic earthquake in A.D. 551 practically ruined the city, and by the time of the Muslim conquest in the 7th century A.D., Petra was beginning to slip into obscurity. There was another damaging earthquake in A.D. 747 that further structurally weakened the city, after which there was silence until the early 12th century and the arrival of the Crusaders, who built a small fort inside the city. After the Crusaders left in the 13th century, Petra was left in the hands of sandstorms and floods, which buried a large part of the once great city until even its ruins were forgotten.

It was not until 1812 that an Anglo-Swiss explorer named Johann Ludwig Burckhardt rediscovered the lost city of Petra and brought it to the attention of the western world. Burckhardt had been travelling in the near east disguised as a Muslim trader (under the name of Sheikh Ibrahim Ibn Abdallah) in order to acquire knowledge and experience oriental life. While in Elji, a small settlement just outside Petra, Burckhardt heard talk of a lost city hidden in the mountains of *Wadi Mousa*. Posing as a pilgrim wishing to make a sacrifice at the ancient site, he persuaded two of the Bedouin inhabitants of the village to guide him through the narrow *siq*. Burckhardt seems only to have managed a brief tour of the remains of Petra, before sacrificing a goat at the foot of the shrine of the prophet Aaron and making his way back to Elji. The explorer did, however manage to produce a map of the ruins and made an entry in his journal to the effect that he had rediscovered Petra.

Since the time of Burckhardt, the purpose of the rock-cut city of Petra, hidden away in such a secret location, has puzzled many a traveler, scholar, and archaeologist. The romantic ancient atmosphere of the site was evocatively captured in the famous line describing Petra as a "rose-red city half as old as time," from the poem "Petra," written in 1845 by John William Burgon. But what exactly was the function of this strange place—was it a fortress, a commercial center, or a sacred city? There are many royal tombs throughout the site, as well as public tombs and shaft tombs (the latter places are apparently where criminals were buried alive). But evidence from archaeological investigations over the past decade or so suggests Petra may have had many different functions over the hundreds of years it was inhabited. The magnificent entrance to the site is the more than a mile-long *siq*, or narrow gorge that winds through the soaring golden-brown sandstone cliffs. There are many small Nabatean tombs carved into the cliff walls of the *siq*, as well as evidence for the skill of the Nabateans as hydraulic engineers, in the form of channels—once containing clay pipes—which originally carried drinking water into the city. A further example of the engineering abilities of the Nabateans can be seen at the right of the entrance to the *siq*. Now, as 2,000 years ago, after heavy rain, water flows down the *Wadi Mousa* (or Valley of Moses) into the *siq*

and threatens to flood the site of the city. There was a catastrophic flood at Petra in 1963, after which the government decided to construct a dam to redirect the flood water. During building, the excavators were astonished to discover that the Nabateans had already built a dam, probably around the second century B.C., to redirect the flood water away from the entrance and to the north, via an ingenious system of tunnels, which eventually diverted the water back into the heart of the city for the use of the population.

The *siq* eventually opens out dramatically to reveal the best known and most impressive of the monuments of Petra, the classically influenced Treasury (*El-Khazneh* in Arabic). The name *Treasury* originates from a Bedouin legend that a pharaoh's treasure was hidden inside a huge stone urn which stands at the top of the structure.

© *Thanassis Vembos.*
The Treasury Monument at Petra.

The Bedouins, believing the story, would periodically fire their rifles at the urn hoping to break it open and recover the treasure. The many bullet holes still visible on the urn are proof of this practice. The well-preserved façade of the Treasury, carved out of the solid sandstone rock, is decorated with beautiful columns and elaborate sculptures showing Nabatean deities and mythological characters, and stands 131 feet high and about 88 feet wide. The structure may have served as a royal tomb, perhaps with the king's burial place in the small chamber at the back, and also seems to have been used as a temple, though to which specific god or gods it was dedicated is not known. The exact date of the *Khazneh* is not certain, though construction somewhere in the 1st century B.C. is the most likely.

One of the few remaining freestanding buildings at Petra is the huge masonry-built Temple of Dushares, also known mysteriously as *Qasr al-Bint Firaun* (The Castle of Pharaoh's Daughter). This extensively restored large yellow sandstone temple stands upon a raised platform and has massive 75 feet high walls. The temple, built sometime between 30 B.C. and A.D. 40, was dedicated to Dhushares, the chief god of the Nabateans, and has the largest façade of any building in Petra. Inside, the building is separated into three rooms, the middle room serving as the sanctuary, or holy of holies.

Facing this structure is the Temple of the Winged Lions, named after two eroded lions carved on either side of the doorway. This structure, the most important Nabatean temple ever discovered, has been the subject of more than 20 years of research and excavation by the American Expedition to Petra. Apparently the temple was dedicated to the pre-Islamic Arabian fertility goddess Allat, who was one of the three chief goddesses of Mecca. Rather than a single building, the Temple of the Winged Lions is really a temple complex including workshops and living areas. (One of the workshops even manufactured souvenirs!) The temple is almost certainly the one described in the Dead Sea Scrolls as the Temple of Aphrodite at Petra. As the site has produced such a huge amount of excavated material the exact dates of its habitation are known. The temple was founded in August A.D. 28 and was destroyed in the May A.D. 363 earthquake that brought down many of the city's buildings.

The largest monument in Petra and one of the most striking is *El-Deir* (the Monastery), acquiring the name from its use as a church during the Byzantine period (c. A.D. 330–A.D.1453). The spectacularly situated structure, high up on the mountain, is 164 feet wide and 148 feet high, with its great doorway measuring around 26 feet in height. The structure is carved, as with the Treasury, into the side of a cliff face. In fact, the Monastery is similar to a larger, rougher, weather-beaten version of the more famous Petra monument. Archaeologists believe that construction of *El-Deir* began during the reign of Nabatean king Rabel II (A.D. 76–106), but was never completed.

Petra was brought back to the center of public attention in 1989 with the release of *Indiana Jones and the Last Crusade,* starring Harrison Ford.

© *Thanassis Vembos.*
The Monastery at Petra.

Lama led a host of Nobel Prize winners who, together with actor Richard Gere, organized a two-day conference at the rose red city entitled "A World in Danger." The fortunately excellent state of preservation of much of the ancient city can be explained by the fact that most of its structures have been carved out of solid rock. However, as with many ancient monuments, the sandstone buildings at Petra are in constant danger from excessive tourism, and the free-standing buildings in particular are suffering from salt, water, and wind erosion. On December 6, 1985, Petra was recognized as a World Heritage Site by UNESCO (the United Nations Educational, Scientific, and Cultural Organization), and for the past few years conservationists have been at work on the monument filling in the holes and cracks in the stone with a specially designed mixture, as close as possible to the original sandstone of the 2,000-year-old plus structures. Hopefully, one of the world's most beautiful and spectacular ruined cities will be around for at least another 2,000 years.

In the film, it served as a secret temple hidden for hundreds of years, and the place where Harrison Ford finally locates the Holy Grail. It was in the news again in 2005, when the Dalai

The Silbury Hill Enigma

Photograph by the author.
Silbury Hill, barely reaching the height of the surrounding hills.

Lying low in the Kennet valley in Wiltshire, southern England, looms the mysterious Silbury Hill, the largest man-made mound in Europe and one of the biggest in the world. The site stands amid the prehistoric sacred landscape surrounding the present day village of Avebury, and contains a complex of Neolithic monuments, including an enormous henge (a roughly circular flat area enclosed by a boundary earthwork), stone circles, stone alignments, and burial chambers. The imposing earthwork structure of Silbury Hill stands at 128 feet high, its flattened top is 98 feet across, and its diameter at the base is 547 feet. The huge 125 foot wide ditch that surrounds Silbury was the source of much of the material which makes up the mound, an amazing 8,756,880 cubic feet of chalk and soil. It has been estimated that construction of the monument would have taken the efforts of 1,500 to 2,000 men working for a year, 300 to 400 men working for more than five years, or 60 to 80 men working for more than 25 years. In all, an estimated 4 to 6 million man hours, though some have suggested a figure as high as 18 million hours. Because of its dimensions, Silbury has often been compared with the Great Pyramid in Egypt, which is roughly contemporary with the huge English earthwork. According to a radiocarbon date recently obtained from an antler pick fragment, Silbury probably achieved its final form between 2490 B.C. and 2340 B.C. But what was the purpose of such a massive undertaking of organization and manpower?

There is at present no consensus of opinion amongst archaeologists as to how many building phases there were at the huge earthwork at Silbury, though we know its builders used tools of stone, bone, wood, and antler in its construction. The late Richard Atkinson, who excavated the mound in the late 1960s, hypothesized three separate phases. In the first of Atkinson's phases (Silbury I), dated to around 2700 B.C., the earthwork consisted of a low gravel-built mound covered in alternating layers of chalk rubble and turf, around 18 feet high and about 115 feet across. Atkinson believed that Silbury II was begun about 200 years later, and consisted of a much larger mound constructed over the top of Silbury I. In this phase, the earthwork had a diameter at its base of about 246 feet, with a height of 66 feet. Silbury III was the hill's final form, basically the earthwork we see today. Atkinson thought that the structure of Silbury III had been built up in tiers of chalk, only the upper two of which are now visible on the monument. Each of these horizontal steps was inclined inwards at an angle of 60 degrees, to provide the monument with stability; the tiers were then filled in with soil, probably from the ditch at the base of the mound. Despite Atkinson's three-phase theory, the latest evidence from surveys of parts of Silbury has revealed the possibility of

there being only one construction phase at the site. Only a complete survey of the whole monument will decide this issue.

There have been three main excavations undertaken at Silbury Hill in an attempt to fathom its mystery. The first of these was carried out by the Duke of Northumberland in 1776, who hired a team of Cornish miners to dig down from the top of the mound. However, they found nothing of note, and as the workers did not fill in the shaft properly after investigations were finished, their excavation led ultimately to the partial collapse of the summit of the mound in 2000. Antiquarian Dean Merewether supervised the excavation of a tunnel from the side of the hill to its core in 1849, but this shed little light on the function of Silbury Hill. Professor Richard Atkinson's BBC-sponsored excavations of the enigmatic earthwork, which took place from 1968 to 1970, have been the most comprehensive investigations of the site to date. One of Atkinson's three trenches followed Merewether's tunnel, but there were no sensational finds. In fact, precious few artifacts at all, no burials, and no clues to the function of the structure were found. However, from his work at the site, Atkinson was able to arrive at his theory about how the mound had been constructed. Atkinson's excavations also revealed considerable environmental evidence, including the presence of flying ants in the turf of the building, which has been used to suggest that construction of the earthwork was begun in the month of August, interpreted by some as coinciding with the Celtic Festival of Lughnasadh, or Lammas. Even though

Silbury was constructed 2,000 years before, there is evidence of Celtic culture in Britain.

Although most archaeologists are at a loss to explain the function of Silbury Hill, there has been no shortage of theories put forward in the 300 years of investigations at the site. The belief of the 18th and 19th century investigators was that the earthwork represented the burial mound of an ancient British king. In fact, local folklore suggests that the hill is the resting place of an unknown King Sil (or Zel), or that it contains a life-size statue of Sil sitting on top of a golden horse. Another legend tells that the Devil was about to empty a huge apron full of soil on the nearby town of Marlborough, but was forced to drop it at Silbury by the magic of the priests of nearby Avebury. Though folklore often contains a grain of truth, no human remains have ever been discovered in excavations at the hill, although it has to be admitted that not all of the structure has been investigated. Other theories about the earthwork include that the flattened top of Silbury functioned as a platform for druid sacrifices, or that the structure was a Temple to Mercury, a giant sundial, an astronomical observatory, a symbolic representation of the Mother Goddess, a power source for passing alien spaceships, or a center for meetings and legal proceedings. In fact, fairs did once take place on the summit of the Silbury Hill, but that was in the 18th century.

One feature of the massive earthwork which seems to point to a ritual function is a possible spiral path climbing up the structure. A new theory (evidence for which was revealed by a 3-dimensional seismic survey undertaken in 2001) goes against Richard Atkinson's hypothesis of construction in flat layers for the mound, suggesting rather that Atkinson's steps may actually be a spiralling ledge. This spiral may have served the dual purpose of an access route to the summit during construction and a pathway to the top for ritual processions. This idea would also link with the profusion of the spiral motif in Neolithic art, as seen for example at the temple/tomb at Newgrange in Ireland. That the mound had some

Close-up of the mysterious Silbury Hill.
Photo by the author.

kind of religious significance is given credence by its setting within the complex of ritual, funerary, and ceremonial monuments in the area around Avebury; which itself lies only 20 miles north of the roughly contemporary monument at Stonehenge.

The huge ditch surrounding Silbury, probably once intentionally filled with water, may be further evidence of a ritual function. In the early summer of 2001, a huge straight-edged 33 foot wide mark in the vegetation was identified, extending towards the ditch of the Silbury mound. The vegetation or crop mark indicates a deep man-made ditch under the soil, possibly—as some archaeologists believe—built to channel water from local springs into the moat at Silbury Hill. Ditches around prehistoric sites, such as henges and hillforts, may not have always been dug for practical purposes, but could also have had a less tangible function, such as a barrier to separate the religious from the mundane, or to protect the site from malign influences. The site of the Silbury monument is also interesting. When originally built, Silbury Hill would probably have been a brilliant white structure surrounded by a shimmering moat. However, rather than placing such an awe-inspiring structure on a hill where it could be seen for miles around, its builders placed Silbury in a valley, so it barely protrudes above the horizon, and is hardly visible from most of the surrounding monuments. Perhaps this indicates that the ground on which the structure was erected was as important as the building itself, though its lowland setting does emphasise its huge size.

Intriguingly, Silbury Hill seems to have retained its importance as a sacred site long after it was built. Excavations at the hill have revealed a large amount of Roman finds, including a ritual platform cutting into the mound, more than 100 Roman coins in the surrounding ditch, and many Roman shafts and wells. On the adjacent Waden Hill, a Romano-British settlement has been discovered, which suggests (along with the finds on Silbury Hill itself) that Silbury was still a sacred site in the Roman period. There are fascinating parallels here with Newgrange, which also retained ritual significance into the Roman period. The religious attraction of Silbury seems to have continued into the medieval period, as is suggested by finds of pottery, iron nails, an iron spearhead, and a coin of King Ethelred II (dating to A.D. 1010) at the site. The iron nails were found inside small holes that had been dug for wooden posts, at first thought to indicate a defensive structure—perhaps a fort on the hill. However, these post holes were located on the inside of the terraces, which would mean that they served as revetment rather than defense. Further work on the hill will surely reveal more evidence of medieval interest in Silbury.

Unfortunately, the recent history of Silbury Hill has been rather worrying. In 2000, the collapse of the 1776 excavation shaft (due to heavy rainfall) produced a substantial hole in the top of the earthwork. The one positive aspect of this disaster was that it enabled the English Heritage Society to undertake a seismic survey of the mound to probe the extent of the damage caused by the collapse. Fortunately, the ensuing repair work led to further archaeological investigations of the earthwork, which revealed the possible spiral staircase mentioned previously, and the first secure radiocarbon date from the site. Since this collapse, in order to preserve the long-term stability of the site, the Silbury mound has been off limits to the public. But despite the signs prohibiting the act, people continue to attempt to break in to the site and climb to the top. The worst offenders so far have been the Dutch couple Janet Ossebaard and Bert Janssen, professional crop circle enthusiasts and alien hunters. Suspecting Silbury was some kind of ancient power plant, the couple, along with another crop circle hunter, tunnelled under the temporary roof installed by English Heritage and abseiled into the shaft, damaging the mound in the process. There is even a commercially available video of the couple's investigation inside Silbury, which shows "the descent into the hole, the spontaneous burning of a cell phone display, the appearance of beautiful colored balls of light, and the discovery of secret chambers inside Silbury Hill." The couple later receieved a £5,000 fine for their act of vandalization and trespassing.

In November 2005, new plans to stabilize Silbury Hill were revealed by English Heritage. Their strategy includes the infilling with chalk of various shafts and cavities caused by the often clumsily performed investigations of the site in the 18th and 19th centuries. Over the coming years, English Heritage will also investigate the erosion on the monument resulting from the thousands of years of enthusiastic visitors climbing on the mound. Unfortunately, while there remains no supervised access to the site, there will always be people willing to ignore the warning signs and attempt a climb to the summit. Hopefully English Heritage will take this into consideration when they implement their new strategy. All this brings us no closer to finding an explanation and a meaning behind the construction of Silbury Hill. Most importantly, the great earthwork needs to be considered in the context of the sacred area of Neolithic monuments in which it lies. The meaning of the mound may be inextricably linked with the surrounding landscape, and the other neighboring monuments, such as the West Kennet Long Barrow (a rectangular earthen burial mound) and the Avebury Henge and stone alignments. The whole Avebury area functioned as a monumental religious center for generations, and perhaps the method of preserving the memory of ancestors in a preliterate society was to give it material form. Silbury Hill is perhaps one such surviving memory of our remote ancestors.

Troy: The Myth of the Lost City

Photograph by Adam Carr. (GNU Free Documentation License).
Walls of the excavated city of Troy.

The legendary city of Troy, scene of the 10-year-long Trojan War, is inextricably linked with some of the most prominent characters in Greek myth. From the goddesses Hera, Athena, and Aphrodite (and the matchless beauty of Helen) to the action heroes Achilles, Paris, and Odysseus. Most people are familiar with the story of the fall of Troy. But is there any truth to the tale of this mighty conflict caused by the love of Paris for Helen, which only ended when the Greeks introduced the Trojan Horse? Did the war really take place? Was there a city called Troy?

The myth of Troy begins with the marriage celebration of King Peleus, one of the Argonauts who accompanied Jason on his quest for the Golden Fleece, and his wife Thetis, a sea-goddess. The couple neglected to invite Eris, goddess of discord, to the wedding, but she arrived at the banquet anyway, and in her anger threw a golden apple onto the table inscribed "For the most beautiful." Hera, Athena, and Aphrodite all reached for the apple at the same time. To resolve the conflict, Zeus assigned the crucial decision to the most handsome man alive—Paris, the son of Priam, king of Troy.

Hera promised Paris great power if she were his choice, Athena offered him military glory, and Aphrodite promised the love of the most beautiful woman in the world. Paris decided to present the golden apple to Aphrodite, who gave him Helen, the wife of Menelaus, and Paris set off for the Greek city of Sparta to find her. The Trojan prince was welcomed as an honored guest at Menelaus's palace in Sparta. But when Menelaus was absent at a funeral, Paris and Helen escaped to Troy, taking with them a large amount of the king's wealth. On his return, Menelaus was understandably outraged to find his wife had been abducted and his treasures stolen. He immediately gathered Helen's old suitors, who had long before sworn an oath to protect the marriage of Helen and Menelaus, and they decided to raise an army and sail for Troy. And so the seed for the legendary Trojan War was sown.

After more than two years of preparation, the Greek fleet (consisting of more than 1,000 ships under the command of Agamemnon, King of Mycenae) assembled at the port of Aulis in east central Greece, ready for the voyage to Troy. However, there was no wind to carry the ships, so the seer Calchis told Agamemnon that in order for the ships to sail he must sacrifice his daughter Iphigenia to the goddess Artemis. With this barbarous—but apparently necessary—act accomplished, the Greeks were able to leave for Troy. For nine years the battle raged, during which time many great heroes from both sides were slain, including Achilles, who was killed by Paris. But still the Greeks could not breach the great walls of Troy and gain

entrance to the city. In the 10th year of the war, the cunning Odysseus organized the building of a giant wooden horse, the inside hollowed out in order to conceal Greek warriors, including Odysseus, within. The horse was placed outside the gates of Troy, and the Greek fleet in the harbor sailed away, as if in defeat. When the Trojans saw the ships leaving and the huge wooden horse outside the city, they believed victory was theirs and dragged the horse inside the walls of Troy. That night, the Greeks climbed down from the horse and opened the gates of the city, letting in the whole Greek army. The Trojans, caught completely by surprise, were slaughtered. Polyxena, daughter of Priam, was sacrificed at the tomb of Achilles, and Astyanax, son of Hector, was also sacrificed. Although Menelaus had been intent on killing the disloyal Helen, her beauty overcame him and she was spared.

The story of Troy was first told in Homer's *Iliad*, written around 750 B.C. Details were added by later writers, such as the Roman poet Virgil in his *Aeneid*, and Ovid in his *Metamorphoses*. Most ancient Greek historians, such as Herodotus and Thucydides, were convinced of the historicity of the Trojan War. These writers took Homer at his word and placed Troy on a hill overlooking the Hellespont (modern Dardanelles)—the narrow straits between the Aegean and Black Seas. This was a position of great strategic importance in terms of trade. For hundreds of years, explorers and antiquarians fascinated by the legend of Troy searched the area, known in antiquity as the Troad, now part of northwest Turkey. The most famous and successful searcher for the great city of Troy was German businessman Heinrich Schliemann. Guided by the *Iliad* of Homer, he decided that Troy was located on a mound at Hisarlik a few miles from the Dardanelles, and began excavations there in 1870, continuing until 1890. Schliemann discovered the remains of a series of ancient cities beginning in the early Bronze Age (third millennium B.C.) and ending in the Roman period. Believing Troy must be located in the lower levels, Schliemann quickly and carelessly hacked through the upper levels, irrevocably destroying much vital evidence in the process. In 1873 he unearthed a variety of gold artifacts, which he dubbed *Priam's Treasure*. He announced to the world that he had found Homer's Troy.

There has been much debate about whether or not Schliemann actually found the gold artifacts in the place where he claimed, or if he had them planted there to verify his claims that the site was in fact the fabled city of Troy. Schliemann is known to have distorted the facts on more than one occasion. Although he claimed to have discovered the site of Troy at Hisarlik himself, when Schliemann first visited the Troad, English archaeologist and diplomat Frank Calvert had already been excavating on part of Hisarlik for some time, as it was on his family's land. Calvert was convinced Hisarlik was the site of ancient Troy and later collaborated with Schliemann on his early excavation on the hill. However, when Schliemann later received worldwide acclaim for discovering the Homeric city, he refused to admit that Calvert had anything to do with the discovery. Currently, English and American heirs of Frank Calvert are pursuing claims for a portion of the treasure that Schliemann and Calvert recovered from the site of Hisarlik. The spectacular gold finds discovered by

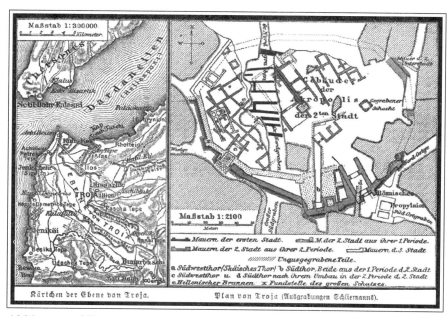

1880 map of Troy.

Schliemann are now believed to have come from a much earlier city on the Hisarlik mound than he believed. The city Schliemann thought was Homer's Troy in fact dates from 2400 to 2200 B.C., at least 1,000 years before the generally accepted date for the Trojan War.

Despite Schliemann's egotistical attitude, he did bring the site of Hisarlik to the attention of the world. After his excavations, further work at Hisarlik was undertaken by Wilhelm Dörpfeld (1893–1894), American archaeologist Carl Blegen from 1932 to 1938, and from 1988 to 2005 by a team of the University of Tübingen and the University of Cincinnati, under the direction of the late Professor Manfred Korfmann. Excavations at Troy have shown that there were nine separate phases and cities at the site, with various sub-phases. These phases begin in the third millennium B.C. (early Bronze Age) with Troy I and finish in the Hellenistic period (323 B.C.– c. 31 B.C.) with Troy IX. The Late Bronze Age phase Troy VIIa (c. 1300– c. 1180 B.C.) is the city usually put forward as the most likely candidate for Homer's Troy, mainly due to its date, which seems to tie in with Homer's descriptions, and the fact that traces of fire indicate that the city was destroyed during a war. Contact between mainland Greece and Troy VIIa is attested to in the form of imported Mycenaean (Late Bronze Age) Greek artifacts, especially pottery. Furthermore, the city of Troy VIIa was of considerable size, and finds including partial human remains and some bronze arrowheads have been made in the fort and city. However, a large part of Troy VIIa remains unexcavated, and

the finds are generally too meager to argue with certainty that the destruction of the site was done by human hands over that of a natural catastrophe, such as a massive earthquake. Nevertheless, if we are to interpret the Homeric city of Troy as a historical truth, then on present knowledge Troy VIIa would seem to fit the facts best. Recently, evidence that would seem to support the view of the Hisarlik mound as the site of Troy was revealed by geologists John C. Kraft from the University of Delaware, and John V. Luce from Trinity College, Dublin. The pair undertook a geological study of the landscape and coastal features of the area around Hisarlik, which revealed that the region's sedimentology and geomorphology are consistent with the features described in Homer's *Iliad*.

There may even be some historical fact behind what is perhaps the most outlandish detail in Homer's narrative—the colossal Trojan Horse. English historian Michael Wood has suggested that rather than being a clever ploy to get inside the city, the Trojan horse might actually represent a large battering ram or primitive siege engine resembling a horse. Such devices are known from Classical Greece. For example, the Spartans made use of battering rams in the siege of Plataea in 429 B.C. Alternatively, it is known that the symbol of the horse was used to represent Poseidon, the terrible god of earthquakes. Perhaps the Trojan horse may be a metaphor for an earthquake that struck the city, fatally weakening its defenses, allowing the Greek armies easy access. Further evidence, though controversial, for the historical existence of Troy comes from letters found in the archives of the Hittite Empire of Anatolia (modern Turkey). These letters, dating to around 1320 B.C., refer to military and political tension with a powerful empire called *Ahhiyawa* over the control of the kingdom of *Wilusa*. Wilusa has been tentatively identified with the Greek *Ilios*; Troy; and *Ahhiyawa* (with the Greek word *Achaea*, the country of the *Achaeans*, as Homer refers to the Greeks in the *Iliad*). These identifications remain controversial, but have been gaining more acceptance among scholars as research into the relationships between Greece and the Near East in the Late Bronze Age progresses. Unfortunately, we still do not possess a Hittite text that makes specific reference to a conflict in the Troad that can definitely be identified with the Trojan War.

So was there one huge extended conflict at Hisarlik around 1200 B.C. that we can say was the Trojan War? Perhaps not. Homer was writing about a semi-mythical age of heroes, the details of which had been passed down orally for at least four centuries. Even if the war happened, much of the story will have been lost and changed over that time. Admittedly there are details in Homer's narrative that seem to date back to the Late Bronze Age, such as various types of armor and weapons that were more at home in 1200 B.C. than 750 B.C., when the poet was writing. Homer also mentions certain Greek cities, little trace of which remained in his own time, as being particularly significant at the time of the Trojan War. Archaeological excavations at some of these sites have often proved that these cities were indeed of major importance during the Late Bronze Age. Nevertheless, given Troy's important location overlooking the Hellespont, on the borders of the Hittite Empire and the Greek world, the area was bound to be the site of armed conflict on more than one occasion during the Late Bronze Age. Perhaps it is more likely that Homer's story is a memory of a number of these conflicts between the Greek World and the inhabitants of the Troad, condensed into one final epic struggle, a war to end all wars. In a sense then, the story of the Trojan War is based roughly on historic events, though embelished by centuries of retelling, during which the supernatural elements of the tale were inserted. Perhaps even the beautiful Helen of Troy was added by a later storyteller to the original semi-historical narrative.

Photograph by Adam Carr. (GNU Free Documentation License).
View from Hisarlik across the plain of Ilium to the Aegean Sea.

Chichén Itzá: City of the Maya

Photograph by Keith Pomakis (Creative Commons License. Attribution- ShareAlike 2.5)
Temple of the Warriors at Chichén Itzá.

The mysterious ruined Mayan city of Chichén Itzá (meaning *at the mouth of the well of the Itzás*) has fascinated and intrigued archaeologists, explorers, and historians ever since it was first encountered and described by Bishop Diego de Landa, who wrote about the history of the Yucatán in the late 16th century. Chichén Itzá was at its height from around A.D. 600 to 1200, and was probably the main political and religious center in the whole of the Yucatán at this time. The site itself consists of many elaborately designed and decorated stone buildings, including temple-pyramids, palaces, observatories, baths, and ball courts, all constructed without the use of metal tools. For reasons not exactly understood, the Maya began to abandon Chichén Itzá around the beginning of the 13th century A.D., and before long the ruins were left to the encroaching jungle.

Although the existence of Chichén Itzá was known about for centuries after its abandonment, there was no exploration of the ruins until as late as the 1830s. From 1839 until 1842, American explorer and writer John Lloyd Stephens, together with English architect and draftsman Frederick Catherwood, made various jouneys through South America visiting countless ancient sites. Their research resulted in two important books, *Incidents of Travel in Central America, Chiapas and Yucatán* (1841) and *Incidents of Travel in Yucatán* (1843), both written by Stephens and illustrated by Catherwood. Between 1875 and 1883, French antiquarian and photographer Augustus Le Plongeon and his wife Alice undertook the first excavations at Chichén Itzá, and made some incredible stereographs of Mayan sites. However, Plongeon's conclusions on the Mayans were clouded by his belief that South America was the origin of all the world's civilizations. In the following decades there were various other expeditions to the site, including that of the Italian-born Teoberto Maler who, in the 1880s, lived at Chichén Itzá for three months, documenting the ruins more comprehensively than anyone before him. In 1889, English colonial diplomat, explorer, and archaeologist Alfred P. Maudslay visited the site and surveyed and photographed the ruins. Maudslay's assistant Edward H. Thompson (the U.S. consul to Yucatán), later moved to Chichén Itzá with his Mayan wife, and spent 30 years carrying out investigations among the ruins, including dredging artifacts of copper, gold, jade, and human bones out of the Sacred Cenote (a water-filled limestone sinkhole).

Professional archaeologists from the Carnegie Insitution at Harvard University began work at Chichén Itzá in 1924. The 20-year-long excavation project was directed by Sylvanus G. Morley, who had been a guest of Edward H. Thompson on his first visit to the ruins in 1907. In 1961, Mexico's National Institute of Anthropology and History undertook a methodical dredging of the Sacred Cenote, recovering 4,000 artifacts in the process. Since 1993, the Mexico-based Chichén Itzá Archaeological Project (under the direction of Dr. Peter Schmidt) has been carrying out excavation, research, and conservation work at the site, in order to map the whole area, examine the pottery, and restore the many structures previously left in a partially excavated state.

The ancient sacred city of Chichén Itzá is located in the jungle of the northeastern Yucatán peninsula, 75 miles southeast of Merida. The reason for the Maya locating their sacred city here can be best explained by the presence of natural sink holes, known in the area as *cenotes*, as the lack of aboveground rivers made an all year round water supply essential. The previously mentioned Cenote of Sacrifice or Sacred Cenote is the most famous of these sink holes, and was used by the Maya as a place for ritual offerings to their rain god Chaac. During periods of extreme drought, it seems that humans were also sacrificed here in order to propituate the god.

Chichén Itzá is generally thought to have been founded in A.D. 514 by the priest Lakin Chan, also known as Itzámna, and at its height comprised several hundred buildings. The ruins of the city can be divided into two groups, one belonging to the Classic

Maya period (A.D. 250–900) and constructed between the seventh and 10th centuries A.D., and the other belonging to the Maya-Toltec period, which lasted from the late 10th century up to the beginning of the 13th century. The Toltecs, another Native American people probably originating in central Mexico, made Chichén Itzá their capital in the late 10th century A.D., though whether this was by force or by some kind of agreement with the Maya is not known. It was during the Maya-Toltec period of the site that Chichén Itzá's most spectacular ruins were constructed.

The structure that people most identify with the Mayans and Chichén Itzá is probably the giant stepped pyramid that dominates the site, called the *Temple of Kukulcan* and also known by its Spanish name of *El Castillo*. The temple is actually composed of two buildings, a larger, more grand pyramid built over an earlier, more modest structure. The whole building is around 180 feet tall and each of its four sides once had 91 steps,

which, in addition to the platform crowning the structure, makes 365 steps, one for each day of the year. Further evidence for the calendrical significance of the temple are its 52 panels (representing the 52-year cycle of the Mayan calendar round), and 18 terraces (for the 18 months in the Mayan religious year). The pyramid is also oriented to accurately mark the occurrences of the equinoxes. Inside the earlier of the two pyramid-temples there are narrow steps leading to a secret chamber at the top of the structure, where archaeologists discovered the stone-carved Throne of the Jaguar, painted in brilliant red with jade spots, and also a sculpture of a Chac Mool figure. This latter object is a type of stone altar consisting of a reclining figure holding a bowl or tray over its stomach. It is thought that this tray was used for offerings of incense to the figure, who would act as a messenger to the gods. The bowl may also have been used to hold human hearts cut from sacrificial victims. During the spring or autumn equinox (March 21st

Photograph by Aaron Logan (Creative Commons License. Attribution- ShareAlike 1.0) El Castillo (the Castle) at Chichén Itzá.

and September 21st) when the sun's light hits the steps on the northern side of the pyramid, it creates the spectacular illusion of the shadow of a moving serpent slithering up the pyramid as the sun moves across the sky.

East of El Castillo stands the *Templo de los Guerreros* or Temple of the Warriors, a huge, flat-topped, pyramidal structure, which originally possessed a wood and plaster roof. The temple has pillars sculpted in bas-relief in the likeness of warriors, many of which still retain some of their original color. Surrounding the temple are hundreds of columns, the remains of ruined buildings known as the Group of a Thousand Columns.

On the western side of the site is The Temple of the Jaguars. This structure derives its name from the procession of jaguars carved on the front of the upper part of the building, and was constructed in the Maya Toltec architectural style from around A.D. 900 to 1100. Inside the temple are some of the most fascinating mural paintings in Chichén Itzá, including one example which depicts an ancient battle between the Mayas and the Toltecs. Adjacent to the Temple of the Jaguars is the Ball Court Complex (*Juego de Pelota*), one of seven courts for playing the Meso-American ballgame discovered at Chichén Itzá. The dimensions of this particular court, however, are 544 by 223 feet, making it the largest ball court ever built in central America, as well as the best preserved. No one is quite sure how this ballgame, called *Pok-Ta-Pok* by the Maya, was played, though it was probably more of a ritual ceremony than a recreational game. Consensus of opinion is that in order for a team to score, one of their players had to pass a firm leather or rubber ball through the openings of the stone scoring rings, located on opposite walls of the court, without using his hands or feet. This could be a deadly pastime, as it is believed that the captain of either the winning or losing team (researchers are not quite sure) was decapitated at the end of the game as an offering to the gods. However, the size of this particular ball court at Chichén Itzá has persuaded a number of scholars that actually playing the game there would have been out of the question. Due to the enormous size of the court it would not have been possible for a player to hit the ball from one end to the other, and as the stone rings are located almost 20 feet up on the vertical walls, they would have been completely out of reach for the players.

One hypothesis which has been put forward is that the ball court area was utilized as a ritual space where ceremonies were performed, which carried a similar meaning to the actual ball game. Panels along the side walls of the ball court are decorated with events from ball games, including scenes of players dressed in heavy padding and a particularly gruesome illustration depicting the beheading of a player in front of both teams. Much of the Mayan creation story (the *Popol Vuh*) is concerned with a ball game played in this world and also in the world of the dead, indicating the religious significance of the game. In one part of the myth, the hero twins play the game for their lives against the lords of the underworld. In another, the use of a ball comprised of a decapitated head encased in rubber is described.

More graphic illustrations of the relevance of the human head in Mayan ritual is provided by the *Tzompantli*, or the Wall of Skulls, a large, centrally-located T-shaped stone platform 198 feet long and 40 feet wide. This structure was used as a base for wooden stakes on which the decapitated heads of enemy warriors and sacrificial victims were impaled for public viewing. Its walls are covered in bas-relief sculptures of skulls, as well as carvings of eagles, feathered serpents, and Mayan warriors carrying human heads. This Wall of Skulls was probably designed to display the strength of the Maya and must have presented a fearsome site to invading armies.

In the southern part of the city stands one of the highest accomplishments of Mayan architects at Chichén Itzá. This is the 74 foot high Observatory, or *El Caracol* (the Spanish word for *snail*, referring to the resemblance of the building's internal spiral stairway to a snail's shell). The Observatory, as it stands today, is actually the ruins of a cylindrical structure, and consists of a tower built on top of a rectangular platform. The building has openings at several points, which probably served as small windows to enable the observing and tracking of stars and planets. South of *El Caracol* is the Nunnery, also known by its Spanish name of *Las Monjas*, a colossal structure measuring at its base 230 by 115 feet with a height of 59 feet. This elaborately decorated building was constructed over a period of several centuries, but functioned as the city's government palace.

It is recorded in the Mayan Chronicles that in A.D. 1221 the Maya revolted against the Maya-Toltec lords then ruling at Chichén Itzá. Evidence of destruction has been found by archaeologists in the form of the burning of the Great Market and the Temple of the Warriors. Civil war subsequently broke out, and control of Yucatán moved to Mayapan, 30 miles southeast of Merida. The city of Mayapan became the most important center of the Mayan civilization before the arrival of the Spanish in 1519. After this shift of power in the early 13th century, Chichén Itzá went into decline, its citizens moving elsewhere, and when the Spanish came upon the site in 1517 they found only a city of ghosts, its past glories long vanished.

The Sphinx: An Archetypal Riddle

Photograph by Michael Reeve. (GNU Free Documentation License.)
The Great Sphinx at Giza.

*The purpose of the Sphinx had now
become a little plainer. The Egyptian
Atlanteans had built it as their
grandest statue, their sublimest
figure of remembrance, and they had
dedicated it to their Light-god, the
Sun.*

—Paul Brunton

*A knoll of rock, which had been left
by the builders of the Great Pyramid
when quarrying stone for its inner
core, was fashioned in the time of
Chepren (Cheops) into a huge
recumbent lion with a human head...*

—I.E.S. Edwards

These quotes illustrate the contrasting interpretations of the Great Sphinx: the wildly mystical with the coldly pragmatic. Buried for most of its life in the sand, an air of mystery has always surrounded the enigmatic Sphinx, causing speculation about its age and purpose, method of construction, concealed chambers, role in prophesy, and relationship to the equally mysterious pyramids. Much of this theorizing is to the despair of Egyptologists and archaeologists, who alone seek to own the Sphinx and lay claim to its secrets. Perhaps the primary role of this national symbol of ancient and modern Egypt, which stands guard over the Giza plateau, is as it has always been: to stir the imagination of poets, scholars, mystics, adventurers and tourists for century after century. The Sphinx of Giza represents the essence of Egypt.

Facing the rising sun, the Great Sphinx is located on the Giza plateau, about 6 miles west of Cairo, on the west bank of the Nile River. Egyptian rulers worshipped it as an aspect of the Sun God, calling it *Hor-Em-Akhet* (Horus of the Horizon). The Sphinx sits in part of the necropolis of ancient Memphis, the seat of power for the pharaohs, a short distance from three large pyramids—the Great Pyramid of Khufu (Cheops), Khafre (Chephren), and Menkaura (Mycerinus). The monument is the largest surviving sculpture from the ancient world, measuring 241 feet in length and in parts 65 feet in height. Part of the uraeus (a sacred cobra that protected from evil forces), the nose, and the ritual beard are missing; the beard is now displayed in the British Museum. The extensions at the side of the head are part of the royal headcloth. Although the head of the Sphinx has been badly affected by thousands of years of erosion, traces of the original paint can still be seen near one ear. It is thought that originally the Sphinx's face was painted dark red. A small temple between its paws contained dozens of inscribed stelae, placed there by the pharaohs in honor of the Sun God.

The Sphinx has suffered greatly from the ravages of time, man, and modern pollution. In fact, the only thing that has saved it from complete destruction is that it has been submerged beneath the desert sand for most of its life. There have been various attempts at restoration over the millennia, beginning in c. 1400 B.C.with the pharaoh Tuthmosis IV. After falling asleep in the shade of the Sphinx when out hunting, the pharaoh dreamt that the great beast was choking from the sand engulfing it, and that it told him if he cleared the sand he would obtain the crown of Upper and Lower Egypt. In between the front paws of the Sphinx is a granite stela, now called the Dream Stela, which is inscribed with the story of the pharaoh's dream.

Despite this clearing, the colossal sculpture soon found itself beneath the sand once again. When Napoleon arrived in Egypt in 1798, he found the Sphinx without its nose. 18th century drawings reveal that the nose was missing long before Napoleon's arrival; one story goes that it was the victim of target practice in the Turkish period. Another explanation (and perhaps the most likely), is that it was pried off by chisels in the eighth century A.D. by a Sufi who considered the Sphinx a sacrilegious idol. In 1858, some of the sand around the sculpture was cleared by Auguste Mariette, the founder of the Egyptian Antiquities Service, and between 1925 and 1936, French engineer Emile Baraize excavated the Sphinx on behalf of the Antiquities Service. Possibly for the first time since antiquity, the Great Sphinx was once again exposed to the elements.

The explanation for the enigmatic sculpture (favored by most Egyptologists) is that Chephren, a Fourth Dynasty pharaoh, had the stone shaped into a lion with his own face at the same time as the construction of the nearby Pyramid of Chephren, around 2540 B.C. However, there are no inscriptions anywhere that identify Chephren with the Sphinx, nor is there mention anywhere of its construction, which is somewhat puzzling when considering the grandness of the monument. Despite many Egyptologists claims to the contrary, no one knows for sure when the Sphinx was built or by whom. In 1996, a New York detective and expert in identification concluded that the visage of the Great Sphinx did not match known representations of Chephren's face. He maintained that there was a greater resemblance to Chephren's elder brother, Djedefre. The debate is still continuing. The mystery of the Sphinx's origin and purpose has often given rise to mystical interpretations, such as those of English occultist Paul Brunton, and, in the 1940s, American psychic and prophet Edgar Cayce. While in a trance, Cayce predicted that a chamber would be discovered underneath the front paws of the Sphinx, containing a library of records dating back to the survivors of the destruction of Atlantis.

The Great Sphinx was excavated from a relatively soft, natural limestone, left over in the quarry used to build the Pyramids; the forepaws being separately made from blocks of limestone. One of the main oddities about the sculpture is that the head is out of proportion to its body. It could be that the head was re-carved several

The Great Sphinx in 1867, in its unrestored original condition, still partially buried in the sand.

times by subsequent pharaohs since the first visage was created, though on stylistic grounds this is unlikely to have been done after the Old Kingdom period in Egypt (ending around 2181 B.C.). Perhaps the original head was that of a ram or hawk and was re-cut into a human shape later. Various repairs to the damaged head over thousands of years might have reduced or altered the facial proportions. Any of these explanations could account for the small size of the head in relation to the body, particularly if the Great Sphinx is older than traditionally believed.

There has been lively debate in recent years over the dating of the monument. Author John Anthony West first noticed weathering patterns on the Sphinx that were consistent with water erosion rather than wind and sand erosion. These patterns seemed peculiar to the Sphinx and were not found on other structures on the plateau. West called in geologist and Boston University professor Robert Schoch, who, after examining the new findings, agreed that there was evidence for water erosion. Although Egypt is arid today, around 10,000 years ago the land was wet and rainy. Consequently, West and Schoch concluded that in order to have the effects of water erosion, the Sphinx would have to be between 7,000 and 10,000 years old. Egyptologist's dismissed Schoch's theory as highly flawed; pointing out that the once prevalent great rain storms over Egypt had stopped long before the Sphinx was built. More seriously, why were there no other signs of water erosion found on the Giza plateau to validate West and Schoch's theory? The rain could not

have been restricted to this single monument. West and Schoch have also been criticized for ignoring the high level of local atmospheric industrial pollution over the last century, which has severely damaged the Giza monuments.

Someone else with his own theory regarding the Sphinx's date is author Robert Bauval. Bauval published a paper in 1989 showing that the three Great Pyramids at Giza—and their relative position to the Nile—formed a kind of 3-D hologram on the ground, of the three stars of Orion's belt and their relative position to the Milky Way. Along with best-selling *Fingerprints of the Gods* author Graham Hancock, Bauval developed a theory that the Sphinx, its neighboring pyramids, and various ancient writings, constitute some sort of astronomical map connected with the constellation Orion. Their conclusion is that the best fit for this hypothetical map is the position of the stars in 10,500 B.C., pushing the origin of the Sphinx even further back in time. There are various legends of secret passages associated with the Great Sphinx. Investigations by Florida State University, Waseda University in Japan, and Boston University, have located various anomalies in the area around the monument, although these could be natural features. In 1995, workers renovating a nearby parking lot uncovered a series of tunnels and pathways, two of which plunge further underground close to the Sphinx. Bauval believes these are contemporaneous with the Sphinx itself. Between 1991 and 1993, while examining evidence for erosion at the monument using a seismograph, Anthony West's team found evidence of anomalies in the form of hollow, regularly shaped spaces or chambers, a few meters below the ground, between the paws and at either side of the Sphinx. No further examination has been allowed. Could there have been a grain of truth in Edgar Cayce's library of records prophecy after all?

Today, the great statue is crumbling because of wind, humidity, and the smog from Cairo. A huge and costly restoration and preservation project has been underway since 1950, but in the early days of this project, cement was used for repairs, which was incompatible with the limestone, and so caused additional damage to the structure. Over a period of 6 years, more than 2,000 limestone blocks were added to the structure, and chemicals were injected into it, but the treatment failed. By 1988, the sphinx's left shoulder was in such a state of deterioration that blocks were falling off. At present, restoration is still an ongoing project under the control of the Supreme Council of Antiquities, which is making repairs to the damaged shoulder and attempting to drain away some of the subsoil. Consequently, today the focus is on preservation rather than further explorations or excavations, so we will have to wait a long time before the Great Sphinx gives up its secrets.

The Knossos Labyrinth and the Myth of the Minotaur

© *Thanassis Vembos.*
Ruins of the palace at Knossos, showing some of Arthur Evans's reconstruction.

The archaeological site of Knossos is situated on a hill 3.1 miles southeast of the city of Heraklion, the modern capital of the Aegean island of Crete. Knossos was constructed by the Bronze Age Minoan civilization, named for the legendary King Minos of Crete. The Minoan culture existed on the island for around 1500 years, from 2600 to 1100 B.C., and was at its height from the 18th to 16th centuries B.C. The main feature of the extraordinary site at Knossos is the Great Palace, a huge complex of rooms, halls, and courtyards covering approximately 205,278 square feet. The Palace of Knossos is closely associated in Greek myth with Theseus, Ariadne, and the dreaded Minotaur. In fact, the legend of the labyrinth constructed by Daedalus to conceal the dreaded man-beast has been understood by some to originate with the complex layout of the palace itself. There are even dark hints in archaeological findings at Knossos (and elsewhere on Crete) of the practice of human sacrifice, as is suggested by the myth of Athens sending 14 girls and boys every seven years to be devoured by the Minotaur.

The site of Knossos was first discovered in 1878 by Cretan merchant and antiquarian Minos Kalokairinos, who excavated a few sections of the west wing of the palace. But systematic excavations at the site did not begin until 1900, with Sir Arthur Evans, director of the Ashmolean Museum in Oxford, who purchased the whole area of the site and continued his investigations there until 1931. The work of Evans and his team at Knossos revealed (among other things) the main palace, a large area of the Minoan city, and various cemeteries. Evans carried out much restoration work at the Palace of Minos, as he called it, much of it controversial, and the palace in its present form has been said by some archaeologists to be as much due to Evans's imagination and preconceptions as to the ancient Minoans. Since Evans's time, further excavations at Knossos have been undertaken by the British School of Archaeology at Athens and the Archaeological Service of the Hellenic Ministry of Culture. The hilltop on which Knossos is situated has an extremely long history of human habitation. People were living there from Neolithic times (7000 B.C.–3000 B.C.) continually up until the Roman period. The name *Knossos* derives from the Linear B word for the city: *ko-no-so*. Linear B is the oldest surviving example of the Greek language, and was in use on Crete and the Greek mainland from the 14th to the 13th centuries B.C. Examples of Linear B script were found at Knossos in the form of clay tablets, which were used by palace scribes to record details of the workings and administration of their main industries, such as the production of perfumed oil, gold and bronze vessels, chariots and textiles, and the distribution of goods such as wool, sheep, and grain. Clay tablets inscibed with the earlier undeciphered Cretan Linear A script were also found by Evans at Knossos.

The first Minoan Palace was built on the Knossos site around 2000 B.C. and lasted until 1700 B.C., when it was destroyed by a huge earthquake, thus bringing to an end what is referred to by archaeologists as the Old Palace Period. A new, more complex palace was erected on the ruins of the old; this structure heralded the Golden Age of Minoan culture, or the New Palace Period. This Great Palace, or Palace of Minos, was the crowning achievement of Minoan culture and the center of the most powerful city state on Crete. The timber- and stone-built multi-storied complex acted as an administrative and religious center, with perhaps as many as 1,400 rooms. The plan of the Knossos Palace was similar to other palaces of this period on Crete, such as that at Phaistos in the south-central part of the island, though Knossos seems to have been the capital. Minoan palaces generally consisted of four wings arranged around a rectangular, central court, which acted as the heart of the whole complex. Each section of the Knossos Palace had a separate function; the western part contained the shrines, suites of ceremonial rooms, and narrow storerooms, which were full of huge storage jars, known as *pithoi*. The elaborately decorated Throne Room complex was also located in this section of the complex, and had a stone seat built into the wall facing a row of benches. This seat was interpreted by Arthur Evans as a royal

The throne room in the palace of Knossos.

throne, and the name has stuck. In the far west of the complex was the great paved West Court, the formal approach to the palace. The east wing of the structure once had four levels, three of which remain today. Located in this part of the complex were what have been interpreted as residential quarters for the Minoan ruling elite, workshops, a shrine, and one of the most impressive achievements of Minoan architecture: the Grand Staircase. Other parts of the Palace include large apartments with running water in terracotta pipes, and perhaps the first example of flush toilets.

Some of the most extraordinary discoveries at Knossos have been the richly colored frescoes that adorned the plastered walls, and sometimes even the floors and ceilings. These murals show princes, courtly ladies, fish, flowers, and strange games involving young people leaping over charging bulls. When originally found, these wall paintings were fragmentary, often with significant parts missing, and were subsequently reconstructed and replaced by Evans and artist Piet de Jong. Consequently, there has been much controversy over the accuracy of the reconstructions, though there seems to be no doubt that many of the frescoes are of a religious or ritual nature.

Between 1700 B.C. and 1450 B.C., Minoan civilization was at its peak, with the city of Knossos and the surrounding settlement having a population of perhaps as many as 100,000. During this period the Minoan centers survived two major earthquakes, the most serious of which probably occurred in the mid-17th century B.C. (though some researchers date it to as late as 1450 B.C.), and was caused by a massive volcanic eruption on the Cycladic island of Thera (modern Santorini) 62 miles away from Crete. The explosion from this eruption was even greater than the atomic blast at Hiroshima, and blasted the island of Thera into three separate parts. Finally, in the mid-15th century B.C., due to a combination of the accumulative effects of earthquake damage, periodic invasions from the Greek mainland, and the collapse of their trade networks, the Minoan civilization began to decline.

Perhaps its layout is quite complex —resembling a labyrinth—the Palace of Minos is thought by some to be the source of the Theseus and the Minotaur myth. The main part of the myth begins when Theseus is in Athens and hears about a blood payment demanded by King Minos of Crete, for the murder of his son by the Athenians. This payment involves sending seven young Athenian men and seven young virgin girls to Crete every year, where they are given to the terrible half-bull, half-man Minotaur. This beast is kept shut up in a labyrinth designed by the famous architect Daedalus. Appalled at this situation, Theseus volunteers to be part of the yearly sacrifice and kill the Minotaur. As he is about to set off for Crete with the intended victims on a black-sailed ship, his father King Aegeus makes Theseus promise that if he is successful in slaying the Minotaur, he will, on his return, change the ship's black sail to white, as an indication that he is alive and well. When the group arrives at Knossos, King Minos' daughter Ariadne immediately falls in love with Theseus and agrees to help him kill the Minotaur. Ariadne gives Theseus a silk thread, which the hero uses to help him find his way out of the labyrinth after he has killed the monster. The couple subsequently set sail for Athens, but on the way Theseus deserts Ariadne on the island of Naxos, where she is rescued by the god Dionysus. Unfortunately, on his approach to Athens, Theseus forgets his promise to his father and leaves the black sail on the ship. King Aegeus, thinking his son has been killed, leaps to his death from a cliff.

There is evidence that Knossos's link with Theseus and the Minotaur was kept alive long after the Minoans ceased to exist. This comes mainly in the form of coinage, and examples include a silver coin from Knossos dated c. 500 to 413 B.C., which depicts a running Minotaur on one side and a maze or labyrinth on the reverse. Another coin shows the head of Ariadne surrounded by a labyrinth. The Minotaur and labyrinth were also extremely popular in the Roman period, and numerous mosaics illustrate the Knossos labyrinth. The most spectacular of these is probably that from a Roman villa near Salzburg, in western Austria, dating to the fifth century A.D. However, some researchers do not believe the Minotaur originates with the architecture of the Palace at Knossos. They point out the difference between a labyrinth, which has only one path to the center, and a maze, which can have many. Indeed it is tempting to see the labyrinth as relating to the maze as a symbol of the mysteries of life and death: An abstract concept connected with religious ritual, where the Minotaur waiting at the center of the labyrinth represents something concealed in the heart of all of us.

The story of the 14 youths brought from Athens to Knossos as a sacrifice to the Minotaur has always been thought of as simple myth. But there is archaeological evidence that perhaps gives some support to this horrific tale. In 1979, in the basement of the North House within the Knossos complex, excavators discovered 337 human bones. Analysis of these bones showed that they represented at least four individuals, all children. Further examination of the bones revealed the grisly detail that 79 of them showed traces of cut marks made by a fine blade, which bone specialist Loius Binford interpreted as being made to remove the flesh. Ruling out the possibilty that the defleshing of the bones was part of a burial rite (only lumps of flesh had been removed, not every piece), excavator of the site Peter Warren, Professor of Classical Archaeology at the University of Bristol, concluded that the children were probably ritually sacrificed and then eaten.

At the four-room sanctuary at Anemospilia, only 4.3 miles south of Knossos (first excavated in 1979 by J. Sakellarikas) another find suggestive of human sacrifice was made. When investigating the temple's western room, archaeologists found three skeletons. The first was an 18-year-old male lying on his right side on an altar in the center of the room, a bronze dagger at his chest, and his feet tied. Near to the altar there had once been a pillar with a channel running around its base, seemingly intended to catch blood dripping from a sacrifice. Examination of the dead youth's bones revealed that he had probably died from loss of blood. In the southwest corner of the room, the remains of a 28-year-old female were found sprawled across the floor, and near the altar the skeleton of a 5-foot 9-inch tall male in his late thirties was discovered. This man's hands were raised, as if trying to protect himself, and his legs had been broken by falling masonry. A further skeleton, too damaged to identify, was also found in the building. The temple was destroyed in a fire around 1600 B.C., which probably resulted from an earthquake. Three of these individuals had been killed by the collapsing roof and masonry of the upper walls, but it seems that the teenager was already dead by this time.

According to the archaeological evidence, human sacrifice does not seem to have been widespread on Minoan Crete. The examples cited may have been exceptions brought on by a desperate attempt to appease the gods in troubled times, probably during violent earthquake activity. A point worthy of note is that at both the North House at Knossos and at at the Anemospilia temple, the sacrifices were of young adults or children, bringing to mind the seven young men and seven young women sent by Athens to satisfy the Minotaur. Perhaps the origins of the Knossos labyrinth legend were partly in these horrific practices of human sacrifice, made in unstable times, when the safety of the entire community was thought to be at risk.

The Stone Sentinels of Easter Island

© *Thanassis Vembos.*
A group of moai on their ceremonial platforms.

The most isolated inhabited island in the world, Easter Island (nowadays called *Rapa Nui*, which means *Great Island*) is located in the southeast Pacific Ocean, 2,000 miles from the nearest population center. The island is roughly triangular in shape and composed of volcanic rock. It is most famous for its large number of enigmatic giant stone statues scattered along the coast, and perhaps less so for its undeciphered and mysterious script known as *Rongorongo*.

The original inhabitants of Easter Island called it *Te Pito O Te Henua* (Navel of the Earth), but who these first settlers were or where they came from are much debated subjects. Probably the most controversial theory about the peopling of the island was originated by the Norwegian explorer and archaeologist Thor Heyerdahl. According to Heyerdahl, Easter Island was partly settled by a pre-Incan society sailing from Peru in substantial ocean-going rafts, with the help of the prevailing westerly trade winds. In 1947, to prove it was theoretically possible to make it across the Pacific in such a vessel, Heyerdahl built a replica of one of these balsa wood crafts and named it the *Kon-Tiki*, after an Incan Sun God. Once out in the Pacific, Heyerdahl and his team sailed for 101 days across 4,349 miles of open sea before crashing into the reef at Raroia atoll, in the

Tuamotu Archipelago, east of Tahiti. In 1951, the documentary *Kon-Tiki*, relating the expedition, won an Academy Award. The *Kon-Tiki* expedition proved that it was technically possible for South American peoples to have crossed the Pacific in a raft and settled the Polynesian Islands. But there are one or two problems with Heyerdahl's experiment. The *Kon-Tiki* was a type of vessel copied from rafts in the 16th century A.D., after the sail had been introduced by the Spanish. So it is not certain how close his raft was in design to those in use 800 years before the appearance of the Spanish, when the supposed colonizing expeditions to the Pacific took place. Furthermore, when Heyerdahl first attempted to set out on his journey, the offshore currents were so strong that the *Kon-Tiki* needed to be towed out to sea a distance of 50 miles before it could be sailed.

Heyerdahl also included botanical, linguistic, and architectural evidence in his theory of a South American origin for the Easter Islanders, around A.D. 800. However, archaeological evidence gathered in the years since Heyerdahl made his daring voyage has all but disproved his hypothesis, especially as the settlement of the island was already complete by the time of the proposed trans-Pacific journey. So where did the first inhabitants of Easter Island come from? Due to its extremely isolated position, a voyage to Easter Island from anywhere would have taken at least two weeks, over thousands of miles of open sea. Such a journey clearly indicates a maritime people. Polynesian cultures were expert sailors and constructed huge ocean-going canoes and rafts, navigating by using the position of the stars,

wind direction, and the natural movements of birds and fish. Linguistic evidence points to the settlement of Rapa Nui by peoples from East Polynesia between A.D. 300 and A.D. 700, possibly from the Marquesas Islands or Pitcairn Island. The latter is the nearest inhabited land, lying 1,199 miles to the west. This colonization was probably part of a gradual eastward migration, originating in southeast Asia around 2000 B.C. A western origin is also indicated by an Easter Island myth. This myth describes how, around 1,500 years ago, a Polynesian king named Hotu Matua (the Great Parent) came to the island with his wife and family in a double canoe, by sailing in the direction of the sunrise from an unspecified Polynesian island. Just before he died, Hotu Matua traveled to the western extreme of Easter Island to look for the last time towards his homeland. Recent evidence from DNA studies has practically ruled out colonization by South Americans. Skeletons from burial sites on Easter Island have been found to contain a genetic marker, called the Polynesian Motif, proving that the Easter Islanders are descendents of settlers from eastern Polynesia, not South America.

The incredible Easter Island giant statues have puzzled explorers and archaeologists for hundreds of years. There are almost 900 of these statues, known by the islanders as *moai*, averaging 14 feet in height and 14 tons in weight, though the highest was almost 69 feet and weighed around 270 tons. These enigmatic monoliths were carved from hardened volcanic ash and consist of an elongated stylized human head, pointed chin, and a short body with arms lying at the sides. They were set up to face the interior of the island,

© *Thanassis Vembos.*
Detail of some Easter Island moai.

perhaps keeping a silent watch on the population. Some of the statues would originally have had their eyes colored using red and white stone and coral, and there are remaining examples today with their strange staring eyes intact. More than half of the 887 statues are distributed along the island's coast, while the remaining moai are still in Rano Raraku, the quarry where they were made, indicating a fairly sudden end to statue building. Most of the monoliths were erected on ceremonial structures known as *ahu*. These ahu were built from blocks of volcanic rock and consisted of platforms, ramps, and plazas. As many as 15 moai were placed on these structures, which functioned as religious centers for dances and ceremonies related to ancestor worship.

The majority of the moai were carved, transported, and erected in the period between A.D. 1100 and 1600, when the island was well-wooded, and had an estimated population of between 9,000 and 15,000. Most of the statues

were still upright when Dutch explorer Jakob Roggeveen arrived there (by chance) on Easter Sunday in 1722 (hence the name of Easter Island). English explorer and cartographer Captain James Cook also found many still standing when he landed at the island in 1774. One of the great mysteries of Easter Island is how its inhabitants managed to move and set up the giant stone statues. Jo Anne Van Tilburg, of the University of California, Los Angeles, is a specialist in Polynesian studies who has worked on Easter Island for more than 15 years. Using computer simulation, which included data on available manpower and materials, rock type, and the easiest routes for transportation— Van Tilburg arrived at a plausible hypothesis of how the statues were moved. She worked out that the giants would first have been laid on their backs on a wooden sledge and then moved on a wooden canoe ladder (logs spaced three feet apart over which the sledge could slide). Once the statues arrived at the ceremonial platforms, they were levered into an upright position, using the sledge to hold them in place. In 1999, she and a team of 73 people tested this theory with a considerable degree of success, showing that her method is the best suggestion yet for how the huge stone figures were transported and erected.

A much more difficult and complicated question is *why* the people of Rapa Nui undertook the enormous task of carving, transporting, and erecting these giant stone figures. Apart from the undeciphered Rongorongo script, which is probably no earlier than late-18th century, the Easter Islanders left no written record to help us understand their beliefs and the significance of the moai. Various theories have been put forward; perhaps they represent revered ancestors or powerful living chiefs. The statues must also have played an important role as status symbols, embodying the power and organization of the people who created them. Jo Anne Van Tilburg believes that the figures had a dual role. She thinks that they did not represent individual portraits of chiefs, but were standardized depictions of important rulers, as well as being mediators between the people, the chiefs, and the gods.

Easter Island once possessed a thick forest of palms, but by the time the Dutch arrived in 1722, it was a treeless landscape. Pollen analysis has shown that by as early as A.D. 1150 the lowlands of the island had practically been cleared of forest. As the trees vanished, considerable soil erosion took place, leading to problems in growing crops. This ecological collapse resulted in overpopulation, food shortages, civil war, and the eventual downfall of the Rapa Nui society. There is even some evidence of cannibalism from a few sites on the island. Eventually, all of the sacred statues on the coast were pulled down by the islanders themselves during intertribal warfare. Though the Rapa Nui used vast amounts of timber in the transport and setting up of their statues, in canoe building, and in clearing land for agriculture, they may not have been solely to blame for the deforestation. The Polynesian rat, used as a food source in the Pacific, seems to have contributed to the extinction of the native palm tree by eating the palm nuts thus preventing new trees from growing.

The first contact with Europeans proved to be a disaster for the Rapa Nui on almost the same scale as the collapse of their ecosystem. In raids between 1859 and 1862, Peruvian slave traders dragged off every able-bodied man and woman, probably around a thousand islanders, to work in mines on islands off the coast of Peru. After objections were raised by the Bishop of Tahiti, the Easter Islanders were eventually allowed to return home. But when those who had not already died of disease and overwork arrived back on Rapa Nui, they were carrying smallpox and leprosy. The diseases quickly took hold on the island, and by 1877, there were only 110 inhabitants left. As a result of this forced depopulation, a substantial part of the oral history and culture of the Easter Islanders was tragically lost.

In 1888, the island was annexed to Chile and the population subsequently rose again. Though Rapa Nui National Park was created by the Chilean government in 1935, the native inhabitants were confined to a reservation outside the capital, Hanga Roa, while the rest of the land was leased to ranchers who kept sheep. In 1964 an independence movement began, and by the 1980s, sheep ranching had been stopped and the entire island was declared a historic park. In 1992 it had a population of 2,770, which had reached 3,791 by 2002, most of whom live in the capital. Though the official language is Spanish, many native islanders still speak the Rapa Nui tongue. In 1995, Rapa Nui National Park was declared a World Heritage site by UNESCO, recognizing the considerable achievements of this unique and enigmatic culture.

The Lost Lands of Mu and Lemuria

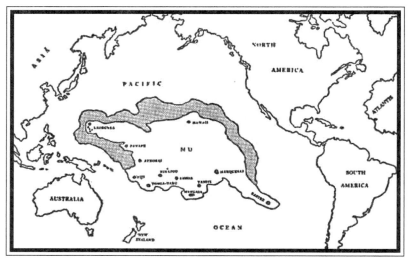

The geographical position of Mu, as shown in The Lost
Continent of Mu, *by James Churchward (1926).*

Lemuria and Mu are interchangeable names given to a lost land supposedly located somewhere in the southern Pacific Ocean. This ancient continent was apparently the home of an advanced and highly spiritual culture, perhaps the mother race of all mankind, but it sank beneath the waves many thousands of years ago as the result of a geological cataclysm of some kind. The thousands of rocky islands scattered throughout the Pacific (including Easter Island, Tahiti, Hawaii, and Samoa) are said to be the only surviving remains of this once great continent. This theory of a physical and spiritual lost land has been put forward by many different people, most notably in the mid-19th century by scientists in order to explain the unusual distribution of various animals and plants around the Indian and Pacific Oceans. In the late 19th century, occultist Madame Blavatsky approached the idea of Lemuria from a spiritual angle and influenced many thereafter to do the same, including psychic healer and prophet Edgar Cayce. The popularization of Lemuria/Mu as a physical place began in the 20th century, with ex-British army officer Colonel James Churchward, and the idea still has many adherents today. But is there any physical evidence to back up these claims of an ancient continent under the Pacific Ocean? Or should these lost homeland stories be interpreted in another way entirely, perhaps as the symbol of a mythical vanished Golden Age of man?

The land of Mu does not actually have a particularly long history, nor is it mentioned in any ancient mythologies, as some writers have suggested. The title *Mu* originated with eccentric amateur archaeologist Augustus Le Plongeon (1826–1908), who was the first to make photographical records of the ruins of the archaeological site of Chichén Itzá in Yucatán, Mexico. Plongeon's credibility was badly damaged by his attempted translation of a Mayan book known as the *Troana Codex* (also known as the *Madrid Codex*). In his books, *Sacred Mysteries Among the Mayans and Quiches* (1886) and *Queen Moo and the Egyptian Sphinx* (1896), Plongeon interpreted part of the text of the Troana Codex as revealing that the Maya of Yucatán were the ancestors of the Egyptians and many other civilizations. He also believed that an ancient continent, which he called Mu, had been destroyed by a volcanic eruption, the survivors of this cataclysm founding the Mayan civilization. Plongeon equates Mu with Atlantis and states that a "Queen Moo," originally from Atlantis, traveled to Egypt, where she became known as Isis, and founded the Egyptian civilization. However, Plongeon's interpretation of the Mayan book is considered by experts in Mayan archaeology and history as completely erroneus. Indeed, much of what he interpreted as hieroglyphics turned out to be ornamental design.

Lemuria, the alternative name for the lost continent, also originated in the 19th century. Ernst Heinrich Haeckel (1834–1919), a German naturalist and supporter of Darwin, proposed that a land bridge spanning the Indian Ocean (connecting Madagascar from India) could explain the widespread distribution of lemurs—small, primitive, tree-dwelling mammals found in Africa, Madagascar, India, and the East Indian archipelago. More bizarrely, Haeckel also suggested that lemurs were the ancestors of the human race, and that this land bridge was the "probable cradle of the human race." Other well-known scientists, such as the evolutionist T.H. Huxley and the naturalist Alfred Russell Wallace, had no doubt about the existence of a huge continent in the Pacific millions of years previously, which had been destroyed in a disastrous earthquake that submerged it beneath the waves, much as Atlantis was thought to have been drowned. Before the discovery of continental drift, it was not unusual in the mid- to late-19th century for scientists to propose submerged land masses and land bridges to explain the distribution of the world's flora and fauna. In 1864, the English zoologist Philip Lutley Sclater (1829–1913) gave the hypothetical continent the name *Lemuria* in an article "The Mammals of Madagascar" in *The Quarterly Journal of Science,* and since then it has stuck.

The lost civilization of Lemuria/Mu was brought dramatically back to public attention in 1931 with the publication of Colonel James Churchward's bizarre *The Lost Continent of Mu,* the first in a series of five books by Churchward about the lost continent. In the book, he claimed that the lost continent of Mu had once extended from an area north of Hawaii southwards as far as Fiji and Easter Island. According to Churchward, Mu was the original Garden of Eden, and a technologically advanced civilization that boasted 64 million inhabitants. Around 12,000 years ago, Mu was wiped out by an earthquake and submerged beneath the Pacific. Apparently Atlantis, a colony of Mu, was destroyed in the same way a thousand years later. All the world's major ancient civilizations, from the Babylonians and the Persians, to the Maya and the Egyptians, were the remains of the colonies of Mu. Churchward claimed he received this sensational information when, as a young officer in India during a famine in the 1880s, he became friendly with an Indian priest. This priest told Churchward that he and two cousins were the only survivors of a 70,000-year-old esoteric order that originated on Mu itself. This order was known as the Naacal Brotherhood.

The priest showed Churchward a number of ancient tablets written by the Naacal Order in a forgotten ancient language, supposed to be the original language of mankind, which he taught the officer to read. Churchward later asserted that certain stone artifacts recovered in Mexico contained parts of the *Sacred Inspired Writings of Mu,* perhaps taking ideas from Augustus Le Plongeon and his use of the Troana Codex to provide evidence for the existence of Mu. Unfortunately, Churchward never produced any evidence to back up his exotic claims: He never published translations of the enigmatic Naacal tablets, and his books—though they still have many followers today—are better read as entertainment than factual studies of Lemuria/Mu.

Zoologists and geologists now explain the distribution of lemurs and other plants and animals in the area of the Pacific and Indian Oceans to be the result of plate tectonics and continental drift. The theory of plate tectonics (and it is still a theory) affirms that moving plates of the Earth's crust supported on less rigid mantle rocks causes continental drift, volcanic and seismic activity, and the formation of mountain chains. The concept of continental drift was first proposed by German scientist Alfred Wegener in 1912, but the theory did not gain general acceptance in the scientific community for another 50 years. With recent understanding of plate tectonics, geologists now regard the theory of a sunken continent beneath the Pacific as an impossibility.

The idea of Lemuria as something other than a physical place, perhaps more akin to a lost spiritual homeland, seems to derive from the writings of colorful Russian occultist Helena Petrovska Blavatsky (1831–1891). Blavatsky was the co-founder (together with lawyer Henry Steel Olcott) of the Theosophical Society in New York, in 1875. The society was an esoteric order designed to study the mystical teachings of both Christianity and Eastern religions. In her massive tome, *The Secret Doctrine* (1888), Blavatsky describes a history originating millions of years ago with the Lords of Flame and goes on to discuss five Root Races which have existed on earth, each one dying out in an earth-shattering cataclysm. The third of these Root Races she called the Lemurian, who lived a million years ago, and who were bizarre telepathic giants, keeping dinosaurs as pets. The Lemurians eventually drowned when their continent was submerged beneath the Pacific Ocean. The progeny of the Lemurians was the fourth Root Race, the human Atlanteans, who were brought down by their use of black magic, when the continent of Atlantis sank beneath the waves 850,000 years ago. Present humanity represents the fifth Root Race.

Madame H.P. Blavatsky, in New York, 1877.

Blavatsky maintained that she learned all of this from *The Book of Dzyan*, supposedly written in Atlantis and shown to her by the Indian adepts known as Mahatmas. Blavatsky never claimed to have discovered Lemuria; in fact she refers to Philip Schlater coining the *name* Lemuria, in her writings. It has to be said that *The Secret Doctrine* is an extremely difficult book, a complex mixture of Eastern and Western cosmologies, mystical ramblings, and esoteric wisdom, much of it not meant to be taken literally. Blavatsky's is the first occult interpretation of Lemuria, but on one level it should not be equated with the physical continent proposed by Churchward. What Blavatsky and other occultists have since suggested concerning Lemuria could be partly interpreted as an ideal spiritual condition of the soul, a kind of lost spiritual land. Nevertheless, there are some psychics and prophets who even today regard the existence of ancient Lemuria or Mu as a physical reality. Indeed, there are a few who, when hypnotically regressed, have recalled former lives as citizens on the doomed continent.

This is not, however, quite the end of the story. In the last 20 years, submerged civilizations have once again been in the news, due to a number of intriguing underwater discoveries. In 1985 off the southern coast of Yonaguni Island, the western-most island of Japan, a Japanese dive tour operator discovered a previously unknown stepped pyramidal edifice. Shortly afterwards, Professor Masaki Kimura (a marine geologist at Ryukyu University in Okinawa) confirmed the existence of the 600 foot wide, 88 foot high structure. This rectangular stone ziggurat, part of a complex of underwater stone structures in the area which resemble ramps, steps, and terraces, is thought to date from somewhere between 3,000 to 8,000 years ago. Some have suggested that these ruins are the remains of a submerged civilization—and that the structures represent perhaps the oldest architecture in the world. Connections with Lemuria and Atlantis have also been mentioned. However, some geologists with knowledge of the area insist that the underwater buildings are natural, and similar to other known geological formations in the region. The debate is still continuing on these controversial structures.

In 2001, the remains of a huge lost city were located 118 feet underwater in the Gulf of Cambay, off the western coast of India. A year later, further acoustic imaging surveys were undertaken, and evidence was recorded for human settlement at the site, including the foundations of huge structures, pottery, sections of walls, beads, pieces of sculpture, and human bone. One of the wooden finds from the city has been given a radiocarbon date of 7500 B.C., which would make the site 4,000 years earlier than the oldest known civilization in India. Research is ongoing at this fascinating site, which—if the dates are proved correct—may one day radically alter our understanding of the world's first civilizations. Whether these underwater finds in the Pacific and Indian Oceans prove to be the remains of forgotten civilizations or not, one thing is certain: Man will always be searching for a lost homeland or a more spiritually satisfying ancient past. In this sense, Lemuria or Mu will always be more than just a physical place.

Stonehenge: Cult Center of the Ancestors

Photograph by the author.
The monumental ruins at Stonehenge brooding mysteriously on Salisbury Plain.

Looming like a group of huddled stone giants on Salisbury Plain, Wiltshire, in southern England, Stonehenge is perhaps the most recognizable ancient monument in the world. The name *Stonehenge* originates from Anglo-Saxon and roughly translates as *hanging stones*. But the history of the great monument dates back thousands of years before the Saxons came to Britain, sometime in the fifth century A.D. Its origins go back beyond the mysterious Celtic Druids of the last few centuries B.C., before iron was known in Europe, and before the Great Pyramid was erected in the sands of Egypt. Who built this enigmatic stone monument and what role did it play in the prehistoric landscape of England and Europe all those thousands of years ago?

What visitors see today when they visit Stonehenge is a circular setting of large standing stones surrounded by earthworks, the remnants of the last in a series of monuments erected on the site between c. 3100 B.C. and 1600 B.C. During this period, Stonehenge was built in three broad construction phases, although there is evidence for human activity on the site both before and after these dates. In fact, one of the most important and fascinating discoveries ever made in the area of

Stonehenge was that of four large Mesolithic pits or post holes dating to between 8500 and 7650 B.C., found beneath the modern carpark at the site. These huge post holes had a diameter of around 2.4 feet, and had once held pine posts. Three of the holes were aligned east to west, suggesting a ritual function—it has been suggested that they may have held totem poles, and indeed it is difficult to see what other purpose they could have served. The area around Stonehenge is full of prehistoric monuments, a number of which were constructed in the early Neolithic period (c. 4000 B.C.–3000 B.C.) and thus predate the Stonehenge monument. Examples include the long barrow (communal burial chamber) at Winterbourne Stoke, 1.4 miles away; the causewayed enclosure (a type of large prehistoric earthwork) known as Robin Hood's Ball, 1.2 miles northwest of Stonehenge; and the Lesser Cursus (a long, narrow, rectangular earthwork enclosure) 1,968 feet to the north. Thus, when the builders of the first stage of construction at Stonehenge began work, they were already operating in a sacred landscape, one that had seen ritual use for more than 5,000 years.

The first of Stonehenge's three construction phases was begun around 3100 B.C. and consisted of a circle of timber posts surrounded by a ditch and bank. This henge, (henge used in the archaeological sense to mean a circular or oval-shaped flat area enclosed by a boundary earthwork) measured approximately 360 feet in diameter, and possessed a large entrance to the northeast and another smaller one to the south. This monument was dug by hand using deer antlers and the shoulder blades of oxen or cattle. Modern excavations of the ditch have recovered antlers used in the construction that were deliberately left behind by the builders of this monument. One odd fact about this phase is that there were other animal bones, mainly from cattle, placed in the bottom of the ditch, which proved to be 200 years older than the antler tools used to dig the structure. It seems that the people who buried the items kept them for some time before burial; perhaps the bones were sacred objects removed from a previous ritual location and brought to Stonehenge. There is little remaining evidence for Phase II at Stonehenge, though judging by finds of cremated bones from at least 200 bodies, the site must have functioned as a cremation cemetary.

Phase III at the site, beginning around 2600 B.C., involved the rebuilding of the simple earth and timber henge in stone. Two concentric circles of 80 bluestone pillars were erected at the center of the monument. These stones, weighing about 4 tons each, were carved and transported from the Preseli Hills, in Pembrokeshire, southwest Wales, and brought by a route at least 186 miles long. Apart from the bluestones, a 16 foot long blue-gray sandstone, now known as the Altar Stone, was brought to Stonehenge from near Milford Haven on the coast to the south of the Preseli Hills. How the bluestones arrived on Salisbury Plain is a subject of much controversy, though most archaeologists nowadays believe that they were brought there by man. The most obvious way for the builders of Stonehenge to transport the stones would have been to drag them down to the sea at

Milford Haven by roller and sledge, and then float them to Stonehenge on rafts by sea and river—an incredible achievement of organization and dedication. An experiment to duplicate this feat was undertaken in 2001, when volunteers managed to pull a 3-ton stone down to the sea from the Preseli Hills in a wooden sledge on rollers, but when the stone was placed on the raft it slipped into the sea and sank. Intriguingly, an old legend held that Stonehenge originated with Merlin the wizard, who had a huge structure known as the Giant's Dance magically transported from Ireland. Could the journey of the bluestones form Wales be a disorted memory of Stonehenge originating in the west?

It was also in Phase III at Stonehenge that the northeastern entrance to the enclosure was widened so that it precisely aligned with the midsummer sunrise and midwinter sunset of the period. Another feature added to the Stonehenge landscape during this phase was the Avenue, a ceremonial pathway consisting of a parallel pair of ditches and banks stretching for 1.86 miles from the monument down to the River Avon.

Around 2300 B.C. the bluestones were dug up and replaced by enormous sarsen stones brought from the Marlborough Downs, 20 miles away. The sarsens, each around 13.5 feet high, 6.8 feet wide, and weighing around 25 tons, were arranged in a 108 foot diameter circle with lintels (horizontal stones) spanning the tops. Within this circle a horseshoe-shaped setting of five trilithons (two large stones set upright to support a third on their top), of dressed sarsen stone, was added, its open end facing northeast. The enormous stones, which made up the central horseshoe arrangement of 10 uprights and five lintels, weighed up to 50 tons each. Later in this period, between 2280 to 1930 B.C., the bluestones were re-erected and arranged at least three times, finally forming an inner circle and horseshoe between the Sarsen Circle and the Trilithons, mirroring the two arrangements of sarsen stones. It is

Photograph by the author.
Detail of Stonehenge, showing the huge sarsen stones.

thought that more bluestones were transported from Wales to the site at this time. Between 2000 and 1600 B.C. a double ring of pits, known as the Y and Z holes, were dug outside the outermost sarsen circle, possibly to take another setting of stones. However, for whatever reason, no stones were added and the pits were allowed to silt up naturally. After 1600 B.C. there was no further construction at Stonehenge, and the monument appears to have been abandoned. Nevertheless, the site was still occasionally visited, as is evidenced by finds of Iron Age pottery, Roman coins, and the burial of a decapitated Saxon man dated to the seventh century A.D.

There has been considerable speculation as to how Stonehenge was built. An experiment in the 1990s showed that a team of 200 people, using a wooden sledge on laid timber rails covered with grease, could have transported all 80 sarsens from the Marlborough Downs to Stonehenge in two years, or longer if the work was seasonal. The experiment illustrated that the maneuvering of the stones into position could have been accomplished using timber A-frames to raise the stones, which could then have been hauled upright by teams of people using ropes. The lintels may have been raised up gradually on timber platforms and levered into position when the primitive scaffolding reached the top of the upright stones. A fascinating aspect of the construction of Stonehenge is that the stones were worked using carpentry techniques. After being hammered to size using stone balls known as *mauls*, examples of which have been found at the site, the stones were fashioned with

mortise and tenon joints so that the lintels could rest securely on top of the uprights. The lintels themselves were joined together using another woodworking method known as the tongue-in-groove joint.

Much more interesting than how Stonehenge was built is *why* it was built. Unfortunately, for such an important structure the archaeological finds from Stonehenge have been relatively meager. This is partly due to the fact that until the last couple of decades research at the site had been, on the whole, poorly performed and insufficiently documented. Skeletons were lost or seriously damaged, artifacts misplaced, and excavation notes destroyed. Despite these losses, the evidence from surviving burials discovered at or near the site gives a fascinating insight into the lives of Early Bronze Age peoples in the area.

The main burials at Stonehenge are all broadly contemporary with each other, dating from 2400 B.C.–2150 B.C. (the Early Bronze Age period). Examination of a skeleton buried in the outer ditch of the monument revealed that the man had been shot at close

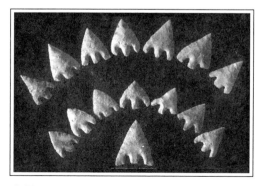

© *Wessex Archaeology*
Flint arrowheads found with the buried Archer.

range by up to six arrows, probably by two people, one shooting from the left, the other from the right. Was this an execution or some form of human sacrifice? Another astonishing burial was found in 2002 at Amesbury, 2.8 miles southeast of Stonehenge, and has become known as either the Amesbury Archer or the King of Stonehenge. The rich goods found with this burial indicate a high-status individual, and include five Beaker pots, 16 beautifully worked flint arrowheads, several boar tusks, two sandstone wristguards (to protect the wrists from the bow string of a bow and arrow), a pair of gold hair ornaments, three tiny copper knives, and a flint-knapping kit and metal-working tools. Not only are the gold objects the oldest ever found in Britain, but this person may have been one of the earliest metalwokers in the islands. Tests on the skeleton show that the Archer was a strongly built man aged between 35 and 45, though he had an abscess on his jaw and had suffered an accident, which had torn his left knee cap off. But the most surprising element of the burial was yet to come.

Research using oxygen isotope analysis on the Archer's tooth enamel found that he had grown up in the Alps region, in either Switzerland, Austria, or Germany. Analysis of the copper knives showed that they had come from Spain and France. This is incredible evidence for contact between cultures in Europe 4,200 years ago. Could the unusually rich burial of the King of Stonehenge, obviously an important person of high rank, mean that he played an important part in the construction of the first stone-built monument on the site? A second male burial, dating from the same period as the Archer, was located near to his grave. This skeleton, which bone analysis has shown may be the Archer's son, had been buried with a pair of gold hair ornaments in the same style as the Archer's, though for some reason these had been left inside the man's jaw. Oxygen isotope analysis revealed that this man had grown up in the area around Salisbury Plain, though his late teens may have been spent in the Midlands or northeast Scotland.

The Boscombe Bowmen are a group of Early Bronze Age burials, found in a single grave at Boscombe Down, close to Stonehenge. Known as bowmen due to the amount of flint arrowheads found in their grave, the burial consists of seven individuals: three children, a teenager, and three men, all apparently related to each other. Finds from the grave are similar in character to that of the Amesbury Archer and include an unusually high amount of Beaker pottery. Again, it was the teeth that provided the clue as to where these people originated. In this case, the men grew up in Wales but migrated to southern Britain in childhood. Given that the Boscombe Bowmen were roughly contemporary with the transport and erection of the Welsh bluestones at Stonehenge, it is believed by many researchers that they may have accompanied the stones on their 186 mile trek to Salisbury Plain. The burials of the Amesbury Archer and the Boscombe Bowmen, then, offer fascinating evidence for some of the people who were involved in the task of constructing Stonehenge, but what purpose did the enigmatic and unique monument serve?

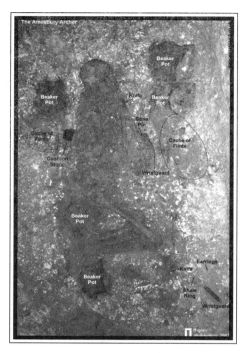

The Amesbury Archer

Beaker Pot

Knife

Beaker Pot

Beaker Pot

Bone Pin

Cache of Flints

Cache of Flints

Cushion Stone

Wristguard

Beaker Pot

Beaker Pot

Earrings

Knife

Shale Ring

Wristguard

© *Wessex Archaeology*
Detail of the Archer burial with
interpretation of the burial goods.

Because Stonehenge is aligned to the midsummer sunrise/midwinter sunset, many researchers (most notably English-born astronomer Gerald Hawkins) have claimed that a number of astronomical alignments are present at the site. However, subsequent analysis of the data assembled to support Hawkins' theory has shown that many of the supposed astronomical alignments were arrived at by joining together features from different periods, as well as natural pits and holes that were not part of the monument.

The most important thing to remember about Stonehenge is that although it is a unique structure, it was not an isolated monument. Stonehenge grew to be the focal point of a vast prehistoric ceremonial landscape, as can be seen from the numerous barrow (burial mound) cemeteries that were built around the monument. We have already seen that the Salisbury Plain landscape had been sacred for thousands of years before the building of Stonehenge. But in what sense was it sacred? One theory, put forward by English archaeologist Mike Parker Pearson and Ramilisonina, an archaeologist from Madagascar, used modern anthropological evidence to suggest that for the Stonehenge people, timber may have been associated with the living, and the permanence of stone associated with the ancestors. As there are two important timber henge sites close to Stonehenge—Durrington Walls and Woodhenge—Pearson and Ramilisonina hypothesized a ritual route for funeral processions, which travelled down the River Avon from wood-built Durrington Walls in the east at sunrise, and then along the Avenue up to Stonehenge, the realm of the ancestors, in the west at sunset. This would have been a sacred journey from wood to stone via water, a symbolic passage from life to death. The paucity of archaeological finds from the central area inside Stonehenge certainly suggests that only a few people had access to the monument; not just anyone could walk inside. Whether these selected few were priests, or included the Amesbury Archer, it is difficult to tell. But the stone structure as a metaphor for the ancestors makes a lot of sense, though it is likely that no single explanation can ever do justice to the remarkable people who built Stonehenge.

El Dorado: The Search for the Lost City of Gold

© Carlos A. Gomez-Gallo.
Lake Guatavita, allegedly the scene of the Golded Man Ceremony of the Muisca Tribe.

"Over the Mountains
Of the Moon,
Down the Valley of the Shadow,
Ride, boldly ride,"
The shade replied
"If you seek for Eldorado!"
"El Dorado" by Edgar Allan Poe (1849)

A city of untold wealth buried deep in the heart of the Amazonian rainforest, a Mexican king or Gilded Man covered from head to foot in powdered gold, an idea, a quest for a Holy Grail always just out of reach of the seeker, a destroyer of lives, and a giver of dreams. El Dorado has been and still is all of these things. In the 16th century, Spanish conquistadors undertook journeys fraught with danger in the hope of glimpsing the fabled city of gold, and English explorer Sir Walter Raleigh wrote in 1596 that he knew its exact location. Even 21st century explorers have not given up hope of finding a physical El Dorado, perhaps in the dense jungles of Peru or at the bottom of a mysterious lake in Columbia. Are all these efforts in vain? Is there an El Dorado to find or does the city only exist in the mythology of the Native American peoples of Colombia?

The legend of the Golden Man (*El Dorado* in Spanish) was well-known in Colombia and Peru when the Spanish arrived in the early 16th century. Some researchers believe that the legend is based on a ceremony performed by an isolated tribe called the Muisca, a highly developed gold-working community who lived around 8,200 feet up in the Andes Mountains. Apparently the ceremony (for the appointing of a new king or chief priest) took place at Lake Guatavita, north of present-day Bogotá. At the beginning of the ritual, the new ruler made offerings to the god of the lake, after which the tribe constructed a raft from rushes and filled it with incense and perfumes. The naked body of the new king was then covered with balsam gum, and a fine gold dust spread on top of it. When the chief was ready, the tribe placed him on the raft along with a great pile of gold and emeralds, and four subject chiefs who brought along gold crowns, pendants, earrings, and other precious items. To the accompaniment of music from trumpets and flutes, the raft left the shore and sailed out into the middle of the lake. Once the vessel reached the center, all was silent, and the king and his subjects cast all their riches into the water as an offering. The new chief was now recognized as lord and king.

John Hemming notes in his book, *The Search for El Dorado*, that in the 17th century it was common among tribes living along the Orinoco River in Venezuela to anoint their whole bodies with a specially made oil, which served as clothing and protection against mosquitoes. On certain feast days the people covered the oil with various multicolored drawings. Even today, tribes of the Amazon paint their bodies with vegetable dyes. If there was an abundance of gold among the tribe it is certainly plausible that it could have been used as body decoration. Perhaps there was some truth in the Gilded Man legend after all, but could it be the origin of the El Dorado story?

There are, however, other elements involved in the beginnings of El Dorado. Another rumor circulating among the Spanish at the time of the conquest was that a rebel group of Inca warriors had managed to elude the conquistadors and escape to the mountains of Venezuela. The rebels allegedly took large amounts of gold and precious stones with them and founded a secret new empire. There were also various stories told by captured Indians of a rich land lying beyond the mountains east of Quito, the modern capital of Ecuador, where the people strolled about covered in gold ornaments. In a letter written in 1542 to Charles V, King of Spain, conquistador Gonzalo Pizarro refers to this rich land as Lake El Dorado, perhaps a reference to the Golden Man ceremonies of the Muisca. Pizarro was one of a number of Spanish invaders who organized expeditions to search for the fabulous lost city. Another element in the El Dorado story is the interest the Spanish had in the cinnamon the Incas used. In Europe, spices were highly valued as a method of preserving food (in the days before refrigeration), and huge profits could be made from trading in the commodity.

The conquistadors found out from the natives that the spice originated with tribes located east of Quito. In February 1541, an expedition headed by Gonzalo Pizarro with Francisco de Orellana as his lieutenant, and including 220 Spanish adventurers and 4,000 mountain Indians serving as porters, left Quito in search of cinnamon and the fabled El Dorado. During his obsessive quest for these valuable commodities, Pizarro would often brutally torture Indians until they told him what he wanted about the existence of hidden gold and cinnamon trees. The expedition followed the courses of the Coca and Napo rivers, but soon began to run short of provisions, and before long more than half of the Spanish and 3,000 of the Indians had perished. In February 1542 the expedition split into two parts, with Francisco de Orellana pursuing a course down the Napo, and Pizarro eventually deciding to struggle back overland to Quito. From the Napo, Orellana and his men finally found their way to the Amazon and sailed its entire length to the Atlantic Ocean, an incredible achievement. But they never found El Dorado.

But this did not deter the Spanish. Driven by their lust for gold and spices, a series of adventurers spent much of the 16th century in search of the vast treasure they believed existed in some hidden location in the jungles or mountains of Ecuador or Columbia. In 1568, wealthy explorer and conquistador Gonzalo Jiménez de Quesada received a commission from King Philip to explore the southern Llanos, a vast expanse of tropical grassland plain situated in Colombia. In December 1569, the expedition, which included 300 Spaniards and 1,500 Indians, set off from the Columbian capital of Bogotá in search of El Dorado. But the expedition, confronted with the harsh mosquito-ridden environment of the dismal swamps and the blankness of the dusty plains, was a disaster. Three years later, Quesada arrived back in Bogotá accompanied by just 64 Spaniards and four Indians.

The original myth of the Muisca ceremony at Lake Guatavita combined with the Lake El Dorado of Gonzalo Pizarro convinced many explorers that the lost city may in fact be located near a lake. English explorer and Courtier Sir Walter Raleigh launched another search for El Dorado in 1595, in an attempt to restore lost favor with Queen Elizabeth I. His expedition sailed along the Orinoco River for many weeks, but found nothing. However, in his book *The Discovery of the Large, Rich and Beautiful Empire of Guyana with a Relation to the Great and Golden City of Manoa,* Raleigh claimed that El Dorado was a city on Lake Parima on the Orinoco in Guiana (modern-day Venezuela). Raleigh's map showing the the city on the lake was so convincing that the mythical Lake Parima was marked on maps of South America for the next 150 years. It was not until the early 19th century, with German naturalist and explorer Alexander von Humboldt, that it was proved that neither the lake nor the city had ever existed.

Though Lake Parima was entirely mythical, there was never any doubt about the existence of Lake Guatavita. Perhaps *this* was, after all, the location of El Dorado. As soon as the Spanish invaders learned that the Muisca deposited precious objects in Lake Guatavita as offerings, they immediately set about organizing the draining of the lake. Wealthy merchant Antonio de Sepúlveda used a workforce of Indians to cut a trench to drain the lake in 1562, but only succeeded in lowering its level slightly. De Sepúlveda did, however, find a number of gold discs and emeralds in the mud at the lake's edge. Nevertheless, the total haul from the drainage was recorded as only "232 pesos and 10 grams of good gold." Another attempt to drain the lake in 1823 by Don 'Pepe' Paris, a prominent citizen of Bogotá, found no precious gold artifacts. Further drainage projects in the early- to mid-20th century discovered a few items of interest, but nothing similar to what would be expected from the repeated deposits of gold supposedly made in the sacred lake. Finally, in 1965 the Colombian Government brought an end to these efforts, which by then had visibly scarred the lake, and put Lake Guatavita under national protection.

In 1969, an exquisitely detailed solid gold model of a raft 10.5 inches in length was found by two farm workers in a cave near the town of Pasca, close to Bogotá. The model raft contains a regal figure towering above 10 attendants, all wearing elaborate head-dresses. It has been interpreted by many as confirming the existence of the Muisca rite at Lake Guatavita. In fact, an almost identical raft was found on the edge of Lake Siecha, south of the village of Guatavita, during a drainage attempt in 1856. This golden raft subsequently came into the hands of a certain Salomon Koppel who sold it to the Imperial Museum of Berlin, from where it disappeared after World War I. These rafts are certainly evidence of a ceremony taking place on a lake, though the Muisca culture not only venerated water, but mountains, stars, planets, and ancestors as well. More importantly, the tribe did not actually produce gold themselves; they obtained it through trade with other tribes. Consequently, their gold objects are small and usually very thin, as is the surviving golden raft. It is unlikely that the Muisca would have possessed gold in enough quantities to either cover their chief in gold dust or tip prodigal amounts into the lake during the ceremony referred to in the myth.

Nevertheless, modern explorers continue to be fascinated by the possibility of finally locating El Dorado. In 2000, the American explorer Gene Savoy announced that he had discovered the lost pre-Columbian city of Cajamarquilla deep in virgin rainforest in eastern Peru. Some members of his team claimed that the site, which includes temples and burial sites, could possibly be the remains of the fabled El Dorado. A Polish-Italian journalist and explorer named Jacek Palkiewicz was not quite so reticent when in 2002 he announced that his expedition had located El Dorado beneath a lake on a plateau next to Manu National Park, southeast of Lima in Peru. Investigations are apparently still ongoing in both of these cases.

Despite more than 450 years of searching, the discovery of the fabulous wealth of El Dorado seems to be no closer than it was for the Spanish of the mid-16th century. The term itself has become a metaphor for the single-minded pursuit of wealth that is always just out of reach, constantly around the next corner. No doubt there are lost pre-Hispanic cities still to be discovered in the vastness of the Amazon rainforest, but El Dorado, whether a Golden Man or a Golden City, only exists in the minds of men obsessed with discovering the quickest path to riches.

The Lost City of Helike

© *Dr. A. Siokou*
The plain of Helike and the Gulf of Corinth from the mountains.

The ancient city of Helike, situated on the southern shore of the Gulf of Corinth, roughly 93 miles west of Athens, was originally founded in the Early Bronze Age (2600–2300 B.C.). The first prehistoric settlement was submerged beneath the waves about 2,000 years before the city was destroyed. In the eighth century B.C. Homer wrote of Helike sending ships to the Trojan War under the command of Agamemnon. By the time of its destruction in the fourth century B.C., Helike had become a wealthy and successful metropolis, the leader of the 12 cities of the first Achaean league (a union of local city states), and founder of colonies abroad such as Priene, on the coast of Asia Minor, and Sybaris in Southern Italy. Helike's temple and sanctuary of Helikonian Poseidon was famous throughout Classical Greece, and was rivaled only by the Oracle at Delphi, across the Gulf of Corinth.

But all this was to change one terrible night in the winter of 373 B.C. For a period of five days, citizens of the city gazed in bewilderment as snakes, mice, martens, and other creatures fled from the coast and made for higher ground. Then, on the fifth night, "immense columns of flame" (now known as earthquake lights) were witnessed in the sky, followed by a massive earthquake, and a towering 32 foot high tsunami wave. The coastal plain was submerged, and as Helike collapsed, the tsunami rushed in and dragged its buildings and its inhabitants out with the retreating waters. The city and its surroundings disappeared beneath the sea, along with 10 Spartan ships that had been ancored in the harbor. The neighboring city of Boura, and the Temple of Apollo at Delphi, were also destroyed.

When a rescue party arrived the next morning, nothing remained of the once great city but the tops of the trees in Poseidon's sacred grove, peeping above the waves. Perhaps because Helike had been a revered center for worship of Poseidon (the god of earthquakes and the sea), a tradition originated among its jealous neighbors that the city's destruction was punishment sent by the angry god for desecrating his sanctuary. Following the disaster, the former territory of Helike was doled out between its neighbors, with the city of Aegio taking over leadership of the Achaean League. Hundreds of years later a Roman city was built on the site, which also appears to have been partly destroyed by an earthquake in the fifth century A.D. For centuries after the disaster ancient writers such as Pliny, Ovid, and Pausanias reported that the submerged ruins of Helike could be glimpsed on the sea floor. The Greek scientific writer, astronomer, and poet, Eratosthenes (276–194 B.C.) visited the site and recorded reports by local ferrymen of an upright bronze statue of Poseidon submerged in an inland lagoon, where it often trapped the nets of fishermen. But soon afterwards the area silted over and the location became lost.

In 1861, German archaeologists visiting the region obtained a bronze coin of Helike featuring a splendid head of Poseidon, but nothing else surfaced from the ancient site. Ancient writers had all stated that the remains of the city lay submerged beneath the Corinthian Gulf, but for decades numerous expeditions searched for it without success. In 1988 the Helike Project was formed to locate the lost city, but a 1988 sonar survey under their auspices revealed no trace beneath the sea. Consequently, director of the Helike Project, archaeologist Dora Katsonopoulou, and Dr. Steven Soter, of the American Museum of Natural History, decided to investigate the coastal plain. In 2001, a few feet beneath the mud and gravel, the team discovered ruins of Classical buildings, which turned out to be the remains of the city of Helike destroyed by the earthquake of 373 B.C. The location of the ruins lay almost half a mile inland, which explains why no one had found them beneath the sea. Analyses of the microscopic organisms preserved in the layer of fine dark clay covering the buildings revealed that the site had been drowned by a shallow inland lagoon, which had subsequently silted up. The discovery of sea shells and the possible remains of seaweed on the site are evidence that Helike's ruins were probably at one time beneath the sea.

The remains of one Classical building graphically illustrated the fate of the city. One of its walls had collapsed in a seaward direction, clear evidence to support destruction by the backwash of a giant wave. Amongst finds of demolished walls, pottery fragments, and terracotta idols, the excavators found a mint silver coin with a representation of Apollo wearing a laurel wreath, cast in the neighboring town of Sikyon a few decades before the earthquake struck. The sad fate of this once great Classical city is thought by many to have been the inspiration for the legend of Atlantis, first recorded by Athenian philosopher Plato a few years after the Helike earthquake, in 360 B.C. A BBC Horizon documentary *Helike— The Real Atlantis*, made in 2002, makes this claim for the site.

The area around ancient Helike is one of the most seismically active in Europe, and at least 4,000 years of ancient settlements on the site have flourished and been destroyed by earthquakes. So it is hardly surprising that the ancient city was the center of a cult dedicated to Poseidon, the god of earthquakes. In August 1817, an earthquake preceded by a sudden explosion destroyed five villages in the place where Helike once stood. In 1861, 8 miles of coastline sunk about 6 feet, and a 597 foot wide coastal belt of coast was submerged beneath the waves. In June 1995, while the Helike Project team were working in the area, an earthquake of 6.2 on the Richter scale struck, killing 10 people in the adjacent town of Aigion, and demolishing a hotel in modern Eliki, killing 16.

Dr. Steven Soter collected many descriptions of odd events preceding this quake, which have overtones of the ancient accounts of the earthquake that destroyed Helike. People heard fierce winds when the air was still outside, dogs howled unaccountably, there were subterranean explosions,

© *Dr. A. Siokou*
The Helike Delta and the Gulf of Corinth.

strange lights in the sky, and fire-balls. Huge numbers of octopuses were seen by local fishermen and, the night before the earthquake, numerous dead mice were found on the road, all of which had been run over by cars while trying to make their escape into the mountains. These incidents are reminiscent of the behavior of animals in the 2004 tsunami that struck Sri Lanka, southern India, and Thailand, caused by a huge 9.15 Richter earthquake in the Indian Ocean. In Sri Lanka, where tens of thousands of people lost their lives, animals appear to have fled inland before the tsunami struck. Even though the tsunami caused a heavy loss of human life in the area of Yala National Park, Sri Lanka's biggest wildlife reserve, no dead animals were found. Experts believe that animals possess a sixth sense with which they sense a natural disaster. This is certainly suggested by their behavior before the Helike earthquakes.

One of the most significant finds from the Helike excavations was of paving stones from what was probably a Classical road. The archaeologists from the Helike Project now hope that following this road will lead them nearer to the heart of the ancient site. However, in terms of finding more complete remains of the Classical city, there is the important question of whether such an immensely destructive tsunami would have left anything behind for the archaeologists to find. Nevertheless, the team from the Helike Project are confident that a major part of the city will still be located. Someone who would certainly have supported this belief was the late Spyridon Marinatos, discoverer of the prehistoric town of Akrotiri on the Greek island of Santorini. One of the earliest modern searchers for the lost city, Marinatos once speculated that hoards of bronze and marble Classical sculptures could lay entombed in the ruins of the city, and fully expected the

© Dr. A. Siokou
The plain of Helike, looking towards the mountains.

discovery of an ancient town surpassing even the archaeological riches of Pompeii.

Apart from the constant danger of further earthquakes in the area, the Helike Project now faces a further threat to the site. In Roman times, a road running from Corinth to the city of Patras passed through Helike. Traces of this road have been found in excavations. Recently, the Greek National Railway began laying a new rail line which will connect Athens with Patras. Trains are currently operating on this railway as far as Corinth, and the line is expected to reach Patras by 2010. At the moment, the route of this rail line is scheduled to run right through the center of the ancient site, probably in the next two or three years. Thus, the remains of ancient Helike will be destroyed before excavations have had the chance to uncover what would surely be priceless evidence of life in prehistoric and Classical Greece.

In order to help protect this important archaeological site from destruction by the railway, the World Monuments Fund has included Helike in its List of 100 Most Endangered Sites. But land along the coast in the region where the Project plans to excavate is being developed quickly, and Dora Katsonopoulou has appealed to the Greek Ministry of Culture to make the area an archaeological zone where new construction is forbidden. Unfortunately, at present, the Greek Archaeological Service and the Greek Ministry of Culture have not acknowledged the importance of the site. Hopefully, the significance of the excavations will be realized before it's too late, and the lost city of Helike will not become lost forever.

The Grand Canyon: Hidden Egyptian Treasure?

Photograph by Scott Catron (GNU Free Documentation License).
View of Grand Canyon from Tiyo Point, North Rim.

On April 5th, 1909, an anonymous front-page story appeared in the Phoenix newspaper the *Arizona Gazette,* with the title "Explorations in the Grand Canyon." The article described a Smithsonian Institute-funded archaeological expedition "under the direction of Prof. S. A. Jordan" accompanied by an explorer in the service of the *Smithsonian* named G.E. Kinkaid. The *Gazette* claimed that the team had found a vast underground citadel within the Grand Canyon which was "not only the oldest archaeological discovery in the United States, but one of the most valuable in the world."

Kinkaid's narration of the discovery in the *Gazette* described how he made the discovery while traveling alone in a wooden boat down the Colorado River from Green River, Wyoming, to Yuma, looking for minerals. According to the article, about 42 miles up from the El Tovar Crystal canyon, (probably around Marble Canyon, in the area of the present-day Navajo Indian reservation), Kinkaid noticed "stains in the sedimentary formation about 2,000 feet above the river bed." He then, with great difficulty, made his way up the canyon wall to arrive at a small cave opening, which had steps leading down from it. Kinkaid then passed through the entrance, and at a cross chamber 100 feet from the entrance, he found a carved image of a cross-legged idol, which he thought resembled Buddha and was probably of Tibetan origin. Several hundred feet along the 12 foot wide passageway he discovered a crypt containing mummies, one of which he stood up and photographed by flashlight. There were numerous side passages, rooms, and various artifacts, including copper tools, urns, and cups of copper and gold, enamelled and glazed pottery vessels, engraved yellow stones strewn all over the floors, and an unknown grey metal resembling platinum. He also found hieroglyphics, which he believed were of an "Egyptian or Oriental type."

Kinkaid surmised that more than 50,000 people could have been comfortably accommodated within the caverns. The newspaper mentioned that some of the artifacts had been shipped off to Washington, D.C., and that the Smithsonian Institute, under the direction of Prof. S.A. Jordan, was carefully investigating the citadel. The discoveries, they claimed, "almost conclusively prove that the race which inhabited this mysterious cavern...was of oriental origin, possibly from Egypt, tracing back to Ramses."

What is the truth behind this amazing story? Is there any other evidence apart from this isolated and anonymous newspaper article? If fact, there *is* a previous article in the same newspaper from March 12, 1909, also relating to G.E. Kinkaid. The article gives a short description of Kinkaid's trip down the Colorado and mentions "some interesting archaeological discoveries" being made, but nothing is indicated of the staggering nature of these finds. For some reason, the *Arizona Gazette* never followed up the story. After May 1909 there is complete silence on the subject until the article was rediscovered by ancient mysteries writer David Hatcher Childress and published in the conspiracy magazine *Nexus* in 1993. It subsequently found its way onto the Internet, and the Egyptians in the Grand Canyon story has now been used by hundreds of Websites. Most of these are merely reprints of Childress' *Nexus* article, and all derive from the original newspaper story. In fact, since 1909, no further evidence at all for truth of the claims has been added to the original source.

In January 2000, researchers into the mystery contacted the Smithsonian Institution on the subject. They were told that over the years the Institution had received many inquiries about the 1909 newspaper article, but that its Department of Anthropology could find no mention in its files of a Professor Jordan, Kinkaid, or a lost Egyptian civilization in Arizona. Researchers did turn up mention of an archaeologist called Prof. S.A. Jordon, spelled with an *o*, not an *a*, but apparently he was European, not American. However, for some researchers this is proof that the entire discovery has been covered up. They point to the many unexplored caves, tunnels, and holes in the canyon and the fact that much of the area around where Kinkaid allegedly made his discovery is now government property and closed to the public. This is certainly true of the 400 foot deep Stanton's Cave, which, when excavated, was found to contain thousands of ancient Indian artifacts, and the remains of 10,000 year old giant California Condors. It is a significant archaeological and palaeontological site, and is now listed on the National Register of Historic Places. This cave, along with others in the area, is now sealed of from the public with a huge steel gate. The sinister reason behind this? To protect the colony of Townsend's big-eared bats living in the cave from being disturbed by visitors.

Another curious feature of the Grand Canyon—which appears to link it to the 1909 newspaper story—is the wide variety of oriental and Egyptian names given to many of its peaks and buttes, particularly in the area of Kinkaid's strange caverns. Around Ninety-four Mile Creek and Trinity Creek there are names such as Isis Temple, Tower of Set, Tower of Ra, Horus Temple, Osiris Temple, while in the Haunted Canyon area there are the Cheops Pyramid, the Buddha Cloister, Buddha Temple, Manu Temple, and Shiva Temple. Perhaps the mysterious origin of these names gives a clue to the location of Kinkaid's hidden treasure?

Unfortunately, the explanation for these names is far more prosaic. It comes in the form of Clarence E. Dutton, Captain of Ordnance in the U.S. Army, whose most important work, *The Tertiary History of the Grand Canyon District*, appeared in 1882. It was Dutton who, noting the similarities between the Grand Canyon peaks and some of the great archi-tectural works of mankind, gave the Grand Canyon most of its exotic names. The remainder were named by Francois Matthes, a government cartographer, who in the spring of 1902 undertook the topographic mapping of the Grand Canyon for the U. S. Geological Survey. There is no mystery about this; most decent histories of the Grand Canyon (*Frommer's Grand Canyon National Park* and Stephen J. Pyne's *How the Canyon Became Grand*, for example) give these facts. Indeed, it is more than possible that the Egyptian and Indian place names of the Grand Canyon provided part of the inspiration for the *Gazette* article.

But is the article anything other than a simple newspaper hoax, akin to that published in *The Dallas Morning News,* of April 19, 1897, telling of a UFO crash in Aurora, Texas? Many details of the 1909 article do suggest this. First of all, nobody has ever seen the photographs Kinkaid is alleged to have taken in the caverns or the artifacts he apparently retrieved. Surely, in more than 90 years someone would have seen them. Another problem is the lack of documentary evidence to back up the existence of either G.E. Kinkaid or Prof. S.A. Jordan. In addition, in the May 1909 article the *Gazette* refers to the Smithsonian as an *Institute* instead of an *Institution* (many Websites using the story have copied this error). It is surely fair to suggest that anyone employed by the Smithsonian would know the difference. A further error in the article is the statement that Kinkaid was "the first white child born in Idaho." In fact, this was Eliza Spalding, born at Lapwai on November 5, 1837, to Henry and Eliza Spalding.

Another interpretation is that the story of the Grand Canyon discoveries were inspired by Hopi Indian legends of ancestors who once lived in an underworld in the Grand Canyon. In fact, a description of this Hopi Indian tradition was appended to the original *Gazette* newspaper article. These legends could be partly responsible for the origin of the story, but there were other inspirations for the anonymous author at this time. In 1869, Major John Wesley Powell led the first successful expedition down the Colorado River and through the (then unknown) region of the Grand Canyon. Interestingly enough, when Powell came upon a huge river cave called Redwall Cavern; he stated that if it were used as a theater it "would give seating to 50,000 people" bringing to mind Kincaid's estimate of 50,000 people being accomodated within the caverns.

The Brown-Stanton expedition of 1889 may also have provided some inspiration. This expedition was undertaken to survey a gorge in the Grand Canyon for possible railroad construction along the Colorado River into California. After three members of the expedition drowned in Marble Canyon, the remainder decided it was impossible to continue and attempted to make their way out of the canyon. They passed the spectacular springs of Vasey's Paradise and, after scaling the limestone wall above the river, discovered "a whole row of cliff dwellings, with pieces of broken pottery all over the cliff." Stanton decided to store the remaining supplies, and explore. He found a cave in the limestone rock face about 160 feet above the river (the Stanton's Cave mentioned previously).

From there they followed a prehistoric trail up South Canyon and to safety.

It also must be remembered that in the late 19th and early 20th century, stories about fantastic lost lands such as Atlantis, Lemuria, and Mu were rife. Kinkaid's supposed career also seems to be partly based on the explorer/antiquarian type of the era, exemplified in traveler, photographer, and amateur archaeologist Augustus Le Plongeon (1825–1908). The idea of the lost land of Mu first appears in the works of Le Plongeon. Born in Jersey, off the coast of Normandy, France, he led a colorful life, which included photographing Mayan ruins in the Yucatán Peninsula, working as a surveyor in San Fransisco, and studying photography in London. There were also great archaeological discoveries being made at this time, and their larger than life discoverers were often in the news. Examples include Heinrich Schliemann, who investigated the supposed site of Troy in northwest Turkey and the palace of Mycenae, Greece, in the 1870s. Other examples include the English Egyptologist, Flinders Petrie, who began excavating in Egypt in 1884, and Arthur Evans, who started work at the prehistoric palace complex of Knossos, on Crete, in 1900. Some, or all, could have provided part of the stimulus for the story.

It is in such accounts of the early explorers of the Grand Canyon, the intrepid archaeologists and antiquarians of the era, and in the Indian and Egyptian place names of the Grand Canyon, that the origins of G.E. Kinkaid and the 1909 newspaper article can be found, rather than in real discoveries inside a mysterious, lost cavern.

Newgrange: Observatory, Temple, or Tomb?

© *Government of Ireland*
Aerial view of Newgrange.

Brú na Bóinne (Dwelling on the Boyne) is an area located on a hilltop overlooking a loop in the River Boyne, in County Meath, Ireland. It consists of various prehistoric archaeological sites, including a cemetery containing around 40 Passage Graves. A Passage Grave is a tomb, usually dating to the Neolithic period (c. 4000 B.C.–c. 2000 B.C.) where the burial chamber is reached along a low passage. The most well-known and impressive of the sites within the Brú na Bóinne complex are the passage graves of Newgrange, Knowth, and Dowth, of which Newgrange is perhaps the finest.

One of the greatest prehistoric monuments in the world, the huge Neolithic tomb of Newgrange (*Si An Bhru* in Irish—perhaps meaning fairy dwelling) was probably built around 5,100 years ago, making it more than 600 years older than the Great Pyramid of Giza in Egypt, and 1,000 years earlier than the Stonehenge trilithons. It is roughly circular, with a diameter of around 264 feet and covers an area of more than one acre. The mound of the monument was constructed from small stones layered with turf and is surrounded by 97 large stones known as kerbstones, some of which are elaborately ornamented with megalithic art. On top of the kerbstones is a high wall of white quartz. The large slab which now stands against the wall outside the passage entrance was originally used to block the passage when construction of the tomb was complete. The 62 foot long passageway, covering only a third of the length of the mound, is lined with roughly hewn stone slabs, and leads to a cross-shaped chamber with a magnificent steep corbelled roof, 19 feet in height. The recesses in the cruciform chamber are decorated with spirals and contain three massive stone basins, two carved from sandstone and one from granite, which archaeologists think once contained cremated human remains.

It was not until 1699, when the overgrown hill of Newgrange was being used as a source of small stones to build a nearby road, that the Newgrange passage tomb was rediscovered. One of the first people to enter the tomb, which he described as a cave, was Welsh antiquary and one time keeper of the Ashmolean Museum in Oxford, Edward Lhuyd (1660–1709). He made the first study of Newgrange, which consisted of descriptions and drawings that were published in 1726 by Thomas Molyneux. In 1909, George Coffey, Keeper of Irish Antiquities in the National Museum, Dublin, catalogued numerous Passage Graves including Newgrange, which he published in 1912 as "New Grange and other Incised Tumuli in Ireland." However, it was not until 1962 that the first major excavations at the site took place under Professor Michael J. O'Kelly from the Department of Archaeology, University College, Cork. During a program of excavation which lasted from 1962 to 1975, the massive passage grave underwent extensive restoration, including the rebuilding of the supposedly original facade of sparkling white quartz using stones found at the site. This restoration, however, has not been without its critics, who see it as a 20th century view of how someone *thought* the building would have appeared c. 3200 B.C.

It has been estimated that the Newgrange Passage Tomb contains around 200,000 tons of material and would have taken 300 workers a minimum of 20 to 30 years to construct. Rounded stones from the River Boyne were used in the construction, but the white quartz pebbles used as facing stones come from the Wicklow Mountains, 50 miles away, and were probably brought by boat down the Boyne.

© *Government of Ireland*
Interior of the monument, showing megalithic art.

The large slabs of rock which make up the walls and ceiling of the passageway were probably transported on wooden rollers from a quarry 8.7 miles away. This huge investment in time and labor indicates a socially advanced and well-organized people, as well as a society of superb craftsmen.

The Passage Graves of Newgrange, Knowth, and Dowth are justly famous for their wealth of megalithic (c. 4500 B.C.–1500 B.C.) rock art. In fact, Knowth alone contains a quarter of all the known megalithic art in Europe. At Newgrange, several of the stones inside the monument are decorated with spiral patterns and cup and ring marks, as are some of the kerbstones. Many of these stones are carved on their hidden sides so as not to be visible to anyone in the tomb. But the most spectacular piece of megalithic art is on the superb slab lying outside the entrance to the tomb. This recumbent stone is profusely decorated with lozenge motifs and one of the few known examples of a triple spiral, the other two examples being inside the monument. Such motifs are found on stones in other passage tombs on the Isle of Man and the island of Anglesey in North Wales. Although these motifs were also used in later Celtic art, it is not known what they represent, though perhaps they recorded astronomical and cosmological observations.

Surrounding the Newgrange mound is a ring of 12 upright stones up to 8 feet in height. Originally, there were perhaps around 35 of these standing stones, but they have been removed or destroyed over time. Representing the final building stage at the site, the circle was erected around 2000 B.C., long after the great passage tomb had gone out of use, although its presence shows that the area itself still retained some importance for the local population, perhaps connected with astronomy or ancestor worship.

Newgrange is perhaps most famous for a spectacular phenomena that occurs at the site every year for a few days around the 21st or 22nd of December. The entrance to the Newgrange passage tomb consists of a doorway composed of two standing stones and a horizontal lintel. Above the doorway is an aperture known as the *roof box* or *light box*. Every year, shortly after 9 a.m. (on the morning of the winter solstice, the shortest day of the year) the sun begins its ascent across the Boyne Valley over a hill known locally as Red Mountain, the name probably taken from the color of the sunrise on this day. The newly risen sun then sends a shaft of sunlight directly through the Newgrange light box, which penetrates down the passageway as a narrow beam of light illuminating the central chamber at the back of the tomb. After just 17 minutes the beam of light narrows and the chamber is once more left in darkness.

This spectacular event was not rediscovered until 1967 by Professor Michael J. O'Kelly, though it had been known about in local folklore before that time. Newgrange is one of only three known sites with such light boxes, the other two being *Cairn G*, at Carrowkeel Megalithic Cemetery, County Sligo, Ireland, and the passage tomb at *Bryn Celli Ddu* on Anglesey, North Wales. There may possibly be a fourth, at a chambered tomb at Crantit on the island of Orkney, Scotland, discovered in 1998, but this is still disputed. Newgrange, however, is by far

© Government of Ireland
Entrance to Newgrange with huge
entrance slab displaying megalithic art.

the best constructed and the most complex of these sites, and reveals in spectacular fashion the highly developed knowledge of surveying and astronomy possessed by the Neolithic inhabitants of the area. It also illustrates that for the people who aligned their monument with the winter solstice, the sun must have formed an important part of their religious beliefs.

One major aspect of the Newgrange monument—which is often disputed—is its primary function. Excavations inside the chambers revealed relatively few archaeological finds, probably because the majority had been removed in the centuries that the site remained open (from 1699 until it was examined by O'Kelly in 1962). Finds included two inhumation burials and at least three cremated bodies, all of which were found close to the huge stone basins, which seem to have been used for holding the bones of the dead. Taking into account the removal of much of the material and the fact that all of the human bones recovered were small fragments, thus making it

difficult to clearly identify individual burials, there must have been a lot more than five people originally buried in the chambers. Archaeological finds inside the monument have not been spectacular; though a few gold objects have been found, including two gold torcs (a piece of jewelry worn about the neck similar to a collar), a gold chain, and two rings. Other finds include a large phallus-like stone, a few pendants and beads, a bone chisel, and several bone pins. The lack of pottery finds at Newgrange is typical for passage grave cemeteries, which seem to have been places reserved for certain types of activity and an extremely limited number of people. However, not everyone agrees that Newgrange ever functioned as a tomb at all. In his 2004 book, *Newgrange—Temple to Life*, South African-born author Chris O'Callaghan argues against Newgrange being a Passage Grave. He maintains that there is no real evidence of intentional human burial at Newgrange, and believes that the bone fragments found during excavations were probably brought in there by animals long after Newgrange became disused. O'Callaghan's theory is that the monument was built to celebrate the union of the Sun God with Mother Earth, a symbol of the life force itself. The light box or sun window would have allowed the Sun God to penetrate the passage of the mound (signifying Mother Earth) and reach deep into the chamber (symbolizing the womb). This theory is borne out in part by the winter solstice alignment of the site, and perhaps by the phallic shaped pillar and chalk balls found in the chamber, which possibly represented male sexual organs. However, Newgrange does not need to be confined to one function. And, as pointed out above, the small amount of human bone discovered at the site does not seem to represent the total of Neolithic burials within the chambers, as significant amounts were probably taken out of the monument, perhaps by scavenging animals or people looking for relics. Newgrange has many connections with Irish myth, and was known as a *sidhe* or fairy mound even into the 20th century. A number of illustrious characters from Irish mythology are mentioned in association with it, including the Tuatha Dé Danann, the ancient mythical rulers of Ireland; Aengus Og, its traditional owner; and the hero Cúchulainn. Various mythical interpretations of Newgrange have been put forward. These include that it functioned as a house of the dead, the passage and chambers being kept dry for the comfort of the indwelling spirits, and the roof box being opened and closed to let the spirits in and out of the tomb. It was also thought to be the dwelling place of the great god Dagda, and at specific times during the year valuable offerings would be made to such gods. There is actually archaeological evidence for offerings at Newgrange long after it ceased to function as a tomb and observatory. Various Roman items, including gold coins, pendants, and brooches—some in mint condition—have been found at the monument. Considering the Romans never invaded Ireland, many of these offerings must have been made by Romans or Romano-British visitors from Britain, perhaps they were ancient pilgrims venerating an already 3,000-year-old religious monument.

© *Government of Ireland*
The monument, as seen from a distance.

In 1993, due to their vast cultural and historical importance, Newgrange and the nearby passage tombs of Knowth and Dowth were designated a World Heritage Site by UNESCO. Newgrange now attracts in excess of 200,000 visitors per year, all of which come on guided tours from the Brú na Bóinne Visitor Center, as there is no longer direct access to the site. Anyone wanting to visit around the 21st of December to witness the magnificent midwinter solstice may, however, be in for a long wait. In 2005 there were around 27,000 applications to enter the tomb at this time. Consequently, admission to the Newgrange tomb chamber for the winter solstice sunrise is only by lottery. It is necessary to fill out an application form, available at the reception desk in the Brú na Bóinne Visitor Center, and in early October, 50 names are drawn, 10 for each morning the tomb is illuminated. Two places in the chamber are then given to each of the lucky people whose names are drawn. One can only wonder how the Neolithic peoples of the area chose their watchers of the midwinter solstice at this magnificent site.

© *John Griffiths.*
Overall view of Machu Picchu in its stunning setting.

Machu Picchu: Lost City of the Incas

Probably the most spectacular archaeological site in South America and the most famous symbol of the Incas, *Machu Picchu* (Old Peak), is located in a semi-tropical area 7,000 feet above sea level in the Andes Mountains of Peru. It lies about 300 miles southeast of Lima, the modern Peruvian capital, and 170 miles northwest of Cuzco, the capital city of the Inca Empire. The vast Inca Empire lasted from A.D. 1438 to 1533, and was centered in what is now Peru, but included Ecuador, Bolivia, Chile, part of Argentina, and the southern end of Colombia. The Incas were the last of the advanced native societies of the Andes before the arrival of the Europeans.

Machu Picchu was known only to a few local farmers until it was rediscovered in 1911 by Hiram Bingham, Director of the Peruvian Expedition of the University of Yale. Bingham was led to the site by a local farmer named

Melchior Arteaga, and at first the American thought that he and his team had discovered another lost Inca city called Vilcabamba. Bingham had read about Vilcabamba in 16th century Spanish chronicles as the jungle city to which the Inca fled after their failed rebellion against the Spanish. Bingham's party were surprised to find how remarkably well-preserved the mountain city was, 400 years after it had been mysteriously abandoned by its inhabitants. Hiram Bingham was the first to describe Machu Picchu as "the Lost City of the Incas" and he used it as the title of his first book, a bestseller which brought the site international attention. The lost city received further exposure in 1913 when the National Geographic Society dedicated their whole April issue to the site.

Machu Picchu was built between A.D. 1460 and 1470 by Inca ruler and founding father of the Inca Empire, Pachacuti Inca Yupanqui, and it seems to have been inhabited until just before the Spanish conquest of Peru in 1532. The city, with its approximately 200 buildings (including houses, palaces, temples, observatories, and storage structures) is an astonishing achievement in urban planning, civil engineering, and architecture. The complex covers an area of about half a square mile and can be broadly divided up into three distinct areas or districts—agricultural, urban, and religious. The agricultural section contains a series of terraces and aqueducts, which utilize the natural slopes of the land, and function not only as cultivation platforms but also retention walls to prevent erosion. The area also includes small, humble dwellings built around narrow alleys, thought to have been occupied by farmers. The urban section of the complex is separated from the agricultural by a wall. In the southern part of this area is a series of recesses carved into the rock

© *John Griffiths.*
An Inca wall at Machu Picchu.

and named "the jail" by Bingham because of these small niches, where he thought prisoners' arms were held in place by stone rings. It is more correctly identified nowadays as part of the Temple of the Condor, this complex deriving its name from what is thought to be an Andean Condor carved into a granite outcrop located at its lowest point. The collection of sophisticated structures next to the Temple built in a reddish stone is known as the Intellectuals' Quarters, where there seems to have been accommodation for the *Amautas* (high-ranked teachers), and also a section known as the *Zone of the Ñustas* (princesses).

The religious section contains splendid Inca architecture and masonry work. Its main part consists of the Sacred Plaza, the scene of popular ceremonies, surrounding the most significant buildings at Machu Picchu. The Sun Temple is a semicircular construction cut into the solid rock containing two windows, one facing to the east and the other towards the north. According to modern scientists, these two windows were used as a solar observatory; the east-facing window allowed an accurate measurement of the winter solstice by measuring the shadow cast by the central stone.

The Three-Windowed Temple, named for its three large trapezoidal windows that open onto the main plaza, contains a carved stone with figures symbolizing the three levels of the Andean World: the Hanan-Pacha (the higher world or heavenly paradise), the Kay-Pacha (the earthly world), and the Ukju-Pacha (the inner world where the gods live). The religious section also includes the Sacred Temple, an excellent example of Inca stone-masonry, with large polished stone blocks perfectly joined together, the Priests' House, and an enigmatic shrine known as the *Intihuatana*, or Hitching Post of the Sun. This is one of the most important and mysterious constructions at Machu Picchu. It is composed of a column of granite, probably the gnomon or pointer of a sundial, rising from a huge pyramidal table-stone, and it is thought to have functioned as a solar observatory. At each winter solstice, during the Festival of *Inti Raymi* (or Festival of the Sun), the god would be symbolically secured to the stone by a priest in an attempt to prevent the complete disappearance of the sun.

© *John Griffiths.*
The Intihuatana *(hitching post of the sun), probably used as a solar observatory by the Incas.*

The main feature of Machu Picchu, and one that has amazed countless visitors, is the fine quality of the massive stone walls and buildings, constructed without mortar, using neither the wheel nor draught animals. Much of the characteristically polygonal masonry in these structures locks together so precisely that it is impossible to fit even the thinnest knife blade in between the joints. This Inca design ensures the stability of the structure in an area well-known for earthquakes. Due to the fine quality of the masonry and the apparent difficulty in transporting and erecting such huge stones, some alternative theorists have conjectured that laser technology was employed to build the structures at Machu Picchu, either by some lost ancient civilization or extraterrestrial visitors. The mystery of Machu Picchu's construction is further enhanced by the lack of any documentary evidence to indicate exactly how the buildings were erected. Research has shown that the Incas had a class of professional architects to design and organize the construction of such building complexes as Machu Picchu. When considering Inca architecture, it is vital to understand that these architects were experts at adapting the form of the construction to the landscape in which they were built. Consequently, existing rock formations were utilized in construction, sculptures were carved into rock faces, and water flowed through stone channels. Though it is not known exactly how the Inca moved such enormous blocks of stone, the general belief is that they used all the able-bodied men from captured tribes to push the stones, perhaps after levering them onto smaller

spherical stones, and then rolling them forward, moving the stones from the back to the front as they progressed. Most of the buildings and walls at the site were constructed of granite blocks, and possibly cut with bronze or stone tools, and finally smoothed off with sand.

The actual function of Machu Picchu has been much debated. Was it a great Inca city with a large, thriving population? Probably not. It has been estimated that only about 1,000 people lived in and around Machu Picchu at any one time, which, along with its isolated position, indicates that it cannot really have been a conventional city. Hiram Bingham's excavations in the early 20th century revealed 135 mummified corpses, 109 of which Bingham identified as female. From the predominantly female burials Bingham deduced that the site functioned mainly as a refuge of the *Acllas*, the Inca Virgins of the Sun. However, more recent analysis of the skeletons has indicated that the skeletons were in fact evenly divided between males and females. The current theory is that the complex was a ceremonial city, which also functioned as a royal estate and religious retreat or sanctuary for Inca royalty, priests, and priestesses.

Machu Picchu's sudden abandonment is shrouded in mystery. During the time of the Spanish Conquest the sacred city lay undiscovered, which suggests that it had long been deserted and forgotten. Theories for the unexplained abandonment are legion and include the city running dry in an extended period of drought, a disastrous fire, or because of evacuation during the time of Inca resistance to the Spanish. Probably the most viable theory points to the fact that, prior to the Spanish Conquest, smallpox had been introduced to Peru from Europe; it soon reached epidemic proportions and spread through the country. By 1527, half of the population had fallen victim to the disease, the government began to collapse, and civil war erupted. A lack of social order and a drastically reduced population would explain a relatively swift desertion.

Today, this amazing mountain-top complex of temples, cyclopean walls, fields, and terraces is a Historic National Sanctuary, protected by the Peruvian Government, and since 1983, a UNESCO World Heritage Site. The lost city of the Incas is no longer lost; it attracts around 500,000 foreign visitors per year and is by far the most visited tourist attraction in Peru. Although the Peruvian government maintains that there are no problems resulting from such a vast amount of tourists tramping all over the site, UNESCO has expressed fears about the possible damage caused by this volume of tourism, and in 1998 added Machu Picchu to its list of endangered World Heritage sites. Unfortunately, over the last few years Machu Picchu has become involved in unwanted controversy. During the filming of a beer commercial in September 2000, at the Intihuatana, where Inca priests and priestesses once worshipped the sun, a 1000 pound crane toppled over, breaking off a sizeable piece of the sundial, resulting in criminal charges being filed against the production company by Gustavo Manrique of the National Institute of Culture. In 2005, the same year that Machu Picchu became twinned with the ancient town of Petra in Jordan, Peru began a legal battle for the return of the thousands of artifacts removed from the site by Hiram Bingham 90 years previously.

The Library of Alexandria

Modern Alexandria from one of the windows of Qaitbay's Citadel, to the west of the city.

Once the largest library in the world—and containing works by the greatest thinkers and writers of antiquity, including Homer, Plato, Socrates, and many more—the Library of Alexandria is popularly believed to have been destroyed in a huge fire 2,000 years ago and its collection lost. Since its destruction, this wonder of the ancient world has haunted the imagination of poets, historians, travelers, and scholars, who have lamented the tragic loss of knowledge and literature. Today, the idea of a universal library situated in a city celebrated as the center of learning in the ancient world has attained mythical status. The mystery has been perpetuated by the fact that no architectural remains or archaeological finds that can definitely be attributed to the library have ever been recovered, which is surprising for such a supposedly renowned and imposing structure. This lack of physical proof has even persuaded some to wonder if the fabulous library actually existed at all in the form popularly imagined.

Home to the massive Pharos lighthouse, one of the Seven Wonders of the Ancient World, the Mediterranean seaport of Alexandria was founded by Alexander the Great in 330 B.C., and as with many other cities, took its name from him. After his death in 323 B.C., Alexander's empire was left in the hands of his generals, with Ptolemy I Soter taking Egypt and making Alexandria his capital in 320 B.C. Formerly a small fishing village on the Nile delta, Alexandria became the seat of the Ptolemaic rulers of Egypt and developed into a great intellectual and cultural center. It was perhaps the greatest city in the ancient world. The story of the founding of the Library of Alexandria is obscure. It is believed that around 295 B.C. the scholar and orator Demetrius of Phalerum, an exiled governor of Athens, convinced Ptolemy I Soter to establish a library. Demetrius envisioned a library that would house a copy of every book in the world, an institution to rival Athens itself. Subsequently, under the patronage of Ptolemy I, Demetrius organized the construction of the Temple of the Muses or the Musaeum, from which our word *museum* is derived. This structure was a shrine complex modeled on the Lyceum of Aristotle in Athens, a center for intellectual and philosophical lectures and discussion.

The Temple of the Muses was to be the first part of the library complex at Alexandria, and was located within the grounds of the royal palace, in an area known as the *Bruchion* or palace quarter, in the northeastern, Greek district of the city. The museum was a cult center with shrines for each of the nine muses, but also functioned as a place of study with lecture areas, laboratories, observatories, botanical gardens, a zoo, living quarters, and dining halls, as well as the library itself. A priest chosen by Ptolemy I was the administrator of the museum, and there was also a separate librarian in charge of the manuscript collection. At some point during his reign (from 282 to 246 B.C.) Ptolemy II Philadelphus, the son of Ptolemy I Soter, established the Royal Library to complement the Temple of the Muses set up by his father. It is not clear whether the Royal Library, which was to become the main manuscript library, was a separate building located next to the museum, or if it was an extension of the original building. However, the consensus of opinion is that the Royal Library did form part of the Temple of the Muses.

During the reign of Ptolemy II, the idea of the universal library seems to have taken shape. Apparently, more than 100 scholars were housed within the museum, whose job it was to carry out scientific research, lecture, publish, translate, copy, and collect not only original manuscripts of Greek authors (allegedly including the private collection of Aristotle), but translations of works from Egypt, Assyria, Persia, as well as Buddhist texts and Hebrew scriptures. One story goes that the hunger of Ptolemy III for knowledge was so great that he decreed that all ships docking at the port should surrender their manuscripts to the authorities. Copies were then made by official scribes and delivered to the original owners, the originals being filed away in the library. An often quoted figure for the library holdings at its peak is half a million documents, though whether this refers to the amount of books or the number of papyrus scrolls is unclear. However, in view of the fact that many papyrus rolls were needed to make up an entire book, it is more likely that it refers to the number of scrolls. Even 500,000 scrolls has been thought too high by some scholars, as the construction of a building with such a vast amount of storage space would be an immense—though not impossible—undertaking. Nevertheless, during the reign of Ptolemy II the collection at the Royal Library became so vast that a daughter library was established. This library was situated in the precincts of the temple of Serapis, in the Egyptian district of Rhakotis, in the southeastern part of the city. During the librarianship of the Greek writer Callimachus (c. 305 B.C.–c. 240 B.C.), the daughter library contained 42,800 scrolls, all of which were copies of those in the main library.

The alleged total destruction by fire of the Library of Alexandria, with the consequent loss of the most complete collection of ancient literature ever assembled, has been a point of heated debate for centuries. What exactly happened to this amazing storehouse of ancient knowledge, and who was responsible for its burning? The first point that needs to be mentioned is that "the greatest catastrophe of the ancient world," may never have taken place on the scale often supposed. Nevertheless, the library did disappear practically without a trace, so obviously a disaster of some kind

befell it. The most popular suspect in the case is Julius Caesar. It is alleged that during Caesar's occupation of the city of Alexandria in 48 B.C., he found himself in the royal palace, hemmed in by the Egyptian fleet in the harbor. For his own safety he had his men set fire to the Egyptian ships, but the fire got out of control and spread to the parts of the city nearest the shore, which included warehouses, depots, and some arsenals. After Caesar's death it was generally believed that it was he who had destroyed the library. Roman philosopher and dramatist Seneca, quoting from Livy's *History of Rome*, written between 63 B.C. and A.D. 14, says that 40,000 scrolls were destroyed in the fire started by Caesar. Greek historian Plutarch mentions that the fire destroyed "the great Library." Roman historian Dio Cassius (c. A.D. 165–A.D. 235) mentions a warehouse of manuscripts being destroyed during the conflagration.

In his book, *The Vanished Library*, Luciano Canfora interprets the evidence from ancient writers not to indicate that the great library itself was destroyed, but manuscripts stored in warehouses near the port waiting for export. The great scholar and stoic philosopher, Strabo, was working in Alexandria in 20 B.C., and from his writings it is obvious that the library was not the world-renowned center for learning it had been in previous centuries. In fact, Strabo does not mention a library as such at all, though he does mention the museum, which he describes as "part of the royal palace." He goes on to say that "it comprises the covered walk, the exedra or portico, and a great hall in which the learned members of the museum take their meals in common." If the great library was attached to the museum, then Strabo obviously felt there was no need to mention it separately, and, perhaps more importantly, if he was there in 20 B.C., the library had obviously not been burned down by Caesar 28 years previously. The existence of the library in 20 B.C., though perhaps in a less grand form, means that we have to look to someone other than Caesar as the destroyer of Alexandria's ancient wonder.

In A.D. 391 Emperor Theodosius I, as part of his attempt to wipe out Paganism, officially sanctioned the destruction of the *Serapeum*, or Temple of Serapis at Alexandria. The destruction of the temple was carried out under Theophilus, Bishop of Alexandria, and afterward a Christian church was built on the site. It has been hypothesized that the daughter library of the museum, located close to the Temple, and the royal library itself, were also razed to the ground at this time. However, while it is plausible that manuscripts from the Serapeum library may have been destroyed during this purge, there is no evidence that the Royal Library still existed at the end the fourth century. No ancient sources mention the destruction of any library at this time, though 18th century English historian Edward Gibbon mistakenly attributes it to bishop Theophilus.

The last suggested perpetrator of the crime is the Caliph Omar. In A.D. 640 the Arabs (under General Amrou ibn el-Ass) captured Alexandria after a long siege. According to the story, the conquering Arabs heard about a magnificent library containing all the knowledge of the world and were

Early fifth century illustration of Theophilus and the Serapeum.

anxious to see it. But the Caliph, unmoved by this vast collection of learning, apparently stated "they will either contradict the Koran, in which case they are heresy, or they will agree with it, so they are superfluous." The manuscripts were then gathered together and used as fuel for the 4,000 bathhouses in the city. In fact, there were so many scrolls that they kept the bath-houses of Alexandria heated for six months. These incredible facts were written down 300 years after the supposed event by Christian polymath Gregory Bar Hebraeus (1226–1286). However, while the Arabs may have destroyed a Christian library at Alexandria, it is almost certain that by the mid-seventh century the Royal Library no longer existed. This is made clear by the fact that no mention is made of such a catastrophic event by contemporary writers such as Christian chronicler John of Nikiou (a Byzantine monk), writer John Moschus, and Sophronius (the Patriarch of Jerusalem).

In fact, attempting to identify one devastating fire that destroyed the great library and all of its holdings is a futile task. Alexandria was often a volatile city, especially during the Roman period, as witnessed by Caesar's burning of the ships, and also in the violent struggle between the occupying forces of Queen Zenobia of Palmyra and the Roman Emperor Aurelian in A.D. 270/271. Aurelian eventually recovered the city for Rome from Queen Zenobia's armies, but not before many parts of Alexandria had been devastated, and the Bruchion district, which contained the palace and the library, were apparently "made into a desert." The city was again sacked a few years later by Roman Emperor Diocletian. Such repeated damage, spread over several centuries, along with neglect of the library's contents as opinions and affiliations changed, means that the catastrophe was gradual, taking place over a period of 400 or 500 years. The last recorded director of the great library was scholar and mathematician Theon (c. A.D. 335–A.D. 405), father of the female philosopher Hypatia, who was brutally murdered by a Christian mob in Alexandria in A.D. 415. Perhaps one day, in the deserts of Egypt, scrolls that were once part of the great library will be discovered. Many archaeologists believe that the buildings that once composed the legendary seat of learning at Alexandria, if not buried under the modern metropolis, could still survive relatively intact somewhere in the northeastern part of the city.

In 2004, a Polish-Egyptian archaeological team made the news when they claimed to have discovered a part of the Library of Alexandria while excavating in the Bruchion region. The archaeologists discovered 13 lecture halls, each with an elevated central podium. However, the structures date to the late Roman period (fifth/sixth century A.D.) so are unlikely to represent the celebrated museum or Royal Library, though investigations in the area are still taking place. In 1995, construction work began on the Bibliotheca Alexandrina, a major library and cultural center located close to the site of original library. The huge complex was officially opened on October 16, 2002, and was established to commemorate the vanished Library of Alexandria, and reignite some of the intellectual brilliance that the original center represented. Hopefully, the existence of a new universal library will show that at least the spirit of the ancient library has not been lost.

The Great Pyramid: An Enigma in the Desert

Photograph by Alex lbh (GNU Free Documentation License).
Detail of the Great Pyramid.

The oldest and only survivor of the Seven Wonders of the Ancient World, the Great Pyramid at Giza has become not only a symbol of ancient Egypt but of the mysterious and unknown itself. The pyramid stands on the west bank of the Nile in the necropolis of Giza, a complex of ancient monuments, which in pharaonic times was part of the ancient city of Memphis. Today it is a part of Greater Cairo. In its size and the quality of its design and construction, the Pyramid represents the high point of pyramid building in Egypt.

Egyptologists generally agree that the pyramid was built around 2650 B.C. as a tomb for the Egyptian pharaoh Khufu (Cheops). However, as no burial has ever been found within the structure, and no inscriptions located to identify its function, some researchers have proposed alternative theories for the date and function of the Great Pyramid, which still continues to amaze and confound thousands of years after its construction.

The Great Pyramid is is the oldest and largest of the three pyramids on the Giza Necropolis. Southwest lies the slightly smaller Pyramid of Khafre (Chephren), one of Khufu's sons, and the supposed builder of the Great Sphinx, which lies to the east of his pyramid. Further to the southwest is the much smaller Pyramid of Menkaure, Khafre's son and successor. The Great Pyramid measures 449.5 feet in height and 750 square feet, though when it was originally constructed its height was 478 feet. It was the tallest building on Earth until the 13th century, when the 524 foot tall spire of Lincoln Cathedral in England was completed. Missing from the original pyramid structure is the fine white limestone casing and its gold plated pyramidion, or capstone, which topped the monument. The four sides of the massive pyramid are carefully oriented to the four cardinal points, and are accurate to within 3 minutes of an arc. More than 2 million blocks of stone were used in the construction of the monument, each weighing more than 2 tons. It has been calculated that the vast area covered by the Great Pyramid could contain St. Peter's in Rome, the cathedrals of Florence and Milan, Westminster Abbey, and St. Paul's in London combined.

The entrance to the pyramid is on its north face. Inside, the structure contains three chambers, connected by descending and ascending passageways. The lowest of these chambers is known as the Unfinished Chamber. This structure was roughly hewn into the bedrock 98.5 feet below ground level, and is believed by Egyptologists to represent the proposed initial location of the burial chamber of King Khufu, who apparently changed his mind and had another chamber constructed higher up the pyramid. The middle chamber is known as the Queen's Chamber, a name given to the room in error by the Arabs. The Queen's Chamber lies exactly midway between the north and south sides of the pyramid, and is the smallest of the three, measuring approximately 18.3 by 17.1 feet, with a pointed roof rising to a height of about 20 feet. The rough unfinished floor in the Queen's Chamber has suggested to many researchers that for some unknown reason work on this room was abandoned before completion.

Located at the heart of the Pyramid is the King's Chamber. This structure is built entirely of granite and measures 34.5 feet from east to west, 17 feet from north to south, and 19 feet in height. Near the west wall of the chamber lies the King's sarcophagus, supposedly once containing the body of Khufu, though there is no evidence that anyone was ever buried in it. The sarcophagus was hollowed out of a single piece of Red Aswan granite and is about 2.5 centimeters wider than the entrance into the King's Chamber. Consequently, the sarcophagus must have been placed in position while the chamber was being constructed. Napolean allegedly spent a terrifying night alone in the King's Chamber in the late 1790s, a feat duplicated with similar results by English occultist Paul Brunton in the 1930s.

The other main feature of the interior of the Great Pyramid is the Grand Gallery. This passageway was built as a continuation of the Ascending Corridor and is 152.8 feet long and 27.8 feet high. It is a stunning architectural achievement and possesses an ingenious corbelled vault, formed by the gradual inward projection of its polished limestone walls. As yet unexplained and unique features of the Great Pyramid are the mysterious shafts, two of which slope upwards out of both the King's and Queen's chambers. Thought once to be ventilation shafts, it is now believed that these narrow passageways had some religious significance. The shafts do appear to be astronomically aligned and are probably connected with the ancient Egyptian belief that the stars were inhabited by the gods and the souls of the dead.

Recent archaeological discoveries on the Giza Plateau are shedding much needed light on the people who actually built the Great Pyramid. In 1990, investigations led by Secretary General of Egyptian Antiquities Dr. Zahi Hawass discovered the tombs of the Pyramid Builders close to the Pyramids at Giza. These tombs included the sarcophagus of a man identified by hieroglyphics as Ny Swt Wsrt, thought to be the overseer of the pyramid builders' village. A few years later, in an area near this cemetery, the Giza Plateau Mapping Project, led by archaeologist Mark Lehner, discovered the site of a vast community of as many as 20,000 people, who had lived in the area around 2500 B.C. This has been dubbed "the workers' village" and includes such features as a dormitory or barracks for up to 2,000 temporary workers, as well as evidence for copper-working and cooking facilities.

One of the greatest enigmas of the Great Pyramid is how such a vast engineering project was organized and accomplished. How were such huge stone blocks, some weighing more than 40 tons, transported to the site, raised up, and fitted so precisely into position? Additionally, some of these stones were brought from Aswan, 620 miles south of Giza. How was this managed? Egyptologists believe that the Great Pyramid was constructed over a period of less than 23 years (the reign of King Khufu) finishing around 2560 B.C. There are some clues

© *John Griffiths.*
The pyramids of Giza

to construction methods in Egyptian reliefs from the tomb of the Fourth Dynasty (c. 2489 B.C.–2345 B.C.) official Ti in Saqqara, which show teams of workmen using ropes and sleds to drag giant obelisks and statues into place. The question of transporting the stones, however far, does not seem so difficult when one considers that the Nile could have been used to float the blocks down to Giza. To raise the stones into position, Egyptologists suggest that ramps of mud, brick, and rubble were built on inclined planes. Egyptologist Mark Lehner has hypotheisized that a spiralling ramp, beginning in an adjacent stone quarry to the southeast and continuing around the outside of the pyramid, could have been used. The blocks would then have been dragged up the ramps on sledges to the required height. The remains of such ramps have been discovered at the Sinki pyramid at South Abydos and the Sekhemkhet pyramid at Saqqara. However, building a ramp large enough to support the building of the Great Pyramid would be almost as massive a task as the construction of the pyramid itself.

An alternative theory has recently been proposed by researchers Roumen V. Mladjov and Ian S. R. Mladjov, and also by Dick Parry, Professor of Civil Engineering at Cambridge University. Their idea originated from inscriptions carved into some of the huge blocks used in the construction of the Great Pyramid, which state "This side up." They reason that this instruction would be meaningless if the rectangular stone blocks were only meant to be dragged up ramps. Their ingenious theory is that the stones were literally rolled up the ramps onto the pyramid, using purpose-made wooden devices similar to solid wheels. Evidence for these prototype wheels has been found in the form of a model of a wooden rocker, which consists of a pair of thick boards with curved bottom edges braced with round wooden bars. This model was found by the English archaeologist Flinders Petrie at the Mortuary Temple of Hatshepsut at Deir el-Bahri, on the west bank of the Nile, opposite Luxor. The purpose of these devices is uknown, but the Mladjovs, along with Dick Parry, believe that two semi-circular rockers could have been attached to the stone blocks to form, in effect, a solid wheel—enabling them to be rolled up a ramp fairly easily and thus greatly increasing the speed of construction. The one problem with this theory is that the blocks used to build the Great Pyramid differed significantly in size, which would mean that these rocker devices would only be useful for a limited range of block sizes. Nevertheless, this theory explains—better than any other put forward so far—how some of the difficulties of constructing the Great Pyramid could have been overcome.

Throughout the interior of the Great Pyramid the walls are completely bare of official inscriptions, leading many researchers to propose alternative theories to the accepted explanation that the building was constructed as a tomb for King Khufu. However, the presence of graffiti inside the monument does strengthen the case for an orthodox explanation. This graffiti has been found on stones of all five relieving chambers above the King's Chamber, an area so difficult to access that the stones are unlikely to have been inscribed after they had been put in position, as some have proposed. One important piece of graffiti reads "Year 17 of Khufu's reign." Another refers to "The friends of Khufu." Nevertheless, though these inscriptions do provide evidence that Khufu did indeed have some connection with the pyramid, it is certainly not indisputable proof that the pyramid originated with the Fourth Dynasty pharaoh.

There have been many speculative theories put forward for the purpose of the Great Pyramid, perhaps the best known being that suggested by writer Robert Bauval, who believes that the three main pyramids at Giza represent a map on the ground of the three stars in the belt of the Orion constellation, with the Nile representing the Milky Way. Others have seen the Great Pyramid as an astronomical observatory, an ancient power plant, a Temple of Initiation (proposed by Theosophist Madame Blavatsky and many others), or the legacy of a super race of refugees from the lost continent of Atlantis. This latter idea was proposed by 20th century psychic and prophet Edgar Cayce; Cayce also predicted that a Hall of Records of the Atlantean civilization would be discovered either underneath the Sphinx or inside the Great Pyramid in 1998. The idea of hidden chambers containing vast riches on the scale of Tutankhamun's treasures, or perhaps a hoard of papyrus rolls containing ancient secrets, has an irresistable allure. In 1993, the southern shaft that runs up from the Queen's Chamber was explored by a small remote control robot equipped with a video camera, built by German robotics engineer Rudolph Gantenbrink. The robot climbed up the shaft for a distance of 213 feet before its way

was blocked by a small limestone door with copper handles. The shaft was examined again in 2003, this time by the Egyptian Supreme Council of Antiquities, who sent another robot inside and discovered a further door only 10 inches beyond the first one. The robot also examined the northern shaft of the chamber and discovered the same arrangement of two limestone doors. What lies behind these mysterious doors is a question that may possibly be answered when a new robot, which is being designed and built by the University of Singapore, examines the shafts.

In August 2004, two French amateur Egyptologists, Gilles Dormion and Jean-Yves Verd'hurt, claimed to have found a previously unknown chamber underneath the Queen's Chamber in the Great Pyramid. The pair had been using ground-penetrating radar and architectural analysis and believe that this chamber may well be the final resting place of King Khufu. However, requests to excavate the feature were rejected outright by Zahi Hawass, representing the Egyptian Supreme Council of Antiquities.

It seems that only now, with the aid of 21st century technology, are we beginning to really probe the secrets of the Great Pyramid. However, whether modern investigations will reveal the body of Khufu, a Hall of Records, or a cache of ancient treasure is anyone's guess. When the Egyptians constructed this vast, complicated edifice at least 4,500 years ago, it was their likely intention to build an enigma in stone, an inscrutable symbol of the mysteries of life and death. In this, they succeeded admirably.

PART II

Unexplained
Artifacts

The Nazca Lines

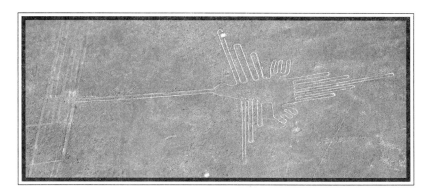

Photograph by Bjarte Sorensen. (GNU Free Documentation License).
Aerial photo of the hummingbird drawing at Nazca.

Etched onto the surface of the desert in a remote part of southern Peru, the Nazca Lines are the world's most remarkable inscriptions. Covering an area 37 miles long and one mile wide, the patterns are only clearly visible from the air. The lines consist of 300 figures made of straight lines, geometric shapes, and pictures of animals and birds. These lines are known as *geoglyphs*—figures or shapes produced on the ground by clearing or arranging stones. For years, scientists and archaeologists have debated why these lines were constructed, and various theories (from the plausible to the extremely implausible) have been put forward. Suggestions have included that the lines functioned as an astronomical observatory, as ritual pathways, a calendar, a landing strip for alien spaceships, or that they were used to map underground water supplies. The investment in time and effort required to draw the shapes in the desert floor so precisely surely indicates that the lines had a vital role in the lives of the Nazca culture. But why are they there and what purpose did they serve?

The Nazca Lines were rediscovered when commercial airlines began flights over the Peruvian desert in the 1920s. Although Julio Tello, the founder of Peruvian archaeology, had recorded the designs in 1926, it was not until American historian Dr. Paul Kosok and his wife first visited Nazca in 1941 that serious research began on the enigmatic inscriptions.

The Nazca Desert is a high arid plateau located 250 miles southeast of the Peruvian capital Lima, between the Pacific Ocean and the Andes Mountains. The desolate plain containing the art is called the *Pampa Colorada* (Red Plain) and covers an area of about 280 square miles stretching between the towns of Nazca and Palpa. Running across this plain is an array of perfectly straight lines of varying widths and lengths, the longest more than 8 miles in length, the shortest just a little more than 1,640 feet. There are also enormous geometric forms including triangles, spirals, circles, and trapezoids, as well as 70 extraordinary animal and plant figures including a hummingbird, a monkey, a spider, lizard, and a pelican of more than 900 feet in length. Anthropomorphic figures are rare at Nazca, though there are a few examples etched onto the slopes of steep hillsides at the edge of the desert, the most well known of which is called the Astronaut, a 105 foot long glyph discovered by Eduardo Herran, chief pilot at Aerocondor, in 1982.

Since the discovery of the lines, many theories have been put forward regarding their construction. Because many of the glyphs are so large and complex and can only be appreciated from the air, it has been proposed by some that manned flight was required to aid in the the planning of the lines. Perhaps the best known proponent of this view is Jim Woodman, a writer and publisher from Miami. In 1974, Woodman, along with English balloonist Julian Nott, tested the theory that the lines had been created with help from the air, by building and flying a balloon made of materials available to the Nazca culture, including reeds for the gondola and cotton for the envelope. The two men managed a short, 300-foot-high flight, and thus proved that it was theoretically within the abilities of the Nazcans to have flown, though there is no evidence whatsoever of such flights.

How the lines were made is actually no great mystery. The iron oxide-coated stones that cover the surface of the desert were simply removed to reveal the underlying lighter colored soil. In this way, the lines were drawn as a groove of a lighter color contrasting with the darker red of the surrounding desert. Sometimes the lines were outlined with stones to provide emphasis to the shape. The Nazca desert is one of the driest places on earth and this, in combination with the flat, stony ground, means that there is very little erosion, so whatever has been drawn onto this giant natural sketchpad has usually remained there. There are fairly simple methods for the creation of straight lines over long distances. One method is to align two ranging poles or wooden stakes in a straight line by eye, which are then used as a guide for the placement of a third stake along the line. It is easy enough if one person sights along the line of the first two stakes and directs another person in the placement of the next stake. This can then be repeated until the desired length is achieved.

The more intricate symbols were probably begun by creating scale drawings and then dividing these drawings up into parts by using grids. These grids could then be recreated on the desert floor and worked on one square at a time. Perhaps even simpler methods could have been used. In 1982, writer Joe Nickel (along with two family members) produced an exact replica of the 440 foot condor figure, in a field near their home. Using primitive technology available to the Nazcan culture, they created the glyph in nine hours, sighting the lines by eye without any aerial help. In his 1987 book *Lines to the Mountain God: Nazca and the Mysteries of Peru,* Evan Hadingham describes an attempt made with Dr. Anthony Aveni, professor of Astronomy and Anthropology at Colgate University, to recreate a desert drawing. The small team, sighting by eye and using such basic equipment as ranging poles and string, produced an impressive spiral glyph in just over an hour. Aveni and his group concluded from their experiments that the creation of one of the most spectacular Nazca Lines, the 2,624 by 328 foot Great Rectangle, could have been accomplished in two months by a team of 100 people. Even so, this is not to say that the construction of the lines did not involve a great deal of planning, ingenuity, and imagination by their creators.

The Nazca Lines are believed to be the creation of the Nazca culture, who lived in the region from around 300 B.C. to A.D. 800. The connection between this culture and the lines is based on Nazcan pottery found in association with the lines, the remarkable similarity between the stylized figures on the desert floor and those from Nazca art, and a radiocarbon date of A.D. 525 from one of the wooden stakes that were used to mark the termination point of some of the longer lines. Lying just south of the Nazca Lines is Cahuachi, a major ceremonial city of the Nazcans, which extends across 370 acres. The city was built about 2,000 years ago and abandoned 500 years later, probably after a series of natural catastrophes. The permanent population of the city was fairly small, but as it served as a center for pilgrims, the amount of people would have increased significantly during major ceremonial events, which were probably connected with the Nazca Lines. But could this ritual function have been the only reason for the creation of the magnificent desert glyphs?

Perhaps the best known researcher associated with the Nazca Lines is the late Maria Reiche, a German mathematician and archaeologist who began her work at Nazca in 1946. Reiche devoted her life to the study and preservation of the lines, living in the desert at Nazca for 50 years. Her theory about the Nazca glyphs, developed from ideas put forward by Paul Kosok (for whom Maria had worked as an assistant) was that they served as an astronomical calendar, and the Nazca plain itself was a huge observatory. In 1968, this theory was tested by American astronomer Gerald Hawkins, well-known for his work on the possible astronomical significance of Stonehenge. Hawkins fed the positions of a sample of the lines into a computer to find out if they matched solar, lunar, or stellar alignments. His results showed that only a minority of the Nazca lines had any astronomical significance, about the same amount as would have occurred by chance, making it unlikely that the lines served any significant astronomical purpose. Soon after the beginning of the flying saucer craze in the late 1940s, the Nazca lines began to attract people's attention as an indication of some sort of connection between Earth and hypothetical alien visitors. In the October 1955 issue of *Fate,* an article by James W. Moseley proposed that, as the markings were only visible from the air, Nazcans must have created their massive glyphs in order to signal alien visitors. This idea was continued by Louis Pauwels and Jacques Bergier in their book *The Morning of the Magicians* published in the early 1960s. (The original was published in French in 1960.) But the best known proponent of the ancient astronaut theory is Swiss author Erich von Däniken. In his 1968 best-seller *Chariots of the Gods*, Daniken suggested that the Nazca Lines had been constructed by ancient astronauts as a landing strip for alien space vehicles. Apart from why supposedly advanced alien space vehicles would require miles of landing strips, another objection put forward to this theory by Maria Reiche, was that with desert's soft clay soil any heavy vehicle, such as a spaceship, would simply sink into the desert on landing. Such speculations that aliens were responsible for the creation of the Nazca Lines are usually indicative of the belief that a supposedly primitive native Nazcan culture had neither the intelligence nor the technology to plan and carry out such sophisticated tasks themselves.

That the lines were constructed by the Nazcans for a ritual purpose is now considered the best explanation. As the Nazca Desert only receives about half an inch of rainfall per year, some researchers have proposed that the lines are pathways connecting shrines which would have been walked—perhaps by priests—in a ceremony that included praying or dancing for rain. Anthony Aveni believes the lines were created as sacred pathways, maintained by local kin groups, and connected with the ritual acquisition of water. Aveni's research has shown that many of the Nazca Lines are located close to watercourses, and in many cases seem to follow the direction of the water. Perhaps part of the function of the lines was to point to sources of water?

An idea linked to the religious road theory was proposed by English explorer and filmmaker Tony Morrison. Morrison carried out extensive research into the ancient folkways of the Nazca people and found a tradition of wayside shrines, often merely a pile of stones, linked together by straight lines. Morrison believes that the Nazca lines represent huge versions of these folkways along which Shamans would walk on a "voyage of the soul." Shamans were members of a tribe who acted as mediums between the visible world and the invisible spirit world, and were prominent in most Native American societies. Perhaps when the Shamans walked along the lines of the animal glyphs, they were attempting to put themselves in touch with potent animal spirits. On behalf of the tribe, the Shaman would (in an altered state of consciousness) make personal contact with the supernatural powers contained within the glyphs and attempt to utilize their energy, perhaps to bring rainfall, or perhaps for a purpose we could never even begin to understand. The experience of Shamans usually involved some sort of flight, so Erich von Däniken may in fact have been partly right when he proposed that the glyphs were designed to be seen from the air. However, there is no need for alien visitors; the motivation for the creation of the Nazca lines was connected with the mountain spirits of the Nazcans high up in the misty Andes, their gods dwelling in the sky, and the mystical flights of their Shamans.

The Piri Reis Map

The Piri Reis map, one of the oldest known surviving maps showing the Americas, first came to light in 1929, when historians working in the Topkapi Palace in Istanbul discovered it in a pile of rubble. It is currently located in the Library of the Topkapi Palace, though it is not usually on display to the public. The map dates to the year 1513 and was drawn on gazelle skin by an admiral in the Ottoman Turkish fleet named Piri Reis. It includes a web of criss-crossing lines, known as rhumb lines, common on late medieval mariner's charts, and thought to have been used in plotting out a course. Close examination of the document has shown that it was originally a map of the whole world, but was torn into pieces at some time in its history.

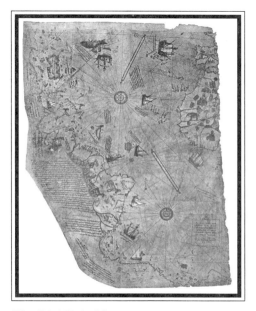

The Piri Reis Map.

The map itself is known as a *portolan* chart, a type common in the 14th to 16th centuries. Such charts were drawn up to guide navigators from port to port, but were not reliable for sailing across an ocean, as they did not consider the Earth's curvature. Such an early map showing America is obviously of considerable historical interest, but some would argue that its importance lies not merely in its depiction of the Americas. In his book *Maps of the Ancient Sea Kings* first published in 1966, Charles Hapgood, a historian and geographer at the University of New Hampshire, put forward the theory that the landmass joined to the southern part of South America at the bottom of the map can only be a depiction of Antarctica, hundreds of years before it was discovered. The apparently detailed rendering of the Antarctic coastline on the chart, including what Hapgood believed was an accurate depiction of Queen Maud Land, shows it *without* glaciers, which would suggest the continent was mapped in remote prehistory, before it became completely covered in ice. But how was Stone Age man able to survey and chart the region of Antarctica at such an early period in human history? Hapgood suggested the existence of now forgotten prehistoric seafaring civilizations, whose achievements included journeying from pole to pole and mapping the entire surface of the Earth at some time in the remote past. Hapgood theorized that these civilizations left a legacy of maps, which were hand copied over thousands of years, perhaps by expert seafaring cultures such as the Minoans and the Phoenicians. For Hapgood, the Piri Reis map was, in effect, a compilation of these ancient maps.

Later, the controversial author Erich von Däniken considered the depiction of a pre-ice-covered Antarctica on the Piri Reis map as evidence to support his ancient astronaut theory, speculating that an extraterrestrial civilization had drawn the original map. In his 1995 book *Fingerprints of the Gods,* Graham Hancock also postulated that a previously unidentified, highly advanced ancient civilization existed in remote prehistory and passed on its sophisticated knowledge of astronomy, architecture, navigation, and mathematics to various ancient cultures including the Olmecs, Aztecs, Maya, and Egyptians. He also speculated that the Piri Reis map-makers may have used source maps compiled by this ancient super-culture. Both Hapgood and Hancock maintain that the Antarctica represented on the Piri Reis map is highly detailed, showing mountains, rivers, and lakes, and that it may have been based on ancient satellite surveys from the sky above Egypt.

Many scientists and archaeologists are sceptical of Hapgood's theory in the first place because there is no record of such an ancient civilization that had the resources, the technology, or most especially the need to undertake a survey of Antarctica. What possible reason could they have had? Allowing for the existence of this advanced prehistoric culture, does the Piri Reis map convincingly show an Antarctica free of ice? Most proponents of the ancient mariner theory emphasize the accuracy of the map, especially the part showing Antarctica, as evidence of lost geographical knowledge. But how accurate is the Piri Reis map? The absence of the Drake Passage between South America and Antarctica means that if the map does show Antarctica, then it depicts it joined to the South American continent, with roughly 932 miles of coast from Brazil to Tierra del Fuego left off. This would be a glaring omission for such a supposedly accurate map.

Examining the rest of the chart, Europe and Africa are shown in a reasonable amount of detail for the time, though peninsulas and inlets are exaggerated, probably due to the necessity at the time of navigating by landmarks. South America is represented as far too narrow although Brazil is fairly accurately shown. North America, on the other hand, is poorly drawn and enormously inaccurate, as if based entirely on hearsay rather than geographical knowledge, something else that would suggest there was no ancient global survey on which to base the map. In fact, there are earlier maps from around A.D. 1500, such as those of Juan de La Cosa and Alberto Cantino, which are more accurate than the Piri Reis map in terms of the positions of islands such as Cuba, Jamaica, and Puerto Rico. One detail, which is alleged to support the extreme antiquity of the map, is that it shows Greenland before it was covered by ice. However, as can be seen from a quick perusal of the map, the top eastern edge clearly shows the western part of France, which is at about 50 degrees north latitude. Consequently, if France is represented as the most northern country on the map, surely Greenland cannot be depicted, and as the map exhibits no islands which are remotely similar to Greenland, it is difficult to know what evidence there is for this suggestion.

To support his theory that the Piri Reis map depicted Antarctica under the ice, Charles Hapgood used sounding data from Antarctic expeditions in the 1940s and 1950s. But Hapgood's hypothesis, once thought by some as scientifically plausible, is now in serious doubt. The insurmountable difficulty with a pre-ice-covered Antarctica being shown on the Piri Reis map is that when Antarctica was last free of ice, its coastal outline would have looked completely different than its current shape. This is because over time, the continental crust has been forced down hundreds of meters, under millions of tons of ice, thus changing the shape of the underlying shoreline completely. A comparison between the Antarctica shown on the Piri Reis map with a relatively recent sub-glacial bedrock topography map of the continent shows no similarities at all between their coastlines. Furthermore, rather than Antarctica being free of ice by 4000 B.C., as claimed by Hapgood, modern geological evidence

now points to the most recent date for an ice-free Antarctica as being more than 14 million years ago.

But perhaps the most convincing evidence against a prehistoric origin for the chart can be found in the notes written on it by Piri Reis himself. In the early 16th century, when the Piri Reis map was drawn, the Portuguese had sailed across the Atlantic and were claiming substantial parts of South America as their own. In relation to the supposed Antarctica land mass, the captions on the map mention that its coast was discovered by Portuguese explorers, whose ships had been blown off course. A particular note on the map refers to a Portuguese ship that landed on this coast and was immediately attacked by unclothed natives; a further caption refers to very hot weather. These descriptions could clearly apply to South America, but hot weather and naked inhabitants in Antarctica are clearly nothing more than fantasy.

The sources for Piri Reis's map have not all been identified by any means, but would likely have included the works of Greek astronomer and geographer Ptolemy (second century A.D.), various Portuguese maps, and Christopher Columbus. In fact, Reis himself notes on the chart that he copied from Columbus's maps. Many features on the Piri Reis map, including place names and representations in the West Indies, show that he was using at least one of Columbus's maps to draw his own chart. Another indication that Reis was using medieval European maps is the depiction, near the top of the chart, of a ship next to a fish, which carries two people on its back.

The note attached to this illustration quotes a medieval story from the life of the Irish saint, Brendan. This has obviously been reproduced by Piri Reis from one of his source maps, proving that one of them, at least, was of medieval European origin.

Greg McIntosh in his *The Piri Reis Map of 1513*, published in 2000, argues that looking at contemporary maps of the period shows that nothing in the Piri Reis map was unknown in 1513. He also suggests that what some have called Antarctica on the Piri Reis map is, in reality, the hypothetical Great Southern Continent, which cartographers had been depicting on maps since Ptolemy's time. The commonly held belief was that a continent must exist in the southern hemisphere to balance the landmasses in the northern hemisphere. McIntosh also demonstrates that all the coasts on the Piri Reis map south of 25 degrees are either inaccurate or wrongly placed, and that the Antarctica depicted on Reis's chart extends north of 40 degrees south latitude, while the actual continent of Antarctica does not extend further than 70. In fact, rather than being a depiction of Antarctica, a close examination of the Piri Reis map reveals that the southern continent bears an extremely close resemblance to the southern half of South America, adjusted width-ways to fit onto the shape of the parchment.

One conspicuously anomalous feature of South America on the Piri Reis map is its apparent depiction of the Andes mountain chain, with the rivers Amazon, Orinoco, and Rio Plata emerging from its base and flowing eastwards to the coast. As the Andes were unknown to Europeans at this time, how did they come to be shown on Piri Reis's map? But Reis's map is not alone in showing a mountain range in the interior of South America; the Nicolo Canerio map, drawn between 1502 and 1504 and now housed in the Bibliotheque Nationale in Paris, depicts the east coast of South America with a tree-topped chain of mountains. From this evidence, it seems likely that the Canerio map was another of Piri Reis's original sources. It is also hard to conceive that if the Piri Reis map were based on the work of an advanced ancient seafaring culture, it would include the Andes but omit the Pacific Ocean. A more plausible explanation is that the mountains depicted in the center of South America on the Piri Reis map are east coast mountains, drawn in the wrong place and at the wrong scale.

Most scholars now believe that the Piri Reis map is no more accurate than would be expected for a 16th century portolan chart, deriving information from existing geographical knowledge and conjecture. There is no reason to believe that Piri Reis based his map on the work of a hypothetical ancient super-culture. Certainly, it is possible that he had ancient source material that is now lost to us, but beyond that, the Piri Reis map should be appreciated for what it is—a strikingly beautiful and historically important document of medieval history.

The Unsolved Puzzle of the Phaistos Disc

Photograph by Maksim. (GNU Free Documentation License).
Replica of the Phaistos Disc.

The undeciphered Phaistos Disc is one of the greatest puzzles in archaeology. Almost everything about this ancient artifact is controversial, from its purpose and meaning to its original area of manufacture. The mysterious clay tablet was found on the Greek island of Crete, at the Minoan Palace site at Phaistos. But who made it, and what was it used for?

The sophisticated Bronze Age civilization of the Minoans reached its height in the period c. 1700 B.C. and began to decline about three centuries later, when many of their palaces were destroyed. The Phaistos Disc was discovered in 1903 by Italian archaeologists excavating at the ruined Minoan palace of Phaistos. The archaeologists came upon the strange object in a basement room in the northeast apartments of the palace, together with a clay tablet inscribed in Linear A (an undeciphered script used on Crete until around 1450 B.C.), and pieces of neopalatial pottery (c. 1700 B.C.–1600 B.C.). The palace had collapsed during an earthquake, which has been linked by some researchers to the massive volcanic eruption on the nearby Aegean island of Thera (modern day Santorini) c. 1628 B.C. The precise age of the Phaistos Disc is disputed; the archaeological context of the find suggests a date not later than 1700 B.C., though the modern opinion is that it could have been created as late as 1650 B.C.

The enigmatic disc is made of baked clay with an average diameter of 6.2 inches, and a thickness of 0.8 inches. Both sides of the disc are covered with a hieroglyphic inscription arranged in a spiral. The inscription was made by impressing wood or ivory hieroglyphic seals or stamps into the wet clay, and then baking the clay at a high temperature to harden it. It has been noted that occasionally on the artifact, a symbol slightly overlaps the one to its right, which demonstrates that the creator was stamping towards the left, that resulted in the text spiraling inwards to the center. The Phaistos Disc represents what is, in effect, the earliest form of printing anywhere in the world.

Printed into the disc are a total of 242 individual impressions divided into 61 groups by vertical lines; there are 45 different signs, including depictions of running men, heads with feather crowns, women, children, animals, birds, insects, tools, weapons, and plants. One or two of these symbols have been identified as vaguely similar to the Cretan hieroglyphs in use during the early to mid-second millennium B.C. What is so puzzling about the artifact is why the Minoans were using a primitive pictographic language at the same time as Linear A, a much more advanced script. Perhaps the primitive nature of the script on the disc points to a much earlier date for the object than is presently accepted. However, this is not necessarily the case, as archaic forms of writing often survive into much later periods, usually in the form of sacred or religious texts, as was the case in ancient Egypt. Furthermore, the text on the Phaistos Disc is unique;

no other examples of the script stamped on it have ever been located. This uniqueness, and the fact that the text is fairly brief, makes it extremely difficult to translate even a small part of it. That the inscription was made using a set of stamps would imply that there was large-scale production of objects impressed with this script, which, for one reason or another, have not yet surfaced in archaeological investigations.

A difficulty with understanding the artifact is that no one knows exactly how the symbols on it are meant to be interpreted. Does the disc contain a hieroglyphic inscription, or are the pictograms meant to be taken at face value? Although some images on the Phaistos Disc are pictures of familiar objects, trying to understand these literally does not help with obtaining any coherent meaning from the disc. Many linguists believe the text is a series of written signs representing syllables (known as a *syllabary*), while others assume it is a syllabary combined with pictorial symbols used to express a concept or idea (known as *ideograms*). The combination of a syllabary and ideograms would make it comparable to all known syllabaries of Greece and the ancient Near East, including Minoan Linear B script, hieroglyphic writing, and cuneiform. (The latter consists of pictograms drawn on clay tablets with a pen made from a sharpened reed, and originated in ancient Sumeria in the late-fourth millennium B.C.) The Palette of Narmer is an interesting example of such texts. It was discovered in Nekhen, (modern Hierakonpolis,) the ancient pre-dynastic capital of Egypt, by English archeologist James E.

Quibell, in 1894. It dates roughly to 3200 B.C. and includes some of the earliest hieroglyphic inscriptions ever discovered. The Palette of Narmer uses a combination of hieroglyphs and pictographic symbols, which are to be taken literally to mean what they depict, indicating a possible parallel with the Phaistos Disc, in the sense that it could be interpreted as containing a mixture of ancient Cretan hieroglyphs and pictographs.

The tremendous difficulty of translation without further examples of the script has not dissuaded both scholars and amateurs from attempting the task. In fact, the unique nature of the text has added to its mystique and enthralled rather than repelled investigators. The distinctiveness of the disc has, unfortunately, meant that there have been a number of highly imaginative and unsubstantiated translations and interpretations of the text. Perhaps the most extreme among them is that the object contains a message left thousands of years ago by extraterrestrial visitors, or an ancient Atlantean civilization, for future generations to discover. The question of what exactly the message contains or why it was written in such a primitive script by supposedly advanced aliens (or Atlanteans) has, of course, never been answered.

Over the last 100 years numerous attempts have been made to try and identify the language on the disc. In 1975, Jean Faucounau published a translation, maintaining that the language was a pre-Greek, syllabic writing of a culture he identifies as Proto-Ionians, a people with closer ties to ancient Troy than to Crete. According to Faucounau's decipherment, the

Phaistos Disc describes the career and funeral of a Proto-Ioanian king named Arion. His translation has, however, not been accepted as sound by most scholars on the subject. In 2000, Greek author Efi Polygiannakis published (in Greek) a book entitled *The Disc Speaks in Greek*, claiming that the inscription on the disc was written in the syllabic writing system of an ancient Greek dialect. Dr. Steven Fischer's *Evidence of Hellenic Dialect in the Phaistos Disk* (1988) also identifies the text as syllabic writing in a Greek dialect.

One clue to the meaning of the object is the context in which it was found. The fact that the Phaistos Disc was unearthed in an underground temple depository has persuaded some researchers of its religious significance, suggesting that the text was possibly a sacred hymn or ritual. Several image groups in the text are repeated, which would suggest a refrain, and perhaps each side of the disc represents a verse from a song, hymn, or ritual incantation. In fact, Sir Arthur Evans, excavator of Knossos (the ceremonial and political center of Minoan civilization), concluded that the disc contained part of the text of a sacred song. The original discoverer of the disc, Italian archaeologist Luigi Pernier, also believed it had ritual significance. Nevertheless, though the Phaistos Disc was found at a Minoan palace site, there is no absolute proof that it originated on Crete at all. It may have been imported from just about anywhere in the Mediterranean, or even from the Near East.

While a religious/ritual explanation is certainly a possibility, it is only one of numerous ideas so far suggested for the Phaistos Disc. Theories include: an ancient adventure story, an ancient calendar, a call to arms, a spell written in Hittite (a language used in Turkey c. 1600–1100 B.C.), a legal document, a farmer's almanac, a schedule for palace activities, and a game board. In his 1980 book *The Phaistos Disc: Hieroglyphic Greek with Euclidean Dimensions,* German author Andis Kaulins claims to have deciphered the mysterious script and maintained that the language of the disc was Greek, and that it contains the proof of a geometric theorem. However, Kaulins' translation has found little support among archaeologists and linguists. In his 1999 book, *The Bronze Age Computer Disc*, author Alan Butler postulated that the Phaistos Disc functioned as an incredibly accurate astronomical calendar/calculating device. However, there is no explicit evidence that the Minoans had any detailed knowledge of astronomy, and even the Egyptian comprehension of astronomy at the time was not detailed enough to support Butler's hypothesis.

Not a single example of the stamped or printed method of writing on the Phaistos Disc has been found in the numerous excavations carried out on Crete over the past 100 years. This complete lack of comparative material has suggested to some that this disc is a forgery. Something that adds to the feeling of unease about the disc's authenticity is that specialists in Mediterranean and Near Eastern archaeology seem unwilling to get involved in the debate about the artifact. A thermoluminescence dating test would certainly prove whether the object was made during the last hundred years, or if it did in fact date to the Minoan period. So far the Greek authorities have been unwilling to submit the disc to such a test. Consequently, the possibility that the object is a forgery made in the early 1900s—using the limited knowledge of the Minoan culture available at the time—is perhaps a far-fetched, but by no means out of the question scenario. In connection with the hoax theory, an intriguing find was made in 1992 in the basement of a house in Vladikavkaz, Russia. This was a fragment of a clay disc, smaller in size than the Phaistos Disc, but apparently a copy of it, though the symbols on this disc were incised rather than stamped. There were rumours of a hoax, but the Russian disc mysteriously disappeared a few years later, and nothing has been heard since.

Despite the apparent thanklessness of the task, many researchers throughout the world still work diligently attempting to decipher the disc. But the extreme variations in the many purported translations have made scholars doubtful of any future success at decipherment, and indicate to many that while it remains an isolated example of its kind, the disc can never be properly understood. We can only hope that future archaeological excavations in Crete, or perhaps elsewhere in the Mediterranean, will turn up further examples of this mysterious script. Until then, the Phaistos Disc, now on display in the archaeological museum of Heraklion in Crete, will remain a unique enigma.

The Shroud of Turin

It is difficult to imagine a more controversial historical artifact than the Turin Shroud. On one side, there are those who believe the shroud to be the actual cloth that was wrapped around the body of Jesus after he was taken down from the cross. Skeptics on the other hand, of are of the opinion that the artifact is a medieval hoax. The vital matters of where, when, and how the image on the cloth was created are subjects of intense debate among historians, scientists, believers, and skeptics. Even the supposedly decisive radiocarbon dating carried out on the shroud in 1988 has ultimately failed to resolve the issue, due to doubts cast on the quality of the sample used in the tests.

The Shroud of Turin is a large, woven linen sheet 14.4 feet long by 3.6 feet wide. The front and back of the cloth bear the image of a naked man with his hands folded across the body, who appears to have suffered injuries

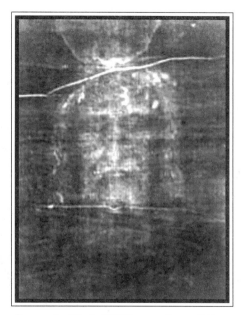

Secondo Pia's 1898 negative of the image on the Shroud of Turin.

consistent with crucifixion. The serene face of the man is bearded, the body at around 6 feet tall, is fairly tall, both for the first century A.D. or medieval times. The cloth contains dark red stains, resembling blood, and on one wrist (the other is not visible) there is a noticeable circular wound. Further wounds are apparent in the side, forehead, and legs. No representative of the church has made any claims about the shroud, but many people are convinced that the picture contained on it is an image of the crucified Christ.

Much of the history of the object is obscure. The first record of it as the Shroud of Turin is not until the 16th century. There are, however, earlier mentions of a cloth bearing the image of Christ. For example, the fourth century church historian Eusebius, Bishop of Caesarea, describes the existence of a miraculous image of Jesus, painted from life, which was supposed to be preserved in Edessa, Syria. A legend recorded by John of Damascus (c. A.D. 676–A.D.749), describes how King Abgar of Edessa, afflicted with an incurable illnes, sent a letter to Jesus asking him to come to Edessa and cure him. Jesus was unable to go, but instead miraculously impressed an image of himself on a piece of cloth and sent it to the king via Thaddeus (also known as Addai), one of the 72 disciples. When Abgar beheld the miraculous image (described by John as an oblong cloth), he was immediately cured. This holy relic became known as the *Edessa Image,* or to Orthodox Christians the *Mandylion.* Although the legend of the Edessa Image describes a facial image on a square or rectangular cloth, researchers (including author Ian Wilson) have suggested that the Edessa Image was folded in a manner that only displayed the face. In A.D. 944, on the arrival of the Edessa Image at Constantinople, Gregory Referendarius, the archdeacon of Hagia Sophia in that city, gave a sermon discussing the artifact. His description makes it clear that the Edessa Image was a full length burial shroud, bearing an image of a whole body and showing bloodstains believed to be from the wounds in Jesus's side. This artifact was subsequently deposited in the Palatine Chapel, where it remained until the city was ransacked and burned by the Crusaders in 1204. The Crusaders brought away a number of treasures from Constantinople, though whether the Image of Odessa was among them is not known. Nevertheless, many researchers believe that the cloth was brought to Europe at this time by the Crusaders, and became known as the Shroud of Turin.

In 1357 the shroud was exhibited by Jeanne de Vergy, widow of the French Knight Geoffroi of Charney, in a church in the small village of Lirey, northeastern France. In 1453 the cloth came into the possession of Duke Louis of Savoy, who kept it in his chapel in Chambéry, the capital of the Duchy of Savoy, in the modern Rhône-Alpes region of France. In 1532 the shroud was damaged in a fire in the chapel where it was stored. (It may also have suffered water damage at this time from attempts to extinguish the fire.) Poor Clare nuns attempted to repair this damage by weaving patches into the cloth. In 1578 the shroud arrived in its present home in Turin, and in 1983 it became the property of the Holy See (Vatican City), after Umberto II, the last of the House of Savoy dynasty, left it to the pope in his will. The shroud remains today in Turin, in the round chapel of the Cathedral of Saint John the Baptist.

In 1988, among much publicity, the Holy See allowed the relic to be independently radiocarbon dated by three separate research institutions: Oxford University, the University of Arizona, and the Swiss Federal Institute of Technology. The laboratories all used parts from the same sample, a piece of cloth just 1 centimeter by 5.7 centimeter, taken from the corner of the shroud, for testing. The conclusion from the tests was that the object dated from sometime between A.D. 1260 and 1390, the era when the shroud was first exhibited, and was therefore not the burial cloth of Christ, but a medieval forgery.

Another piece of evidence which appears to support the theory that the shroud is a medieval forgery comes in the form of a letter from Bishop Pierre D'Arcis of Troyes, in northeastern France. This letter, written in 1389 (ostensibly to the Avignon pope, Clement VII, in southern France) claims that an investigation into the nature of the cloth by his predecessor Bishop Henri of Poitiers had exposed the artist responsible for painting it, and he requested that the relic be removed from display. The letter goes on to say that the cloth could not be the actual burial cloth of Jesus Christ because "the holy Gospel made no mention of any such imprint; while, if it had been true, it was quite unlikely that the holy evangelist would have omitted to record it, or that the fact should have remained hidden until the present time." However, this document appears to be a rough draft of a letter that was never actually sent, and some researchers have questioned the motives of Bishop D'Arcis, suggesting that he coveted the cloth for his own gain.

But if the cloth was a fake, who was responsible and how had they carried it out? In their book *The Second Messiah,* Christopher Knight and Robert Lomas claim that the face on the shroud belongs to Jacques de Molay, the last Grand Master of the Order of the Knights Templar. De Molay was arrested on the orders of Philip IV of France for heresy and burnt at the stake on an island in the river Seine in Paris on March 18, 1314. According to the authors, de Molay was tortured and his arms and legs nailed to a wooden door to parody the sufferings of Jesus. After this, they hypothesize, de Molay was laid on a length of cloth on a soft bed and part of the cloth was draped over his head covering the front of his body. Apparently he was then left, perhaps partly comatised, for

a period of 30 hours, during which time the sweat and blood from de Molay's body imprinted an image on the sheet.

Further evidence, which apparently backs up the de Molay theory, is that the Grand Master was executed together with Geoffroy de Charney, the Templar preceptor of Normandy, whose grandson was Geoffroi de Charney. After the death of Geoffroi de Charney in 1356 at the battle of Poitiers, his widow, Jeanne de Vergy, allegedly discovered the shroud in his possession and put it on display at the church in Lirey. The Knight-Lomas theory relies heavily on the reliability of the radiocarbon dates from the shroud obtained in 1988, and the hypotheses of the authors about the torture methods used on de Molay. Nevertheless, the image on the shroud does bear a resemblance to depictions of de Molay in medieval woodcuts, and to a 19th century color lithograph of him by Chevauchet.

Another candidate for the face on the shroud is the Italian polymath Leonardo da Vinci (1452–1519). Authors Lynn Picknett and Clive Prince have proposed that the shroud actually represents a self-portrait of da Vinci, and is possibly the first example of photography in history. The photograph theory, which has also been proposed by other researchers, suggests that the image on the cloth was constructed with the aid of *camera obscura* (a dark room or box with a hole in one side, through which an inverted image of the scene outside is projected onto an opposite wall, screen, or mirror, and then traced by the artists to make the image). The main objections to this theory is that da Vinci was born almost a century after the appearance of the cloth in historical records, and also that he lived outside the time frame of A.D. 1260 to 1390 given by the radiocarbon dates.

However, recent research has thrown considerable doubt on the validity of the 1988 radiocarbon dates. A paper by chemist Raymond N. Rogers (published in the January 2005 issue of the scientific journal *Thermochimica Acta*) indicates that the original sample of cloth used for radiocarbon dating was invalid. Chemical testing found that the radiocarbon sample had completely different chemical properties than the rest of the shroud, persuading many researchers to believe that the sample used for radiocarbon dating must have been cut from one of the patches used to repair the cloth after the 1532 fire. Rogers concluded from his chemical analyses of the cloth that it was at least 1,300 years old.

In June 2002, a major restoration of the shroud was undertaken, which involved the removal of all the medival repair patches. During this process, expert textile restorer Mechthild Flury-Lemberg found that the fabric of the shroud had been woven in a three-to-one herringbone pattern, a type of weave used for high quality cloths in the ancient world. Flury-Lemberg also pointed out the presence of this same weave pattern on a 12th century illustration depicting Christ's burial cloth, which would suggest that the artist possessed enough knowledge of the shroud to recognize the specific weave pattern of the cloth. She also noted the similarities between an unusual stitching pattern on the seam of one long side of the shroud and that on the hem of a cloth discovered in the tombs of the Jewish fortress of Masada, overlooking the Dead Sea. The Masada cloth dates to between 40 B.C. and A.D. 73, and Flury-Lemberg believes that the Turin Shroud is of roughly the same age, dating to somewhere in the first century A.D.

It was also during the 2002 restorations that the back of the controversial cloth was photographed and scanned for the first time. In 2004, the Institute of Physics in London published an article in the *Journal of Optics A*, revealing the results of the analysis of the photographs. Using image processing techniques, Italian scientists Giulio Fanti and Roberto Maggiolio of Padova University identified a faint, ghostly image on the reverse of the cloth, showing mainly the face and hands. This second image corresponds with that on the front of the cloth, and is entirely superficial, thus ruling out the possibility of paint seeping through from the front. It would also appear to rule out the theory that the image on the shroud was created using early photographic methods.

So does this recent reversal of fortune for the Turin Shroud mean that it really is the burial cloth of Christ? Although many believers are convinced that this new evidence is the final proof of the cloth's authenticity, skeptics refuse to admit to the possibilty of the artifact being the real thing. Many researchers now hope that the Vatican will allow more samples to be taken from the shroud for retesting, though the church at present seems reluctant to do so. Perhaps there will never be any scientific proof that the Turin Shroud is beyond doubt the cloth in which Joseph of Arimathaea wrapped the body of Christ. To believe so may always be a question of faith.

The Stone Spheres of Costa Rica

Photograph by Connor Lee. (GNU Free Documentation License).
Stone sphere in the courtyard of El Musco Nacional.

One of the most enigmatic puzzles of pre-Columbian America is that of the mysterious stone spheres of Costa Rica. Hundreds of these stone balls, varying in size from a few centimeters to 7 feet in diameter and the largest weighing 16 tons, have been found in the Diquis region near the towns of Palmar Sur and Palmar Norte, close to the Pacific coast of southern Costa Rica. The majority are fashioned from granodiorite, a hard, igneous rock similar to granite, but there are a few examples made of coquina, a type of limestone composed mostly of shells and shell fragments.

The spheres first came to light in the 1930s, when the United Fruit Company was clearing jungle to plant banana and other fruit trees. Workers for the company discovered the objects and, remembering a local legend about the spheres being built around a core of gold, blew many of them apart with dynamite looking for the hidden gold. In 1948, Dr. Samuel Lothrop of the Peabody Museum at Harvard University, and his wife, studied the stone balls in context, and in 1963 the final report of the study was published. In his report, Lothrop records a total of 186 examples, although he had also heard of a site near Jalaca that had another 45 balls, before they were taken away to other locations. There have also been finds on Cano Island, 12.5 miles west of the southern Pacific coast. On this evidence it seems that there were once several hundred of these stone sculptures in existence. Since the 1940s, most of the balls have been removed from their original context, often being transported by rail all over the country. Today, only six are known to remain in their original positions. Some can be seen displayed in the National Museum, and several are in parks and gardens in the country's capital, San José.

Scholarly research into the Costa Rica stone spheres has been going on for more than 60 years. It began in 1943 with a study of the objects by archaeologist Doris Zemurray Stone, daughter of Samuel Zemurray, founder of the United Fruit Company. She examined the stones directly after they were discovered by workers for the Fruit Company. Stone, later to become the director of the National Museum of Costa Rica, published her findings in the journal *American Antiquity* in 1943. The study contains plans of five sites, including 44 stone balls, and her interpretation was that the spheres could have served as cult images or cemetery markers, or were perhaps connected with some kind of calendar.

The publication of the Lothrops' study in 1963 includes maps of sites where the spheres were found, and comprehensive accounts of pottery and metal artifacts found in association with and in the vicinity of them. Also included are numerous photographs and drawings of the spheres, including measurements and notes on their alignments.

Further archaeological excavations in the 1950s found the stone spheres associated with pottery and other artifacts known from the pre-Columbian cultures of southern Costa Rica. There have been various other studies made since then, the most thorough being that of archaeologist Ifigenia Quintanilla of the National Museum of Costa Rica, from 1990 to 1995. Archaeologists have long puzzled over the origin of these strange spheres, and whether they were natural or man-made is still a much discussed point. Some geologists have suggested that the stones were formed naturally, theorizing that after a volcano released magma into the air, it settled in a hot, ash-filled valley; the blobs of magma then gradually cooled down to form spheres. Another suggestion is that the original granite blocks were positioned in a man-made pit at the bottom of a powerful waterfall, and the effect of the water continuously flowing over them slowly modeled the stones into near-perfect spheres. Despite these theories, it is more probable that the stones are man-made, especially in view of the fact that the granodiorite from which the majority of them were created does not occur naturally in the area. The quarry from which the rock originated is located in the Talamanca mountain range, about 50 miles from the area where the balls have been found. Archaeologist Ifigenia Quintanilla carried out fieldwork in the area of the finds from 1990 to 1995 and traced the source of the raw material, as well as some boulders that were possibly unfinished examples of the stone spheres. Quintanilla's excavations also revealed flakes from the balls that indicate how they were made. Her findings suggest that the most plausible method would have been to begin by reducing a roughly circular boulder to a more spherical shape by alternative heating and cooling to fracture the rock. The builders could then have smoothed them out using hard stone hammers, possibly of the same material, and finally polished them using other stone tools.

One misconception about the objects is that they are almost perfect spheres, accurate to within "0.5 inch or 0.2 percent" as some have suggested. This is not the case, as there have been no such precise measurements of the spheres. The balls are not flawlessly smooth at all, some can differ more than 5 centimeters in diameter from a true sphere. A problem of a different type is how pre-Columbian societies moved the stones to their required locations. Such a task certainly points to an advanced and organized culture (though if the stones were carved in a mountain quarry, it is obvious that spherical objects roll fairly easily, especially downhill).

The question of who made these mysterious spheres and why is a more complicated issue. According to archaeologists the spheres were shaped during two separate cultural periods. Only a handful of spheres remain from the earlier of these, known as the Aguas Buenas period, which lasted from around A.D. 100 to 500. In the second phase, the Chiriquí period (which dates from around A.D. 800 to 1500), a larger amount of the stone spheres appear to have been manufactured, with a distribution along the lower part of the Terraba River. However, this does not tell us anything about the function of the spheres. Leaving aside helpful intervention by extraterrestrials or Atlanteans, the most unique theory is that they were set up by an extremely advanced prehistoric culture to function as antennae-forming part of an ancient worldwide power grid. However, without concrete evidence, such a theory is baseless, and just as mythical as the local legend that the local people had access to a potion with which they were able to soften the rock. In their 1998 book, *Atlantis in America: Navigators of the Ancient World,* Ivar Zapp and George Erikson suggest that the spheres were set up as navigational instruments by an advanced ancient seafaring race, a race that influenced the Greek philosopher Plato to write about the lost land of Atlantis. However, this theory requires the spheres to be placed close enough to the coast to be seen by navigators, which is not the case. It also presupposes an accuracy in the alignments of the spheres not present in the examples we have left in their original context.

We don't really know why these objects were made, especially as most of them have been moved from their original locations. This is a significant problem, as the placements of the stone balls was probably of vital importance to the people who first positioned them. However, going on the available evidence, the most probable theory for a number of the spheres is that they were used as markers of some kind, perhaps property boundaries or status symbols. Another idea, taking into account that many of the balls were originally found in alignments, is that they represent the sun, moon, and all the known planets at the time of their placement. It has even been suggested that they represent the entire solar system. An interesting fact noted by Lothrop in the 1940s was that several of the balls he examined seemed to have tumbled down from neighboring mounds, which were formerly the sites of houses. Perhaps the spheres had once been contained inside these structures on top of the mounds, though this would make them ineffective for astronomy, and certainly of no use to navigators. It is likely that the spheres had numerous purposes, which perhaps changed over the 1,000 years they were around. One interesting idea is that the laborious manufacture of the spheres may itself have been a significant ritual as important—or perhaps more important—than the finished product.

Ever since their discovery, the stone spheres of Costa Rica have been affected by exposure to temperature changes, damage from rain and irrigation, and periodic burning. In 1997, the Landmarks Foundation was created to conserve sacred sites and landscapes around the world. In 2001, with the cooperation of various governmental organizations, the Foundation and the National Museum of Costa Rica were able to transport many of the spheres from San José across the high mountain range and back to their original homes. They are currently being stored and protected until a Cultural Center can be constructed to house and display them in their original locations in the Diquis Delta.

Archaeologists still occasionally find new examples of the spheres in the mud of the Diquis Delta, and there are probably more out there. In modern day Costa Rica, the stones can be found in museums and adorning the lawns outside various official buildings, hospitals, and schools. Two of them have been transported to the United States: one is on display in the museum of the National Geographic Society in Washington, D.C., while the other is in a courtyard near the Peabody Museum of Archaeology and Ethnography at Harvard University in Cambridge, Massachusetts. The spheres can also be found decorating the gardens of the homes of the rich, where they are regarded as status symbols. In a way then, though many of the stones have long ago been moved from their place of origin, some of them at least may be serving the purpose for which they were originally intended.

Talos: An Ancient Greek Robot?

Photograph by Y. Dondas
The coast of Crete, which was once patrolled by the bronze giant, Talos.

Many people are familiar with the figure of Talos through his depiction as a bronze giant in the 1963 movie *Jason and the Argonauts* using Ray Harryhausen's stunning special effects. But where did the idea for Talos come from, and could he have been the first robot in history?

Originally, Talos was a figure of Cretan legend, though there are many diverse myths to account for his origins. After Zeus kidnapped Europa and took her to Crete, he gave her three presents to demonstrate his love, one of which was the giant bronze automaton Talos. In another version of the tale, the giant was forged by Hephaestus and the Cyclopes and given to Minos, king of Crete. According to yet another myth, Talos was the son of Cris and father of Phaestos, or he was Minos's brother. Others have said that he was in fact a bull, probably identical to the Cretan Minotaur in the Labyrinth. According to the ancient writer Apollodorus of Rhodes's

Argonautica he may have been the last of a generation of men of bronze, originally sprung from the ash trees and who survived to the age of the demigods.

Talos, or Talus, in the ancient Cretan dialect means *sun*, and in Crete the god Zeus was also given the same name, *Zeus Tallaios*. Talos was the guardian of the island of Crete, and made a circuit of the island's coast three times daily, to prevent an enemy invasion, and also to stop the inhabitants from leaving without Minos's permission. He also traveled thrice yearly to the villages of Crete, carrying with him bronze tablets on which were inscribed Minos's sacred laws, and was responsible for these laws being obeyed in the country. Talos was said to hurl enormous boulders and other debris at approaching enemy vessels so that they would not land on the island. If the enemy got through this initial bombardment, the bronze giant would leap into a fire until he glowed red-hot, and would then clasp the strangers in his burning embrace as they landed on the island. It was also said that Talos was once in the possession of the Sardinians, and that when they refused to hand over the brazen man to Minos, Talos leapt into a fire, clasping them to his breast and killing them with their mouths open. From this incident, apparently, comes the expression *sardonic laugh*, which is applied to those who laugh at their own or others' troubles.

Jason and the Argonauts encountered Talos as they approached Crete on their way home from obtaining the Golden Fleece. The giant kept their boat, the *Argo*, at bay by hurling great

boulders towards it, which he had broken off from the cliffs. Medea, the witch accompanying Jason, helped them escape Talos's destructive blows by using her magic. It is recorded that Talos had a single red vein covered by a thin skin running from his neck to his heel, bound shut by a bronze nail. This nail sealed in the divine ichor (an oily substance often referred to as the *blood of the gods*), which enabled his metal limbs to move. This was the one vulnerable spot on his body. In the *Argonautica*, Medea bewitched the giant with a hostile gaze and invoked the Keres (spirits of death) with songs and prayers. As Talos was attempting to hurl boulders to repel these wailing spirits, he accidentally grazed his ankle on a sharp stone at a spot where his vulnerable vein lay concealed. He collapsed to the ground with a great crash, causing the divine ichor to gush out like molten lead. In another version, Medea enchanted the bronze man and deceived him into thinking that she would give him a secret potion to make him immortal if he would let her stop on the island. Talos agreed and drank the potion, which immediately put him to sleep. Medea went to him in his sleep and pulled the plug from his ankle, whereupon he died.

Others believed that the Argonaut Poeas (father of Philoctetes, who was to fight in the Trojan War) pierced the giant's vein with an arrow. After Talos's death, the *Argo* was able to land safely on Crete. Coins depicting Talos, dating from the fourth to the third centuries B.C. have been found in the Cretan city of Phaistos. A late fifth-century A.D. red-figure krater (vase) shows the Dioskouroi (hero-gods Castor and

Polydeukes) catching the dying Talos, as Medea, in Oriental dress, stands at the side in front of the *Argo*, holding an embroidered sack (presumably containing her magic potions and drugs).

There are various ways to interpret the myth of the giant bronze man of Crete. The story certainly has overtones of the very similar fate of Achilles during the Trojan War, and perhaps they had the same source. A political interpretation would suggest that Talos represented the Minoan fleet armed with metal weapons. When the mainland Greeks from the *Argo* defeated Talos, the power of Crete vanished and the control of the Greek world was transferred to the mainland. Or perhaps the harbors of Crete were infested with pirates and Talos represented the Minoan guard against pirates in the form of three watches which sent out patrols. The poet Robert Graves has suggested that Talos's single vein belongs to the mystery of early bronze casting by the *cire-perdue* (lost wax) method, which involves the sculptor producing a model in clay that is then coated with wax. This model is then covered with a perforated clay mold. When heated, the mold will lose the wax (hence the name of the method) as it runs out of the holes in the plaster. The metal in liquid form is then poured into the space formerly occupied by the wax.

A religious/ritual interpretation has been suggested by the discovery of Minoan seal stones dating from c. 1500 B.C., showing a goddess or priestess paddling a boat to seaside shrines, indicating a similar divine circumnavigation of the island to that of the bronze giant. As *Talos* is the Cretan word for the sun, Robert Graves has suggested that he would, as the sun, have circled Crete originally only once a day. And because Talos, a bronze image of the sun, was also called Taurus (the bull) and the Cretan year was divided into three seasons, his thrice-yearly visit to the villages could have been a royal progress of the Sun King, wearing his ritual bull mask.

Another theory is that Talos represents the first fully operational robot in history. It has been calculated that if Talos could circuit Crete three times a day, it would mean that he had an average speed of 155 miles per hour. Proponents of this view point out that when the giant was wounded in the ankle, what poured out seems similar to molten lead. In general, the Greeks were fascinated with automata of all kinds, often using them in theater productions and religious ceremonies. There is some history of ancient robotics, albeit in primitive form. In 350 B.C. the brilliant Greek mathematician Archytas built a mechanical bird, dubbed The Pigeon, that was propelled by steam. It was one of histories earliest studies of flight, as well as possibly the first model airplane. In 322 B.C. the Greek philosopher Aristotle, perhaps foreseeing the development of robots, wrote "If every tool, when ordered, or even of its own accord, could do the work that befits it...then there would be no need either of apprentices for the master workers or of slaves for the lords." In the late third century B.C. the Greek inventor and physicist Ctesibius of Alexandria designed water clocks with movable figures on them, which kept more accurate time than any clock invented until the 17th century.

More than 1,600 years later, around the year A.D. 1495, Leonardo da Vinci designed (and perhaps even built) a mechanical armored knight, probably the first humanoid robot in history. The machinery inside da Vinci's robot, a cable-and-pulley-driven artificial man, was designed to create the illusion that a real person was inside. This robot could sit up, wave its arms, and move its head while opening and closing an anatomically correct jaw. It may even have emitted sounds to the accompaniment of automated musical instruments, such as drums. In fact, there were quite a few inventors in medieval times who built machines similar to this to entertain royalty. Da Vinci's robot was dressed in a typical, late-15th century German-Italian suit of armor. From da Vinci's designs, it appears that all the joints moved in unison, powered and controlled by a mechanical, analogue-programable controller located within the chest. The legs were powered separately by an external crank assembly driving the cable, which was connected to important locations in the ankle, knee, and hip.

In 2005, the Biochemical Engineering Faculty at the University of Connecticut began a recreation of the basic structure of da Vinci's original robot. Their design will incorporate 21st century technology including "vision, speech recognition, and voice command, computer-integrated movements, and a more advanced body structure." The robot will also possess a mobile neck and have the capacity to follow moving objects with its eyes. The recreation will operate in two modes, one which will respond to computer commands and the other to spoken commands. Da Vinci's original pulleys and gears will be utilized in conjunction with muscle models to imitate natural human movements.

It all seems a very long way from ancient Greece. Nevertheless, even though Talos was probably a figure of myth, the giant bronze man of Crete was perhaps the prototype of all modern robots.

The Baghdad Battery

The Baghdad Battery in the Baghdad Museum.

Some researchers have seen in ancient Egyptian wall carvings or in ancient texts evidence for ancient electricity. Though these claims generally lack physical proof, there is one particular ancient artifact that is believed by some scientists to be an example of an electrical power source. Despite its plain appearance, this small, undecorated jar may change the accepted view of the history of scientific discovery.

The object, thought to be a 2,000-year-old electric battery, was found in 1936 by workers moving earth for a new railway in the area of Khujut Rabu, southeast of Baghdad. The battery appears to have been unearthed in a tomb of the Parthian period (247 B.C.–A.D. 228). When found, it consisted of a 13 centimeter tall oval jar of bright yellow clay, inside of which were a rolled up copper sheet, an iron rod, and some fragments of asphalt. The asphalt had been used to seal the top and bottom of the copper cylinder, as well as to hold the iron rod in place in the center of the cylinder. The use of an asphalt sealing indicated that the object had once contained liquid of some sort, as is also suggested by traces of corrosion on the copper tube, which was probably caused by an acidic agent, perhaps vinegar or wine. Similar artifacts were found in the nearby cities of Seleucia (where the jar contained papyrus rolls) and Ctesiphon (where it contained rolled bronze sheets).

In 1938, German archaeologist Wilhelm König, then director of the Baghdad Museum Laboratory, came upon the strange object, or a series of objects (accounts differ) in a box in the museum basement. After a close examination, he realized that the artifact closely resembles a Galvanic cell, or modern electrical battery. König subsequently published a paper suggesting that the object was an ancient battery, possibly used for electroplating (transferring a thin film of gold or silver from one surface to another) gold onto silver objects. He also theorized that several batteries could have been attached to each other to increase their output. The most conservative date for the battery is now thought to be somewhere between 250 B.C. and A.D. 640, but the first known electric battery, the Voltaic pile, was not invented by Italian physicist Alessandro Volta until 1800. So if this was a primitive battery, where did the ancient Parthians acquire the knowledge to assemble it, and how did it work? After reading König's paper, Willard F.M. Gray, an engineer at the General Electric High Voltage Laboratory in Pittsfield, Massachusetts, decided to construct and test a replica of the ancient battery. When he filled the clay jar with grape juice, vinegar, or copper sulphate solution, he found that it generated about one and a half to two volts of electricity.

In 1978, Egyptologist Dr. Arne Eggebrecht, at the time director of the Roemer and Pelizaeus Museum in Hildesheim, Germany, constructed a replica of the Baghdad Battery and filled it with grape juice. This replica generated 0.87 volts, which he used to electroplate a silver statuette with gold; the layer deposited being a mere 1/10,000 of a millimeter thick. As a result of this experiment, Eggebrecht speculated that many ancient items in museums that are presumed to be manufactured from gold may instead be gold-plated silver. More replicas of the Baghdad artifact were made in 1999 by students under the supervision of Dr. Marjorie Senechal, professor of mathematics and the history of science at Smith College in Massachusetts. The students filled one replica jar with vinegar, and it produced 1.1 volts. Judging by these experiments, the Baghdad Battery was obviously able to produce a small current, but what would it have been used for?

The most popular theory is the one originated by König, that when these cells were connected together in a series, the current generated would have been enough for electroplating metals. König found Sumerian copper vases plated with silver, dating back to 2500 B.C., which he speculated could have been electroplated using similar batteries to that discovered in Khujut Rabu, though no evidence of Sumerian batteries has ever been found. König pointed out that craftsmen in modern-day Iraq still use a primitive electroplating technique to coat copper jewelry with a fine layer of silver. He thought it possible that the method was in use in the Parthian period and had been passed on down the years.

In a slightly different form, the technique is known today in a process called gilding, where a layer of gold or silver is applied to a piece of jewelry.

Another theory regarding the electrical use of the batteries is that they were used medicinally. Ancient Greek and Roman writings indicate that there was a fairly sophisticated knowledge of electricity in the ancient world. The Greeks mention how pain could be treated by applying electric fish to the feet; sufferers would stand on an electric eel until the inflamed foot became numb. Torpedo or electric rays possess two electric organs behind their eye, and discharge 50 to 200 volts at 50 amps, which they use as a weapon to stun small prey that swim above them. The Roman writer Claudian described how a torpedo was caught on a bronze hook and emitted an effluence which spread through the water and up the line to give the fisherman a shock. It is recorded that Roman doctors would attach a pair of these electric rays onto a patient's temples in order to treat a range of illnesses, from gout to headaches. Ancient Babylonian doctors are also known to have used electric fish as a local anesthetic. The ancient Greeks also discovered one of the earliest examples of static electricity; when they rubbed amber (in Greek, *electron*) against a piece of fur, they found that the amber would afterward attract feathers, dust particles, and pieces of straw. However, although the Greeks noticed this strange effect, they had no idea what caused it and probably regarded it as a mere curiosity. But not everyone is convinced of the practicality of the battery for the treatment of pain.

The main problem with the theory of medicinal use is the very low voltage the battery produces, which some doubt would have had any noticeable effect on anything other than very minor pain. Again though, if a series of these batteries were connected together, there could have been enough electricity generated. Staying with an medicinal/electrical explanation for the Baghdad Battery, Paul T. Keyser of the University of Alberta in Canada, has postulated another use for the battery based on finds of bronze and iron needles discovered with the other battery-like devices unearthed at Seleucia, not far from Babylon. His suggestion, published in a 1993 paper, is that these needles may have been used for a kind of electro-acupuncture, a treatment already in use in China at the time.

Some researchers favor a ritual use for the Baghdad Battery. Dr. Paul Craddock, an expert in historical metallurgy from the Department of Scientific Research at the British Museum, has proposed that a group of these ancient cells connected together may have been concealed inside a metal statue. Worshippers coming into contact with the idol would get a small electric shock, similar to that of static electricity, possibly when giving the wrong answer to a question posed by the priest. Perhaps this mysterious tingling effect would have been thought of by the worshippers as evidence of magic, and the power and mystique of the particular priest and temple would thus be greatly enhanced. Unfortunately, unless such statues are actually recovered, a ritual use for the cells remains just another fascinating theory.

Despite the repeated tests with replicas of the Baghdad Batteries, skeptics argue that there is no proof that they ever functioned as electric batteries. They note that the ancient people supposedly responsible for this technology, the Parthians, were known as great warriors, but not regarded for their scientific achievements. Skeptics also point to the fact that despite the extensive historical records we have concerning this area and period, there is no mention of anything connected with electricity anywhere. There are also no archaeological finds from the Parthian period that have been proved to be electrogilded, and no evidence of wires, conductors, or more complete examples of ancient batteries. Some researchers have also disputed the results from experiments with replicas of the battery, claiming that they have been unable to duplicate the results themselves. Dr. Arne Eggebrecht's experiments in particular, have come under fire. According to Dr. Bettina Schmitz, a researcher at Roemer and Pelizaeus Museum (the same institution where Eggebrecht did his 1978 experiments with reproductions of the battery), there are no photos or written documentation of the experiments which Eggebrecht undertook.

A favored alternative explanation of those skeptical of the electrical battery theory is that the jars acted as storage vessels for sacred scrolls, perhaps containing rituals of some sort written on organic material such as parchment or papyrus. If such organic materials had rotted away, the sceptics claim, they would leave a slightly acidic organic residue, which would explain the corrosion on the copper cylinder. They believe that an asphalt seal such as that on the Baghdad Battery, while not particularly practical for a Galvanic cell, would be perfect as a hermetic seal for storage over an extended period.

That the Baghdad Batteries would be inefficient compared to to modern devices, even when several were connected together, is not in doubt. But the fact remains that the device does actually function as an electric cell. What is probable is that, similar to the ancient Greeks with amber, the makers of the object did not properly understand the principle involved. But this is not unusual. Many innovations, such as gunpowder and herbal medicines, were developed before their fundamentals were soundly grasped. Nevertheless, even if the Baghdad artifact is one day proved to be an ancient electric battery, it would not be evidence of any genuine comprehension of electrical phenomena 2,000 years ago. The question now remains whether the Baghdad Battery was an isolated find. Can its manufacturers have been the only people in antiquity to discover—probably by accident—electricity? Obviously there is a need for further evidence, whether literary or archaeological, because based on current knowledge, it is likely that the battery is indeed a unique find. Tragically, in 2003, during the war in Iraq, the Baghdad Battery was looted from the National Museum, along with thousands of other priceless ancient artifacts. Its current whereabouts are unknown.

The Ancient Hill Figures of England

Photograph by Dan Huby (public domain).
The Uffington White Horse, as seen from the air.

The cutting of huge figures or geoglyphs into the turf of English hillsides has been going on for more than 3,000 years. There are 56 hill figures scattered around England, with the vast majority on the chalk downlands of the southern part of the country. The figures include giants, horses, crosses, and regimental badges. Though the majority of these glyphs date within the last 300 years or so, there are a few that are much older. The most famous of these is perhaps the mysterious Uffington White Horse in Berkshire, recently redated and shown to be even older than its previously assigned ancient pre-Roman, Iron Age date. More controversial are the Cerne Abbot Giant in Dorset and the enigmatic Long Man of Wilmington in Sussex. What was the purpose of these giant figures? Who carved them? And how have the oldest examples survived for perhaps thousands of years?

The method of cutting the figures was simply to remove the overlying turf to reveal the gleaming white chalk below. However, the grass would soon grow over the glyph again unless it was regularly cleaned or scoured by a fairly large team of people. One reason that the vast majority of hill figures have disappeared is that when the traditions associated with the figures faded, people no longer bothered or remembered to clear away the grass to expose the chalk outline. Furthermore, over hundreds of years the outlines would sometimes change due to the scourers not always cutting in exactly the same place, thus changing the shape of the original glyph. The fact that *any* ancient hill figures survive at all in England today is testament to the strength and continuity of local customs and beliefs which, in one case at least, must stretch back at least a millennium.

The oldest and most famous hill figure in England is the 360 feet long and 131 feet high Uffington White Horse, located 1.5 miles south of the village of Uffington on the Berkshire Downs. This unique stylized representation of a horse consists of a long, sleek back, thin disjointed legs, a streaming tail, and a bird-like beaked head. The elegant creature almost melts into a landscape rich in prehistoric sites. The horse is situated on a steep escarpment, close to the Late Bronze Age (c. seventh century B.C.) hillfort of Uffington Castle and below a long-distance Neolithic track called the Ridgeway. The Uffington Horse is also surrounded by Neolithic and Bronze Age burial mounds. It is only 1 mile from the Neolithic chambered long barrow of Wayland's Smithy, and not far from the Bronze Age cemetery of Lambourn Seven Barrows. The carving has been placed in such a way as to make it extremely difficult to see from close quarters, and, as with many geoglyphs, it is best appreciated from the air. Nevertheless, there are certain areas

of the Vale of the White Horse, the valley containing and named after the enigmatic creature, from which an adequate impression may be gained. Indeed, on a clear day the carving can be seen from up to 18 miles away.

The earliest documentary reference to a horse at Uffington is from the 1070s, when "White Horse Hill" is mentioned in the charters from the nearby Abingdon Abbey, and the first reference to the horse itself is soon after, in 1190. However, the carving is believed to date back much further than that. Due to the similarity of the Uffington White Horse to the stylized depictions of horses on first century B.C. Celtic coins, it had been thought that the creature must also date to that period. However, in 1995 Optically Stimulated Luminescence (OSL) testing was carried out by the Oxford Archaeological Unit on soil sediments from two of the lower layers of the horse's body, and from another cut near the base. The result was a date for the horse's construction somewhere between 1400 and 600 B.C. In other words, it had a Late Bronze Age or Early Iron Age origin. The latter end of this date range would tie the carving of the horse with occupation of the adjacent Uffington hillfort, and may perhaps represent a tribal emblem or symbol marking the land of the inhabitants of the hillfort.

Alternatively, the carving may have been created for ritual/religious purposes. Some see the horse as representing the Celtic horse goddess Epona, who was worshipped as a protector of horses, and also had associations with fertility. However, the cult of Epona was imported from Gaul

(France) probably in the first century A.D., which is when we find the first depictions of the horse goddess. This date is at least six centuries after the Uffington Horse was carved. Nevertheless, the horse was of great ritual and economic importance during the Bronze and Iron Ages, as attested by its depictions on jewelry, coins, and other metal objects. Perhaps the carving represents a native British horse-goddess, such as Rhiannon, described in later Welsh mythology as a beautiful woman dressed in gold and riding a white horse. Others see the White Horse as connected with the worship of Belinos or Belinus, "the shining one," a Celtic Sun God often associated with horses. Bronze and Iron Age sun chariots (mythological representations of the sun in a chariot), were shown as being pulled by horses, as can be seen from the 14th century B.C. example from Trundholm in Denmark. If, as is now believed, Celtic culture had reached Britain by the very end of the Bronze Age, then the White Horse could still be interpreted as a Celtic horse-goddess symbol.

There are some who believe that the great carving does not represent a horse at all, but rather a dragon. A legend connected with Dragon Hill, a low natural flat-topped mound situated in the valley below the White Horse, suggests that the horse depicts the mythical dragon slain by St. George on that hill. The blood of the dying dragon was supposed to have been spilled on Dragon Hill, leaving a bare, white chalk scar where, to this day, no grass will grow. Perhaps the St. George connection with the White Horse is a confused memory of some strange prehistoric ritual performed on Dragon Hill by its creators, perhaps as long as 3,000 years ago. Up until the late 19th century the White horse was scoured every year, as part of a two day Midsummer country fair, which also included traditional games and merrymaking. Nowadays, the accompanying festival is gone, and the task of maintaining the horse is undertaken by English Heritage, the organization responsible for the site. The last scouring took place on June 24, 2000.

A further example of an ancient horse is the Red Horse of Tysoe, which once existed on the Edgehill scarp, above the village of Lower Tysoe in Warwickshire. Unfortunately, this strange creature, actually multiple horses carved in the same area, was ploughed over and disappeared in 1800. The history and design of the Red Horse is obscure. It was first mentioned in 1607 in *Britanica,* written by the English antiquarian and historian William Camden. In the 17th century, the English traveler Celia Feinnes described the horse when travelling through the area, writing, "It's called the Vale of Eshum or 'of the Red Horse' from a red horse cut on some of the hills about it, and the Earth all looking red the horse lookes so as that of the White Horse Vale." Since the 1960s, investigation into the Red Horse using ground survey, aerial photographs, and local archives research has managed to locate as many as six separate horses. At present, the consensus of opinion is that the original Red Horse of Tysoe, or Great Horse, was cut in Anglo-Saxon times around A.D. 600, possibly as a representation of the Saxon war god Tiw or Tiu, from whom the village of Tysoe allegedly takes its name, and from where we get our word Tuesday (Tiw's day).

Almost as well-known as the Uffington White Horse is the 180 foot tall Cerne Abbas Giant, an ithyphallic figure cut into the hillside to the northeast of the village of Cerne Abbas, and to the north of Dorchester, Dorset. The carving is of a giant, round-headed, naked man with a distinct erect penis and testicles, wielding a huge knobbed club in his right hand. As with the White Horse at Uffington, it is not possible to fully appreciate the figure from the ground; only from the air can the giant be seen in all his glory. Above the giants's head lies a rectangular earthwork enclosure, called the Trendle, or frying pan, thought possibly to be an Iron Age temple site, which some researchers believe is connected with the huge chalk figure below it. The favorite interpretations of the Cerne Giant is that he either represents a prehistoric fertility god or a Roman carving of Hercules wielding his giant club. Up

until 1635 there were Mayday fertility celebrations on the hill, with the maypole being erected inside the Trendle, around which locals would dance.

However, unlike the Uffington White Horse, the earliest surviving reference to the Cerne Giant dates only as far back as 1694, when it is mentioned in the village church's accounts. It was subsequently surveyed in 1764, and the results published in the *Gentleman's Magazine* that year. Writing in 1774, John Hutchins in his *History and Antiquities of the County of Dorset*, states that the figure was supposed to have been cut in the middle of the 17th century as a joke, though he also mentions that some of the older residents of the village had in the past claimed it had been there "beyond the antiquity of man." However, the weight of evidence does tend to support a recent origin for the giant. One theory is that although the giant is indeed a depiction of Hercules, it actually represents a caracature of

Photograph courtesy of SacredSites.com.
The Cerne Abbas giant.

Oliver Cromwell, who was sometimes referred to as the *English Hercules*, and was cut on the instructions of local landowner Denzil Holles some time in the 1640s. Another factor that supports this date is that medieval records always refer to the hill on which the giant is carved as Trendle Hill, rather than the modern Giant Hill, making no mention of the huge carving. This would indicate that the giant has only existed for about 400 years. Another interpretation, however, would be that for some reason, perhaps its overt sexuality, writers chose to ignore the Cerne Giant. Perhaps it had even become overgrown and forgotten.

New research into another chalk giant, however, may add support to the more recent date for the Cerne Abbas figure. Carved into the steep slopes of Windover Hill, Sussex, the 226-feet-high Long Man of Wilmington is the tallest hill figure in England, and was, until recently, believed to be of prehistoric origin. But the latest archaeological study at the site (using the same OSL dating technique as on the Uffington White Horse) produced evidence that the earlier theories are wrong and that the figure had been carved as recently as A.D. 1545. Although the new dating of the Wilmington Giant to the medieval period does throw considerable doubt on the prehistoric credentials of the

Cerne Abbas Giant, until OSL dating is carried out on the carving, the giant English Hercules will remain an enigma.

The reasons for the creation of these hill figures are probably as varied as the figures represented. New archaeological and geological evidence is increasingly indicating a medieval date for the giant naked figures, which some historians have argued were products of an age of civil war and extreme political turmoil in England, when satire was sometimes the only weapon. Compared to the huge stone permanence of structures, such as the Avebury Monuments and Stonehenge, hill figures are much more transitory; 10 or 20 years without scouring, and the carving could be lost forever. The fact that the figures could disappear so easily, along with their associated rituals and meaning, indicates that they were never intended to be anything more than temporary gestures, which have only survived either by accident, or, in the case of the Uffington White Horse Abbey, by the continued existence of extraordinarily tenacious local tradition. But this does not lesson their importance. These giant carvings are a fascinating glimpse into the lives and minds of their creators and how they viewed the landscape in which they lived.

The Coso Artifact

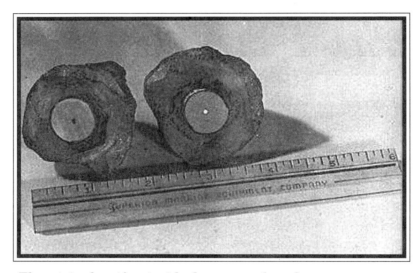

The original artifact inside the supposed geode.

For some people, out of place artifacts (objects found in contexts that are out of sync with the accepted chronology of human history) seriously question what we think we know about the world and its history. Some argue that these discoveries offer persuasive evidence that in remote antiquity, mankind was significantly more advanced than we could ever imagine. They insist that at various times in prehistory we have reached a high level of civilization, only for it to be subsequently destroyed, without a trace, by natural or man-made catastrophes. The evidence for such hypothetical ancient civilizations consists mainly of what appear to be fossilized human footprints, such as those discovered in the 1880s at the summit of Big Hill in the Cumberland Mountains in Jackson County, Kentucky (*The American Antiquarian*, January 1885), and apparently man-made objects enclosed in pieces of coal or rock. The Coso Artifact is such an example.

On February 13, 1961, Wallace Lane, Virginia Maxey, and Mike Mikesell (co-owners of the LM&V Rockhounds Gem and Gift Shop in Olancha, southern California) were out in the Coso Mountains looking for interesting mineral specimens, particularly geodes (hollow, usually spheroid rocks with crystals lining the inside wall, cmmonly around 500,000 years old) for their collection. At lunchtime, after they had been collecting rocks, close to the top of a 4,265 foot peak, overlooking the dry bed of Owens Lake, they put their specimens in the rock sack and headed home.

The next day, while attempting to cut through one of the finds that appeared to be a geode, Mikesell severely damaged a practically new diamond saw. Finally, when the nodule was opened, he found a thick circular section of white porcelain material, in the center of which was a 2 millimeter rod of bright metal. This metal proved to be magnetic. The porcelain cylinder was itself enclosed by a hexagonal sheath of decomposing copper and another unidentifiable substance. The discoverers noticed other strange qualities about the stone. Its outer layer was encrusted with bits of fossil shell, hardened clay, and pebbles, and more surprisingly, two nonmagnetic metal objects which looked similar to a nail and a washer. Puzzled by the find, the group began showing it to friends and associates, though little record remains now of original examinations of the object. One of the discoverers, Virginia Maxey, said that a geologist who examined the object gave its age, based on the fossils encrusted in its shell, as at least 500,000 years old. However, this unnamed geologist has never been traced and the conclusion was never published. But if these conclusions could be supported, then the implications are clear. If the Coso Artifact is a genuine example of unknown technology from millennia before the accepted emergence of *Homo sapiens*, then obviously it would turn accepted thought about the past of the human species on its head.

The only other person known to have physically inspected the artifact was creationist Ron Calais, who was allowed to take photographs of the nodule in both X ray and normal light. The X ray of the upper end of the object revealed that the metallic shaft was attached to what looked similar to some kind of tiny spring. This led to the object being categorized as some type of electrical mechanism. Paul Willis, publisher of paranormal magazine *INFO Journal*, examined the X rays of the mysterious artifact and concluded that it could be "the remains of a corroded piece of metal with threads," and noted the similarity between the object and a modern spark plug. In 1963, the artifact was apparently displayed for three months at the Eastern California Museum in Independence. The spring 1969 issue of *INFO Journal* stated that Wallace Lane, one of the original discoverers of the object, was then its owner, and that it was on display in his home. Lane steadfastly refused permission for anyone to examine it, but was reportedly offering to sell it for $25,000. Some time after 1969, the Coso Artifact seems to have disappeared. In September 1999, a national search undertaken to trace any of the original discoverers proved unsuccessful. It seems likely that by then Lane had died and the whereabouts of Mikesell were unknown. To this day, Virginia Maxey, who is known to be still living, refuses to comment publicly about the artifact, the location of which remains unknown.

Because of the mystery surrounding its whereabouts, and the lack of a published report on the object, speculation is rife about the Coso Artifact. A mechanical object encased in a geode apparently more than half a million years old. How had it gotten there? Was it the product of some unimaginably ancient technologically-advanced culture, all traces of which have now disappeared? The Internet has many Websites that include speculations on the purpose and origin of the mechanism, while offering no new evidence to support their claims. Opinions on its function include a super-antenna, a small capacitor, or an ancient spark plug. The latter suggestion is the most widespread: a spark plug produced by an advanced civilization as part of some mysterious technological apparatus.

Curiously enough, *INFO Journal* editor Paul J. Willis has conjectured that the artifact was some kind of spark plug, but was unable to understand the function of the spring on the object, which did not match up with contemporary spark plugs. Around the time of the original discovery of the Coso Artifact, Virginia Maxey speculated that it was possible that the object was a mere 100 years old. She thought that if it had lain in a mud bed, and afterwards become baked and hardened by the sun, it could have ended up in the condition in which they found it. But it was also Maxey who stated that the artifact was possibly 500,000 years old and "an instrument as old as legendary Mu or Atlantis. Perhaps it is a communications device or some sort of directional finder or some instrument made to utilize power

principles we know nothing about." Thus began the fantastic speculations about the artifact.

The crux of the mystery seems to be that the object was found encased in a 500,000-year-old geode, which included fossil shells. However, the exterior of the object was mainly composed of hardened clay with a mixture of organic matter, whilst a geode has an outer shell composed of dense chalcedonic silica. When broken open by Mike Mikesell the day after the discovery, the inside of the object proved to be of a different composition to that of a geode; it did not possess a hollow center filled with a layer of quartz crystals, as with most geodes. However, this still leaves the problem of what fossil shells were doing encrusted into the surface of the object. But the value of these fossil shells for dating the object is negligible if one remembers the original discoverers identified a nail and washer on the same surface as the fossil shells.

X ray of the Coso Artifact.

Investigations into the origins of the Coso Artifact by writer Pierre Stromberg and geologist Paul V. Heinrich discovered that mining operations were being carried out in the Coso Mountains early in the 20th century. Perhaps, they conjectured, internal combustion engines were being used in these operations, and the ancient spark plug proponents might have been at least partly right after all. In order to test their tentative theory, the duo attempted to have the object identified by contacting an organization known as the Spark-Plug Collectors of America. They sent letters and copies of X rays of the artifact to four different spark-plug collectors, who had no knowledge of the case and had never seen the pictures before. The collectors independently came to the same conclusion—they were certain that it was a 1920s era Champion spark plug, one that probably powered a Ford Model T, and had possibly been modified to serve the mining operations in the Coso mountain range. The amount of decay in the artifact was an almost perfect match for the rates of decay that would occur in a spark plug from this era. So, the Coso Artifact had been lying on the mountain for no more than 40 years.

It seems clear that the spark plug was not actually embedded in rock, but in an iron oxide nodule. The formation of this nodule was probably accelerated by corrosive "mineral dust" blown off of the dry lake bed of Lake Owen by local windstorms, and onto the neighboring uplands where the artifact was found.

The Coso Artifact is not the only spark plug to have been found in a strange place. The summer 1998 number of *The Igniter*, published by the Spark-Plug Collectors of America, featured a discovery made while scuba diving, of what looked like "a ball of barnacles and shells," but with a spark plug top sticking out of it. A spark plug apparently embedded in a melted lump of rock was washed up on a beach in Delaware, but the "rock" was found to be composed of a combination of mud and rust (as with the Coso Artifact), the combination of which, once baked solid in the sun, became almost as hard as rock. In the end the Coso Artifact is more a case of wishful thinking (and at times, wilful secrecy) than an outright hoax. There is no evidence that the original discoverers planned to deceive anyone from the start, though they may have thought otherwise as more attention was placed on the object (as Wallace Lane, offering the artifact for sale at $25,000, suggests). Unfortunately, though it has been proved almost beyond doubt that this controversial artifact is a 1920s spark plug, it is still possible to surf the Inter-net and quite easily find Websites using the Coso Artifact in support of a theory of technically advanced civilizations in the impossibly remote past.

The Nebra Sky Disc

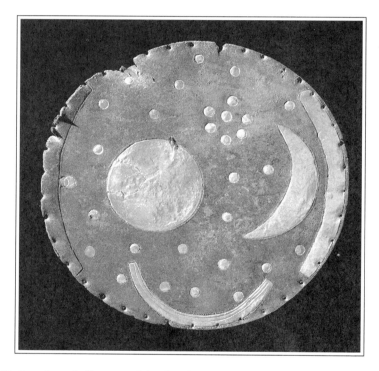

© *Landesamt für Denkmalpflege und Archäologie Sachsen-Anhalt (State Office for Heritage Management and Archaeology Saxony-Anhalt), Juraj Lipták.*
The Nebra Sky Disc.

The Nebra Sky Disc is one of the most fascinating, and some would say controversial, archaeological finds of recent years. Dated to 1600 B.C., this bronze disc has a diameter of 32 centimeter (about the size of a vinyl LP) and weighs around 4 pounds. It is patinated blue-green and embossed with gold leaf symbols, which appear to represent a crecent moon, the sun (or perhaps a full moon), stars, a curved gold band (interpreted as a sun boat), and a further gold band on the edge of the disc (which probably represent one of the horizons). Another gold band on the opposite side is missing.

The object was discovered in 1999 by treasure hunters using a metal detector at a prehistoric enclosure encircling the Mittelberg hill, near the town of Nebra in the Ziegelroda Forest, 112 miles southwest of Berlin, Germany. Unfortunately, the treasure hunters caused considerable damage to the disc during its crude removal from the ground, which included splintering its outer rim, losing one of the stars, and chipping a large piece off the gold disc. The looters subsequently attempted to sell the disc, along with two swords, two axes, a chisel, and fragments of armlets, to local archaeologists. But they discovered that, by law, the objects belonged to the state of Sachsen-Anhalt, where they were unearthed, so they could not be sold legally. In February 2003, they tried selling the disc to an antiquities collector in Switzerland for $400,000. However, the collector was actually working for the Swiss police as part of a sting operation to trap the group, which played out in the basement bar of the Hilton hotel in Basle. The group was subsequently arrested and the disc was recovered. It is now the property of the state of Sachsen-Anhalt.

The disc illustrates the crescent moon, a sun or full moon, three arcs, and 23 stars dotted around (apparently at random). There is a further cluster of seven stars, identified as the Pleiades constellation. X-rays have revealed two more stars underneath the gold of the right arc, suggesting that the two arcs were added later than the other features. The blue-green background of the night sky was once colored a deep violet-blue, apparently by applying rotten eggs, causing a chemical reaction on the bronze surface. Running along the edge of the disc is a ring of holes punched through the metal, probably for attaching the disc to something, perhaps a piece of heavy cloth.

So what exactly is the Nebra Sky Disc and what was it used for? Many researchers believe it is the oldest known realistic representation of the cosmos yet found, perhaps a kind of astronomical calculation tool to determine planting and harvest times. For thousands of years, all across northern Europe, monuments were aligned to mark the summer and winter solstices: Stonehenge in England, and Newgrange in Ireland, are good examples. As Bronze Age people were an agricultural society, a method for finding out the time of year (and thus the correct times for planting and harvesting crops) was obviously vital. One way of doing this was to identify the position of the sun at sunrise and sunset. Intrigued by the possibility of the Nebra Disc as an astronomical device, Professor Wolfhard Schlosser of the University of Bochum measured the angle between the pair of arcs on either side of the disc, and found that it was 82 degrees. Fascinatingly, at Mittelberg hill, between the high midsummer sunset and the low midwinter sunset, the sun appears to travel around 82 degrees along the horizon. This angle would vary from place to place. Further north, for example, it would be 90 degrees, and to the south, 70. But in a restricted belt of central Europe, the suns passage across the sky measures precisely 82 degrees. Schlosser concluded that the pair of arcs along the circumference of the Nebra Disk did indeed depict the sun solstices accurately for its location. This would suggest that the Bronze Age agricultural societies of central Europe made sophisticated celestial measurements far earlier than has been suspected.

Some have pointed to the presence of the Pleiades star cluster on the disc as further evidence of Bronze Age astronomical knowledge. Although nowadays there are only six stars in the Pleiades visible to the naked eye, in the Bronze Age one of the stars may have been much brighter, thus accounting not only for the depiction of seven stars on the disc, but also for the ancient Greek name for the cluster: the Seven Sisters. The Pleiades was an important constellation for many ancient civilizations, including those of Mesopotamia and Greece. The constellation would have appeared in their skies in the autumn, showing that it was time to start bringing in the harvest, and disappeared in the spring, indicating the time for planting crops. This evidence for the importance of the disc in connection with prehistoric agriculture may mean that the (third) golden arc underneath the crescent moon and golden disc represents a harvest sickle.

Others have suggested that the disc actually represents the daytime sky and that the unexplained arc depicts a rainbow. But the majority of researchers believe this third arc to be a sun ship. There are depictions of a disc in a ship from Bronze Age Scandinavia, and a Danish artifact dating to the 15th or 14th century B.C., the Trundholm Sun Chariot, depicting a horse drawing the sun in a chariot. But the main source of the symbol and the

ancient belief that a ship carried the sun across the night sky from the Western to Eastern horizon is Egypt. Their belief was that Rah, the Sun God and their most potent deity, journeyed through the night sky on a ship in order that in the morning, at sunrise, he could be reborn. If the golden arc at the bottom of the Nebra Disk does in fact represent a sun ship traveling across the night sky, then it will be the first evidence of such a belief in central Europe.

There is further proof of prehistoric celestial knowledge in the area, a mere 15 miles distant from where the Nebra Disc was discovered. Lying in a wheat field near the town of Goseck, and first identified from aerial photographs, is the remains of what is thought to be Europe's oldest observatory. Germany's Stonehenge, as it has become known, consists of a huge a huge circle, 246 feet in diameter, and was built by the earliest farming communities in the area around 4900 B.C. Originally, the site consisted of four concentric circles, a mound, a ditch, and two wooden palisades about the height of a person. Within the palisades were three sets of gates, facing southeast, southwest, and north, respectively. The two southern gates marked the sunrise and sunset at the winter solstice. At the the winter solstice, watchers at the center of the circles would have witnessed the sun rise and set through the southeast and southwest gates. It is surely safe to assume that if these southern gates marked the sunrise and sunset at the winter and summer solstice, then the inhabitants of Goseck were able to accurately determine the course of the sun in its journey across the sky. In fact, the angle between the two solstice gates in the Goseck circle corresponds with the angle between the gilded arcs on the rim of the Nebra Disk. Although the Nebra Disk was created 2,400 years later than the Goseck site, Professor Wolfhard Schlosser believes there may be some connection between the two in the astronomical knowledge they both display. Schlosser has even suggested that the details on the disc were based on previous astrological observations, possibly made at the primitive observatory at Goseck.

In late 2004, the Nebra Disc became enmeshed in controversy. German archaeologist Professor Peter Schauer, of Regensburg University, claimed that the disc was a modern fake, and any idea that it was a Bronze Age map of the heavens was "a piece of fantasy." Professor Schauer stated that the supposedly Bronze Age green patina on the artifact had probably been artificially created in a workshop "using acid, urine, and a blowtorch" and was not ancient at all. The holes around the edge of the disc, he insisted, were too perfect to be ancient, and must have been made by a relatively modern machine. His own conclusion was that the object was a 19th century Siberian Shaman's drum. However, it later emerged that Schauer had never studied the artifact himself prior to making his claim, nor did he publish any of his theories in a peer-reviewed journal. But Schauer's objections still shocked the German archaeological community and raised some important questions about the authenticity of the disc. The first was that, because of the circumstances of its discovery, the Nebra Disc had no secure archaeological context. Thus, it was extremely difficult to date

accurately, especially as there was nothing similar with which to compare it. The dating that was done on the object depended upon the typological dating of the Bronze Age weapons that had been offered for sale with it, and were supposed to be from the same site. These axes and swords were dated to the middle of the second millennium B.C.

Solid evidence for the antiquity of the disc was provided by the Halle Institute for Archaeological Research in Germany. The Institute submitted the artifact to an exhaustive series of tests that confirm its authenticity. For example, the copper used on the disc has been traced to a Bronze Age mine in the Austrian Alps. Tests also discovered that a practically unique mixture of hard crystal malachite covers the artifact. In addition to this, microphotography of the corrosion on the disc has also produced images that proved that it was a genuinely ancient artifact, and could not be have been produced as a fake.

The latest examinations of the disc, by a group of German scholars in early 2006, came to the conclusion that it was indeed genuine, and had functioned as a complex astronomical clock for the synchronization of solar and lunar calendars. The Nebra Sky Disc is thus the earliest known guide to the heavens, and certainly, along with the Goseck site, the first examples of detailed astronomical knowledge in Europe. But perhaps that is not the end of the story. Wolfhard Schlosser believes, intriguingly, that the disc (currently valued at $11.2 million) was one of a pair, and that the other is still out there waiting to be found.

Noah's Ark and the Great Flood

A painting by the American artist Edward Hicks (1780–1849) showing Noah's Ark.

The story of Noah's Ark and the great flood is found in the book of Genesis in the Bible. According to the story, when God saw the corruption in the world, he decided to bring floodwaters to destroy His creation. Of all human life, only the righteous Noah and his family would be allowed to survive. God instructed Noah to construct a huge ark, large enough so that two of every living species on the planet could be accommodated within it. It is said that the rains sent by God lashed the earth for 40 days and 40 nights, until the entire land surface of the planet was submerged. When the rains finally abated and the floodwaters began to recede, Noah's ark came to ground in the area of Mount Ararat (in modern Turkey). Noah sent out a dove to see if there was anywhere for it to land, but the dove returned. After seven more days, Noah sent it out again, and this time it returned carrying an olive leaf. Waiting another week, the dove was again sent out, and did not return. Noah now knew there was dry land and it was time to leave the ship. After disembarking, Noah offered sacrifice. God approved, and then concluded a covenant with Noah, in which He agreed to never again to flood the Earth because of the sins of mankind, symbolizing his promise with a rainbow in the sky.

The ark itself, according to the Bible, was akin to a huge barge, probably constructed of cypress wood and sealed with bitumen to make it watertight. Genesis only mentions one window, though perhaps there would have been more, and a door set in the side of the ark; the vessel contained a number of rooms spread over three interior decks. The dimensions of the ark were roughly 450 feet in length, 75 feet in width, and 45 feet in height; proportions making it the largest seagoing ship prior to the 20th century, with a displacement similar to that of the *Titanic*. Its length surpasses that of any other wooden vessel ever built. A much debated question is whether such a ship could possibly have carried two specimens of every species of animal, not to mention how Noah and his family could have collected them all in the first place. The accepted theory today is that if the Noah's Ark story is to be taken literally, then the vessel may have contained kinds instead of species—so rather than every type from the cat family (lions, tigers, and leopards), there were perhaps a male and female representing the whole cat group.

The search for the remains of the elusive ark has been going on for perhaps 2,000 years, and such a find, were it ever made, would be extraordinary proof for the literal reality of the Bible. Genesis 8:4 states that the ark came to rest on "the mountains of Ararat," which indicates not a particular mountain, but a region. Unfortunately, in the modern era the search for the ark, or arkaeology as it is sometimes called, is peppered with dubious research and outright hoaxes. One of the first claims to have seen the ark in the 20th century came from French explorer Fernand Navarra. In 1955, Navarra apparently climbed more than 2.5 miles up Ararat and discovered hand-hewn wood in a wall of ice. He claimed he was able to remove a sample of the wood, which he brought back down with him. In a further expedition in 1969 he found more wood. The samples of wood from the two expeditions were later submitted to six different laboratories and produced dates from 1,190 to 1,690 years ago. But those dates are far too recent to have any connection with Noah's Ark, even if the material was genuinely found on Ararat. There are, however, serious reasons to doubt this. Navarra has specified several different locations where he was supposed to have discovered the wood, and it has also been suggested, by one of his expedition members and his guides, that he actually bought the wood from natives in town and took it up the mountain himself. Ararat's position on the extremely sensitive Turkish/Soviet (now Armenian) border has limited the number of modern ark-hunting expeditions, although it is becoming increasingly likely that there is little to find up there anyway. Beginning in 1973, former NASA astronaut James Irwin led several expeditions to Mount

Ararat, but, as with scores of climbers and explorers before and since, failed to find any evidence of the ark. There is, however, another possibility for the final resting place of the Noah's Ark. The site lies about 19 miles south of the Greater Ararat summit, near the city of Dogubayazit, just over 1.8 miles north of the Iranian border. An aerial photograph taken by a Turkish Air Force pilot in 1959 (while on a NATO mapping mission) revealed a canoe or boat-shaped object sticking out of the rock, 1.19 miles up in the Akyayla mountain region. However, a subsequent expedition to the site in 1960, which included the dynamiting of one side of the supposed ark, discovered no persuasive evidence that the object was not a naturally formed feature. Despite these negative conclusions, adventurer and nurse anaesthetist Ron Wyatt gained a huge amount of publicity in the 1980s and 1990s when he claimed that this geological feature was in fact the true ark. During his first trip to the summit, he managed to discover an impressive-sounding array of artifacts. Among these were stone sea anchors marked with crosses (which he believed were used by Noah to steer the great vessel), iron rivets, washers, and petrified timber belonging to the ark.

The stone anchors have been explained by Armenian archaeologists as pre-Christian Armenian stelae (standing stones) recarved in the Christian period, probably between A.D. 301 and 406. The rock specimens containing Wyatt's so-called petrified wood were later examined by geologists, and no trace whatsoever of wood was found. As for the metal artifacts, they proved to be naturally occurring pieces of iron oxide. When the site was reexamined in 1987 using ground penetrating radar, the results again indicated a feature geological in nature.

In 1993, CBS in America aired a documentary made by Sun International Pictures entitled *The Incredible Discovery of Noah's Ark*. In this program, George Jammal, an Israeli actor living in Long Beach, California, claimed to possess a piece of ancient timber from Noah's Ark. The show was apparently watched by 40 million viewers, who naturally assumed that it was a serious documentary about the biblical Noah's Ark. Later, Jammal admitted that the story was a complete hoax and that he had never even been to Turkey. The ancient timber, which the researchers on the documentary had never even bothered to have tested, was actually a piece of wood taken from the railroad tracks near his workplace in Long Beach. More recently, Daniel McGivern of the Hawaii Christian Coalition, claimed to have discovered the ark on satellite pictures of Mount Ararat. He stated that he was "98 percent sure" that it was the ark, and one image even showed the actual beams of wood on the vessel.

In 2004, McGivern announced a much publicized $900,000 expedition to Ararat, to take place that July, to prove that the Ararat anomaly, as the image has become known, is actually Noah's Ark. McGivern was subsequently refused permission to enter the area by the Turkish government as the summit of Ararat is inside a restricted military zone. But some suspected that this proposed expedition had not been genuine anyway. The choice of Ahmet Ali Arslan, an English professor at Seljuk University in Turkey, as expedition leader, caused many searchers for the ark to become suspicious. Arslan had previously been involved in the hoax documentary aired by CBS in 1993, and has also been accused of faking photographs of the ark. Many now consider McGivern's abortive $900,000 expedition to have been a publicity stunt. Nevertheless, despite the numerous hoaxes and exaggerations surrounding the subject, and the repeated failures to find any physical evidence of the Ark, many still believe the story of Noah's Ark is the literal truth, and that one day its remains will be located in the region of Ararat.

The legend of a great flood and a specially chosen hero who lives through it to bring new life to the world is not confined to the Bible. The story has parallels in many mythologies of the ancient world, and shares numerous features with accounts in Assyro-Babylonian mythology in particular. The best known of these is the *Epic of Gilgamesh,* a story originating from Babylon, but in its most complete version preserved on clay tablets from the collection of the seventh century B.C. Assyrian king named Ashurbanipal. The earliest Sumerian (from southern Mesopotamia) modern day versions of the epic date back to the third dynasty of Ur (2100 B.C.–2000 B.C.). The tale tells of Ellil, chief of the gods, who is about to destroy mankind with a flood. A man named Utnapishtim is warned by the god Ea (the god of water) of this forthcoming deluge and instructed to pull down his reed dwelling and construct a great boat or ark to save himself. He is to fill this ark with his family and representatives of each species of animal. After a ferocious seven-day storm and 12 days floating around on the floodwaters, the ship comes to ground on Mount Nisir. Waiting seven days, Utnapishtim releases a dove which comes back, then a swallow, which also returns, and finally sends out a raven, which does not come back. Utnapishtim then makes a sacrifice to the god Ea and he and his wife are granted immortality. The similarities with the biblical flood story are plainly obvious, but is there any archaeological evidence that such a world flood actually took place at some time in the remote past?

The Deluge *by Gustave Doré.*

There is certainly a considerable amount of evidence for prehistoric flooding in Mesopotamia, an area that included parts of modern day Iraq, Turkey, and Syria. (For example, at the site of Ur, on the Persian Gulf, in southern Mesopotamia.) In his 1999 book *Noah's Ark and the Ziusudra Epic: Sumerian Origins of the Flood Myth,* Robert M. Best cites a six-day flood on the Euphrates River around 2900 B.C. as an explanation of the biblical deluge. His ingenious theory is that Noah was actually a historical person called Ziusudra, a king/priest of the Sumerian city-state Shuruppak. He suggests that Ziusudra and his family were swept down the Euphrates River into the Persian Gulf on a kind of commercial river barge. They were then set adrift for almost a year before eventually grounding in an estuary near the mouth of the river. This particular flood has been archaeologically confirmed, but again, it was a local river flood, not a global inundation.

Another flood theory has been put forward by Walter Pitman and William Ryan, two geologists at Columbia University in New York. In their book, *Noah's Flood*, published in 2000, Pitman and Ryan claim that the biblical account of Noah's flood is based on a cataclysmic flooding of the Black Sea, which took place in the early Neolithic period, about 5600 B.C. The Black Sea, then a freshwater lake, was flooded when the level of the Mediterranean Sea rose at the end of the last ice age, and millions of gallons of its waters poured through the narrow Bosporus Strait. The Black Sea rapidly filled and overflowed into large parts of the surrounding area. It has been estimated that the low-lying land around the lake would have vanished at the incredible rate of about a mile per day. At the time of this great catastrophe there would have been a considerable agricultural population inhabiting the area, who would have had to flee for their lives as a result of this great deluge. Such a cataclysmic occurrence would certainly have etched itself into people's memory, and would subsequently have been handed down from generation to generation, probably with various mythical elements being added over time, until it attained the form we recognize today. Although such an explanation does not by any means prove the literal truth of the biblical flood story, it does provide a catastrophic event upon which many of the flood stories found in the mythology of Near Eastern civilizations, may have been based.

The Mayan Calendar

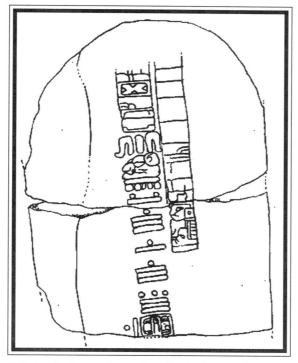

Drawing of the back of Stela C, from the archaelogical site of Tres Zapotes. This stone shows the oldest Mayan-style long-count date yet unearthed, equivalent to September 3, 32 B.C. in our present-day calendar.

The Maya were a remarkably sophisticated Meso-American civilization whose territory included present day Guatemala, Belize, Honduras, El Salvador, and the southeastern Mexican states of Tabasco, Yucatán, and Quintana Roo. The six centuries from about A.D. 250 to 900 was the Classic period of Mayan culture, when their artistic and intellectual achievements were the equal of any pre-Columbian civilization in the Americas. The Maya were the first people of the Americas to keep historical records, most of which adorned stelae (stone monuments), and contain records of civil events and Mayan calendric and astronomical knowledge. Perhaps the supreme example of the Mayan's cultural accomplishments is their extraordinarily intricate calendar system, which had a major influence on the later Aztec calendar. This calendar has become ominously significant in the early 21st century as, according to one reading of its dates, on the winter solstice (around the 21st of December) in 2012, there will be a catastrophic flood and the world will be destroyed.

Calendars are generally based on astronomical events, such as the cycles of the sun, moon, planets, and stars. Ancient civilizations depended on the perceived movement of these bodies across the sky to establish their seasons, months, and years, with priest-astronomers pronouncing the advent of a new period. Such calendars were, and still are, used to organize farming, hunting, and migrating activities, as well as to determine dates for religious and public events. One of the first cultures to create a calendar were the Sumerians, who inhabited southern Mesopotamia around 5,000 years ago. The Sumerian calendar, later inherited by the Babylonians, divided the year into 30-day months, separated the day into 12 periods (each one equivalent to two hours), and split these periods into 30 parts (each equal to four minutes).

The original Egyptian calendar seems to have been derived from the cycles of the moon, but was later replaced when the Egyptians noticed that the Dog Star (Sirius, in the constellation Canis Major), rose with the sun every 365 days, preceding the annual flooding of the Nile by a few days. Based on the knowledge of the heliacal rising of Sirius, they instituted a 365 day calendar that seems to have begun in 4236 B.C., possibly the first recorded date in history. The Egyptian year consisted of 12 months of 30 days each, as well as five additional days at the end of the year. Their months were divided into three periods or weeks, of 10 days each. The Julian calendar, a solar calendar established in 46 B.C. by Julius Caesar, contained a regular year of 365 days divided into 12 months, with a leap day added to

Photograph by Ancheta Wis. (Creative Commons Attribution—ShareAlike License v. 2.5). Aztec Stone of the Sun replica in El Paso, Texas. The stone, based in part on the Mayan Calednar, represents how the Aztecs measured days, months, and cosmic cycles.

February every four years. This was the standard European calendar until the more accurate Gregorian calendar was established in 1582.

The calendars of pre-Columbian America, including those of the Maya and the Aztecs, shared many basic characteristics, such as a 260-day ritual year. The Mayan calendar, the center of their life and culture, was based not only on the sun and moon, but also the cycles of the planet Venus and the constellation of the Pleiades. In fact, what we know as the Mayan calendar is a series of three different calendar systems used in parallel, the most ancient and most important of which was the *Tzolkin* (sacred calendar). There was also the *Haab* (a solar agrarian/civil calendar) and the *Long Count* system. The Tzolkin, or Sacred Year, was a religious calendar used to name children, predict the future, and decide on favorable dates for such things as battles and marriages. The Tzolkin consisted of a 260-day short year (13 months of 20 days), each day of the month having a name, similar to our days of the week, and its own symbol. The Maya day names were Imix, Ik, Akbal, Kan, Chicchan, Cimi, Manik, Lamat, Muluc, Oc, Chuen, Eb, Ben, Ix, Men, Cib, Caban, Eiznab, Cauac, and Ahau. Each of these names was symbolized by a god who carries time across the sky, thus indicating the journey of night and day. This Tzolkin short year system seems to have been taken over by the Mayans from the Zapotec civilization, a native culture of south central Mexico dating back to at least 1500 B.C., and who began to record information in this form around 600 B.C. The Tzolkin is based on the cycles of the Pleiades star cluster, a significant constellation for the Maya, who used pyramids and observatories to track their movement. Indeed, the pyramid and temple complex of Teotihuacán, near Mexico City, is oriented to the position where the Pleiades set along the horizon. The Maya later combined the Tzolkin with a lunar calendar known as the *Tun-Uc*, which used 28 day cycles that reflect the women's moon cycle.

The *Haab* or *Vague Year* (called *vague* because it was a quarter of a day short of the solar year), was a solar calendar in some ways similar to our own, and was connected primarily with agriculture and the seasons. During the Classic Maya period, the days of the *Haab* were numbered from zero to 19, and the first day of the year related to zero. In fact, the Maya invented the concept of the number zero. Their counting system was based on the number 20, instead of the number 10 as with our own, so they counted from zero to 19, rather than zero to 10, before moving to the next order. The Haab calendar consisted of 18 months of 20 days, followed by a further "unlucky" five day month called *Uayeb*, making a total of 365 days to match up with the solar year. The Tzolkin and the Haab calendars were combined to form a co-ordinated 52-year cycle known as the *Calendar Round*. At the beginning of these Calendar Rounds, there were ritual celebrations that included the extinguishing of old fires and the lighting of new, and the consecration of new temples.

The *Long Count* calendar, allegedly more accurate than the Julian calendar of 16th century Europe, seems to have been created around the first century B.C., and was used to record dates over long periods of time. In essence, the Long Count totals the number of days since August 3114 B.C., a date when the Mayan Fourth Creation or present Great Cycle was supposed to have begun. This was in effect the Mayan year zero, akin to our date of January 1, A.D. 1. So 3114 B.C., the start date of this time cycle, is written 0-0-0-0-0, and 13 cycles of 394 years will have passed by the time the next cycle begins, which is in year A.D. 2012 (13-0-0-0-0). The Long Count basically consisted of a *tun* of 360 days, 20 tuns constituting a *katun* (7,200 days), 20 katuns forming a *baktun* (144,000 days), and 13 *baktuns* making a *Great Cycle* (1,872,000 days, or around 5,130 years). At the conclusion of this Great Cycle, the Maya believed that the world as we know it will cease to exist.

The incredible complexity of the Mayan calendrical systems can perhaps be explained in part by a need for power and influence. Decisions about dates for sacred events and the agricultural cycle were in the hands of Mayan priests, who decided by consulting the calendars when the time was right to perform certain tasks. Their abilities to decipher meaning from the calendars in terms of (for example) when to sow and reap, or which were favorable days for marriage or war, meant that they were able to exercise an immense amount of control over the population. As the average citizen was not required to comprehend this complex calendar, the priests basically had a free reign to make the system as intricate as it suited them.

The winter solstice of A.D. 2012 in the Mayan Long Count signifies the end of the 13th baktun cycle that began in 3114 B.C. The conclusion of the Mayan calendar on this date has alarmed many people, who believe that this signifies the violent destruction of the world. But did the Maya actually predict such a cataclysm with their calendar? One of the most important beliefs of the Maya was the idea of a cyclical universe, where the Earth goes through recurring creations and destructions. In the *Popol Vuh* (*Book of Council*), the sacred book of the Maya, probably written in the late 16th century A.D. but dating back much earlier, descriptions of successive creations and destructive floods are prominent. There are also descriptions of the 3114 B.C. creation on various Mayan monuments, such as the monolith known as Stela C at the city of Quirigua, Guatemala. Such texts describe creation, including the organization of the gods, for example, and not destruction, and also relate mythical events much further back in time than 3114 B.C. The Mayan Calendar also determines dates far into the future, such as a royal anniversary which will occur in October of A.D. 4772. This is hardly something they would have done if the world was supposed to have already ended by then. What the Mayan calendar indicates for the winter solstice of 2012 should be interpreted as the conclusion of an old and the beginning of a new cycle, rather than the end of the world. The ancient Mayan calendar cycle still survives today in southern Mexico and the Guatemalan highlands, where it is looked after by calendar priests, or day keepers, who still maintain the 260-day sacred count for divination and other ritual activities.

The Antikythera Mechanism: An Ancient Computer?

© *Rien van de Weygaert, Kapteyn Institute, Groningen, the Netherlands.*
http://www.astro.rug.nl/~weygaert/antikytheramechanism.html.
The Antikytheran Mechanism is on display in the National Archaeological Museum of Athens. Detail showing central gearhouse.

On Easter of 1900, Elias Stadiatos and a party of Greek sponge fishermen were fishing off the coast of the tiny, rocky island of Antikythera, between the southern Greek mainland and Crete. Surfacing after one of his descents, Stadiatos began babbling about a "heap of dead naked women" on the sea bed. Further investigation by the fishermen revealed the 164 foot long wreck of a sunken Roman cargo ship, about 140 feet down. The buried objects from the ship included first century B.C.

marble and bronze statues (the dead, naked women), coins, gold jewelry, pottery, and what appeared to be lumps of corroded bronze, which broke into pieces shortly after being brought to the surface.

The finds from the wreck were subsequently examined, recorded, and sent off to the National Museum in Athens for display or storage. On May 17, 1902, Greek archaeologist Spyridon Stais was looking through the odd lumps from the shipwreck, covered in marine growth from 2,000 years beneath the sea, when he noticed that one piece had a gear wheel embedded in it and what looked like an inscription in Greek. There had been a wooden case associated with the object but this, as well as the wooden planks from the ship itself, had subsequently dried out and crumbled. Further examination and meticulous cleaning of the corroded broonze lumps revealed additional pieces belonging to the mysterious object, and soon an elaborate geared mechanism made of bronze, and measuring about 33 by 17 by 9 centimeters, was revealed. Stais believed the mechanism to be an ancient astronomical clock, but the prevailing opinion at the time was that the strange object was too intricate to belong to a wreck dated by the pottery on board to the early first century B.C. Many researchers thought that the mechanism was the remains of a medieval astrolabe, an astronomical device for observing planetary movements, and used for navigation. (The earliest known example of which is from the ninth century A.D. in Iraq.) But no general agreement on the date or purpose of the artifact was reached, and the enigma was soon forgotten.

In 1951, Derek De Solla Price, an English physicist, and at the time professor of the history of science at Yale University, became fascinated by the complexity of the shipwreck mechanism, and began what was to be eight years of detailed study using x-ray photography. In June 1959, the conclusions of his analyses were published as an article in *Scientific American* entitled "An Ancient Greek Computer." X rays of the mechanism

revealed at least 20 separate gears, including a differential gear, previously thought to have been invented in the 16th century. The differential gear allowed the rotation of two shafts at different speeds, as used on the rear axle of automobiles. Price deduced from his research that the Antikythera find represented the remains of a "great astronomical clock," which had close ties to "a modern analogue computer." These conclusions met with some unfavorable reactions from scholars. A certain professor refused to believe in the possibility of such a device, and hypothesized that the object must have been dropped into the sea in medieval times and somehow made its way into the wreck.

In 1974, Price published the results of more complete research based on further X rays and gamma radiographs by Greek radiographer Christos Karakalos, as a monograph entitled *Gears from the Greeks. The Antikythera mechanism, a calendar computer from ca. 80 B.C.* Price's further study showed that the ancient scientific instrument actually contained at least 30 gears, although most of them were incomplete. However, enough of the gearing remained for Price to work out that when its handle was rotated, the mechanism was meant to show the motion of the moon, sun, probably the planets, and the rising of the major stars. The device was in effect a complicated astronomical computer, a working model of the solar system, which had once been contained inside a wooden box with hinged doors to protect the mechanism inside. From the inscriptions and the position of the gears (and year-ring on the object), Price concluded that it had a close connection with Geminus of Rhodes, a Greek astronomer and mathematician who lived from approximately 110 to 40 B.C. Price believed the Antikythera Mechanism to have been built and designed on Rhodes, a Greek island off the coast of Turkey, probably by Geminus himself around 87 B.C. Indeed, the shipwreck had contained storage jars from the island of Rhodes in its cargo, and was thought to have been journeying from Rhodes to Rome when it sank. The date of the vessel's sinking has been fairly securely tied to somewhere around 80 B.C., so presuming that the object was already a few years old when it was lost, a date for the construction of the Antikythera Mechanism of around 87 B.C. is now generally accepted.

It is conceivable then—in terms of date—that the device could have been made by Geminus on the island of Rhodes, especially as Rhodes is known to have been a center of astronomical and technological research in this era. The second century B.C. Greek writer on mechanics, Philo of Byzantium, describes the *polybolos*, which he witnessed on Rhodes. This amazing catapult had the capacity to fire repeatedly without the need to reload, and possessed two gears linked by a chain drive powered by a windlass (a lifting device consisting of a horizontal cylinder rotated by a crank). Rhodes was also the place where the Greek Stoic philospher, astronomer, and geographer Poseidonius (c. 135 B.C.–51 B.C.) established the nature of the tides. In addition, Poseidonius made a fairly accurate (for the time) measurement of the size of the sun, and also calculated the size and distance of the moon. The astronomer Hipparchus of Rhodes

(c. 190 B.C.–120 B.C.) is credited with the invention of trigonometry and was the first to scientifically catalogue the positions of the stars. Furthermore, he was one of the first Europeans to use observations and information from Babylonian astronomy for his own research into the solar system. Perhaps elements of Hipparchus's knowledge and ideas were used in the construction of the Antikythera Mechanism?

The Antikythera Device is the earliest surviving item of complex mechanical technology. The use of gear wheels more than 2,000 years ago is nothing less than astonishing, and its fine workmanship is as highly developed as any 18th-century clock. In recent years, a number of working reconstructions of this ancient computer have been assembled, one being a partial reconstruction by Australian computer scientist Allan George Bromley (1947–2002) of the University of Sydney, together with clockmaker Frank Percival. Bromley also made more accurate x-ray images of the object, which were the basis of a 3D model of the mechanism produced by his student Bernard Gardner. A few years later, English orrery maker (an *orrery* is a mechanical model of the solar system) John Gleave constructed a full working model, with the front dial depicting the yearly progress of the sun and moon through the Zodiac against a representation of the Egyptian calendar.

The most recent study and reconstruction of the object was made in 2002 by Michael Wright, the curator of mechanical engineering at the Science Museum in London, working together with Allan Bromley. Although some of the conclusions of Wright's

© *Rien van de Weygaert, Kapteyn Institute, Groningen, the Netherlands.*
http://www.astro.rug.nl/~weygaert/antikytheramechanism.html.
Detail showing front dial of the device with ancient Greek inscription.

new study disagree with certain aspects of Derek De Solla Price's work, Wright does imply that the mechanism is even more ingenious than Price thought. To arrive at his theories, Wright used X rays of the object using a method known as linear tomography. This technique can show detail from a single plane or region of an object in sharp focus. Wright was thus able to study the gears in great detail and found that the device would have been able to accurately replicate not only the motions of the sun and moon, but those of all the planets known to the ancient Greeks: Mercury, Venus, Mars, Jupiter, and Saturn. So it is possible that by making use of bronze indicators on a circular face, which depict the constellations of the Zodiac around its edge, the mechanism would have been able to (fairly accurately) calculate the positions of the known planets for any specific date. In September 2002, Wright's completed reconstruction went on display as part of the exhibition of Ancient Technology at Technopolis, a museum in Athens.

Despite the years of study and the various reconstructions and theories, nobody really knows how the Antikythera Device was used. It has been suggested that it had an astrological function and was used for computerized horoscopes, that it functioned as a planetarium for teaching purposes, or even that it was a complicated toy for the wealthy. Derek De Solla Price believed that the mechanism was evidence of an ancient Greek tradition of highly intricate mechanical technology. His opinion was that this skill and knowledge was not lost when ancient Greece went into decline, but was passed on through the

Arab world, which possessed similar mechanisms at a later date, and became the foundation of European clock-making techniques in the Middle Ages. Price felt that originally the device had been permanently mounted, conceivably in a statue, and put on display. Perhaps it was once contained inside a structure similar to the intriguing Tower of Winds, an octagonal marble tower that functioned as a water-powered timepiece in the Roman agora at Athens.

The discovery and reconstructions of the Antikythera Mechanism have also persuaded scholars to look at descriptions in ancient texts of such devices in a different light. Previously, it was believed that the mentions of mechanical astronomical models scattered over the works of several ancient writers should not be interpreted literally. The Greeks, it was felt, had the theory, but not the mechanical knowledge. But after the discovery and testing of the Antikythera Mechanism, this line of thought will surely have to change. Roman orator and writer Cicero, writing in the first century B.C. and living at the time of the Antikythera shipwreck, mentions an invention of his friend and teacher, the previously mentioned Poseidonius. Cicero notes that Poseidonius had recently constructed a device "which at each revolution reproduces the same motions of the sun, the moon, and the five planets that take place in the heavens every day and night." Cicero also mentions that the Sicilian astronomer, engineer, and mathematician Archimedes (c. 287 B.C.–212 B.C.), "is said to have made a small planetarium." In connection with this device, the orator also remarks that the Roman consul Marcellus took great

Detail showing door plate of the device.

pride in the possession of a planetarium designed and built by Archimedes himself, which he had taken as booty from the captured city of Syracuse, on the eastern coast of Sicily. In fact, it was during this siege of this city in 212 B.C. that Archimedes was killed by Roman soldiers. Some researchers have even proposed that it was an astronomical device designed and built by Archimedes that was rescued from the Antikythera shipwreck.Without doubt, one of the most amazing and intriguing artifacts of the ancient world, the original Antikythera Mechanism is currently on display in the collection of the National Archaeological Museum in Athens, accompanied by a reconstruction. There is also a replica of the ancient device displayed at the American Computer Museum in Bozeman, Montana. The discovery of the Antikythera Mechanism has challenged our perception of the scientific and technological capabilities of the ancient world in no un-

certain terms. Reconstructions have proven that the design functions as an astronomical computer, and shows that the scientists of the Greek and Roman world of the first century B.C. were perfectly capable of designing and building complicated mechanisms, which would not be equalled for 1,000 years. Derek De Solla Price commented that the civilization that possessed the technology and knowledge to construct such a mechanism "could have built almost anything they wanted to." Unfortunately, most of what they created has not survived. The fact that the Antikythera Mechanism is not specifically mentioned in any of the ancient texts that have come down to us proves how much has been lost from this important and fascinating period in European history. In fact, if it wasn't for the curiosity of Greek sponge fishermen more than 100 years ago, we would not even have this eloquent proof of the advanced scientific achievements of the Greeks of 2,000 years ago.

Ancient Aircraft

© *David Hatcher Childress*
Strange hieroglyphs in the Temple of Osiris in Abydos.

On December 12, 1903, the Wright brothers made the first sustained and controlled flight by powered airplane in history at Kitty Hawk, North Carolina. At least, this is the accepted story. But had man mastered the power of flight much earlier, perhaps hundreds or even thousands of years earlier? Some researchers believe that there is evidence to suggest that this is indeed the case, but that the knowledge has been lost to history. The physical evidence for this ancient flight comes mainly in the form of enigmatic South American and Egyptian artifacts and Egyptian carvings.

The first examples are the so-called gold aircraft from Colombia. Some of these artifacts date to about A.D. 500 and are attributed to the Tolima culture, which inhabited the highlands of Colombia from around A.D. 200 to 1000.

Traditionally described by archaeologists as animal or insect figurines, the objects seem to display features compatible with airplane technology, such as delta wings, vertical stabilizers, and horizontal elevators. A further example, a stylized gold alloy flying fish pendant, comes from the Calima culture of southwest Colombia, (c. 200 B.C.–A.D. 600). A photo of such a pendant was included in Erich Von Däniken's 1972 book, *The Gold of the Gods*, and he believed the object represented an airplane used by outer space visitors. Although the figure is thought by archaeologists to represent a stylized version of a flying fish found in the region, there are some features, particularly those around the tail, which appear significantly different from anything found in nature.

More gold examples were fashioned by the Sinú culture of coastal Colombia, a gold-working community that existed between about A.D. 300 and A.D. 1550. These objects were about 5 centimeters long and were worn as pendants on neck chains. In 1954, some examples of the Sinú models were among the collection of ancient gold artifacts sent by the Colombian government on a United States tour; 15 years later a modern reproduction of one of the artifacts was given to zoologist and author Ivan T. Sanderson to examine. Apparently, his conclusion was that the object was not characteristic of any known winged animal. The front wings were delta-shaped and straight edged, for example, not like an animal or insect. Sanderson thought that it appeared more mechanical than biological, and even went as far as to suggest that it represented a high-speed aircraft at least 1,000 years old. In fact, the airplane-like appearance of the objects encouraged Dr. Arthur Poyslee to conduct wind-tunnel experiments at the Aeronautical Institute of New York, where he came to a positive conclusion about the object's ability to fly. In August 1996, a reproduction of one of these gold models, built at a scale of 16:1, was flown successfully by three German engineers: Algund Eenboom, Peter Belting, and Conrad Lübbers. From their research, they concluded that the original artifact resembled a modern space shuttle or the supersonic Concorde rather than an insect.

Most of these intriguing South American pendants have four wings (or two wings and a tail) and do not look similar to any known insects or birds. Granted, they are stylized models, but the resemblance to an airplane, and even the space shuttle, is surprising. However, if we are to believe that the objects are supposed to represent some kind of aerial vehicle that

© *David Hatcher Childress*
A gold insect model from a tomb in Columbia.

actually flew, there are one or two problems with many of them. First, on the majority of the models the wings are depicted too far back from the object's center of gravity to allow for stable flight; second, the nose does not resemble anything on an aircraft.

Amazingly little original research into the origin of these artifacts has been done by advocates of the ancient airplane theory. Most of the Web articles about pre-Columbian airplanes mention "South American" or "Central American" models found in tombs, but no exact provenance is given for most of them, and usually no exact dates are mentioned. Perhaps this is partly due to the prolific looting of ancient tombs in Colombia, and the subsequent appearance of their contents on the antiquities market in South America, that still continues to this day. However, the vast majority of Internet sites devoted to the subject of South American ancient aircraft merely reproduce a 1996 article by Lumir G. Janku of the *Anomalies and Enigmas* Website. Without further research into their exact origin and cultural context, the labeling of these intriguing artifacts as ancient airplane models seems ill-advised, to say the least.

Another small plane-like model, believed by Egyptologists to be that of a hawk with outstretched wings, comes from Saqqara in Egypt. It was apparently first discovered in 1898 in the tomb of Pa-di-Imen in north Saqqara, which dates to the fourth or third century B.C. The object is made of sycamore wood, with a length of 14.2 centimeters, wingspan of 18.3 centimeters, and weight of about 39 grams. There are hieroglyphs on the tail that read "The Gift of Amon." The

god Amon in ancient Egypt was usually associated with the wind. After its discovery, the object was stored in the Cairo Museum until 1969, when Khalil Messiha, an Egyptian professor of anatomy and student of ancient models, noticed its resemblance to a modern airplane, or glider. He also perceived that whereas other bird models in the Museum had legs and painted feathers, this one did not. Messiha was of the opinion that the design exhibited many aerodynamic qualities. After his brother, a flight engineer, made a balsa wood model of the object which flew successfully, Dr. Messiha was convinced that the Saqqara Bird represented an ancient scale model of a glider.

However, Martin Gregorie of Harlow, in Essex, who has designed, built, and flown gliders for more than 30 years, disagrees. Experimenting with the design he found that without a tailplane (the fixed horizontal tail surface of an airplane) which he believes the model never had, the model was totally unstable. Even after he had fitted a tailplane to the model, the results were unconvincing. Gregorie suggested that the model may have functioned as a weather vane or perhaps a child's toy. Larry Orcutt, of the *Catchpenny Mysteries* Website, believes the object could have been a weather vane to indicate wind direction on a boat. He bases his idea on bird figures on the mastheads of boats and ships shown on reliefs from the Temple of Khonsu at Karnak, dating to the late New Kingdom (c. 12th century B.C.). Orcutt also notes that there are in fact traces of paint on the beak and tail, which indicates that it was

© *David Hatcher Childress*

Wooden model, probably of a bird, from Saqqara, Egypt dated to the fourth or third century B.C.

once a richly painted model of a bird. The black eyes on the object, actually the ends of an obsidian bar which has been fitted through the head, are not shown in many of the photos circulating of the model, thus significantly increasing its resemblance to an airplane. Consequently, while the Saqqara Bird seems to possess one or two aerodynamic qualities, the possibility that it is the sole surviving scale model of an Egyptian aircraft seems unlikely. Rather, the available evidence of well-crafted Egyptian game boards and toys would point to the object being a model of a bird, or perhaps a child's toy.

Probably the most controversial evidence for ancient flight comes from the puzzling carvings on a panel from the 19th Dynasty Temple of Seti I, at Abydos, Egypt. These incredible glyphs appear to show a helicopter, perhaps a tank, and what looks similar to either a space ship or a jet plane. In fact, one of these glyphs has achieved legendary status as "The Abydos Temple Helicopter." So do these amazing hieroglyphs show that the Egyptians of the 13th century B.C. possessed 21st century technology?

Unfortunately, some of the photos of the glyphs doing the rounds on the Internet have been digitally altered to emphasize the aircraft-like features. Nevertheless, there are still some untouched photos in existence showing these extraordinary hieroglyphs of apparently modern aerial vehicles.

However, Katherine Griffis-Greenberg of the University of Alabama at Birmingham, as well as many other archaeologists and Egyptologists, maintain that the extraordinary carvings are palimpsests—newer writing inscribed over old. The Egyptologists theory is that, in this particular case, plaster has been added over the old inscription and a new inscription made. The plaster subsequently fell out due to time and weathering, leaving bits of the old and new glyphs overlapping and causing images that resemble modern aircraft. It is certainly a fact that a considerable amount of recarving of inscriptions took place in ancient Egypt, as ruling pharaohs attempted to claim the work of previous kings, or to destroy their reputation. It seems that in the case of the Abydos Helicopter panel what has happened is that King Ramesses II, well known for appropriating the work of his predecessors, has covered the panel of his predecessor, King Seti I, with his own inscription. More specifically, the hieroglyph text actually consists of part of the title of Ramesses II, translated as "The one of the Two Ladies, who suppresses the nine foreign countries." This overlies the royal title of Seti I that was originally carved into the stone.

Nevertheless, believers in the Abydos Helicopter argue that overlying inscriptions resulting in such striking images of modern aircraft would be too much of a coincidence. But there are other factors which make ancient airplanes in Egypt improbable. One is the complete lack of any flying machines whatsoever in the entire ancient Egyptian corpus. There should be more related inscriptions, but there's nothing. In addition—and this applies to all the ancient aircraft theories—there is a complete absence of evidence for the necessary support technology required of a flight industry. If Egyptian and South American cultures had developed and assembled such things as helicopters and airplanes, they would have needed a huge manufacturing industry for the vehicles themselves, not to mention provision for fuel production, mines to obtain metal, and storage facilities. Where is it all? If the ancients were flying around in modern airplanes and helicopters, surely there would be more evidence than a collection of dubious models and a solitary panel of hieroglyphs carved over a temple doorway. There is no denying that the idea of human flight must certainly have occurred to many ancient cultures, as witnessed by the literature of India, for example, and perhaps this was part of the inspiration for the enigmatic South American models. However, at present, the physical evidence that they ever achieved it is debatable at best.

The Dead Sea Scrolls

Photograph by Grauesel (GNU Free Documentation License).
Caves at Qumran, in the area where the Dead Sea Scrolls were found.

The Dead Sea Scrolls are, without doubt, the most significant and exciting manuscript find of the last 100 years. The cache of scrolls and scroll fragments were discovered in 11 caves in the area of Qumran, 13 miles east of Jerusalem, close to the Dead Sea in Israel. This extraordinary library of Jewish documents dates from between the third century B.C. and A.D. 68, and consists of scrolls made from animal skins (parchment), a few of papyrus, and one extremely unusual example in copper. The texts are written using a carbon-based ink, and are written mostly in Hebrew, with some in Aramaic (a Semitic language allegedly spoken by Jesus), and a small number in

Greek. Research into these mysterious documents and their authors has been ongoing since their initial discovery in the late 1940s and has thrown some fascinating light, not only on the Bible, but also on a shadowy brotherhood of men and women known as the Essenes.

In 1947, Bedouin goat hearders were searching for a stray goat among the cliffs overlooking the Dead Sea when they came upon a hitherto unexplored cave. Inside the cave, the Bedouins discovered a number of ancient clay jars along the walls, which were filled with manuscripts and wrapped in linen. In all, seven clay jars were recovered from the cave (known as Cave 1) and thus began the nine-year-long investigation of the caves around the northwest shore of the Dead Sea. During the search for scrolls, archaeologists often had to deal with the problem of local Bedouins plundering the caves, eager to make a profit by selling the manuscripts to Arab antiqities dealers in Bethlehem. Eventually, however, the investigations produced approximately 800 documents from 11 different caves at Qumran. A few of these caves, particularly Cave 4, appear to have functioned as permanent libraries with built-in shelves.

Although some of the Qumran Scrolls were written during the time of Jesus, none of them refer directly to him, or to any of his apostles. This may be because the scrolls as a whole only consist of a fraction of what was probably once a huge library of manuscripts, most of which is now lost. One of the most fascinating aspects of the scrolls is that they contain the oldest group of Old Testament texts ever found, the only other Hebrew document of similar antiquity is the second century B.C. Nash Papyrus from Egypt, which contains a Hebrew text of the Ten Commandments. The Dead Sea Scrolls can be separated into two categories—the biblical, which consist of copies of the actual books of the Hebrew Scriptures and commentaries on these texts, and the non-biblical, which consist of the prayer books and rules of life of the community that wrote the scripts. In the Biblical texts, every book of the Old Testament is represented, apart from the Book of Esther and the Book of Nehemiah. There are prophecies by Ezekiel, Jeremiah, and Daniel as well as traditional stories involving Biblical figures such as Noah, Abraham, and Enoch, none of which are recorded in the canonical Hebrew Bible. Some of the most important texts discovered in the caves at Qumran include the Great Isaiah Scroll, which contains the entire 66-chapter book of Isaiah; a commentary on the Book of Habakkuk—one of the books of the Old Testament Minor Prophets; a book of community rules known as the Manual of Discipline, consisting mainly of a summary of the responsibilities of the Master of a sectarian Jewish community and his disciples; and the controversial Temple Scroll. The Temple Scroll is the longest and probably the best-preserved of all the Dead Sea Scrolls, and focuses on the ideal design and operation of a new and perfect temple, including its laws and sacrificial procedures.

The question of who wrote the Dead Sea Scrolls and subsequently hid them away in the caves around

Qumran is a controversial issue. Researchers have christened the probable authors of the text, a small Jewish group who lived at the nearby settlement of Qumran, the Dead Sea Sect. The Dead Sea Sect are often identified as the Essenes, credited with introducing monasticism, and one of the three leading Jewish sects discussed by Jewish historian Josephus (c. A.D. 37–c. A.D. 100), the others being the Pharisees and the Sadducees. The Essenes do appear in other contemporary sources, such as Josephus Flavius, Philo of Alexandria, and Pliny the Elder, though they are not mentioned at all in the New Testament. Apparently the Essenes left Jerusalem in protest at the way the Temple, the central institution of Judaism, was being run, and set themselves up in the Judean Desert, away from what they saw as the worldliness of Jerusalem. They became an ascetic monastic community, though there seems to have been women among them, and were strict observers of the Torah, or the Written Law (usually the the first five books of the Hebrew Bible).

Close to the caves where the scrolls were found lie the ruins of Qumran, an abandoned fortress thought to have been reestablished as a settlement between 150 and 130 B.C. Investigations at the site have revealed that a group of Jewish ascetics inhabited the settlement, which included an assembly hall, ritual immersion pools, aquaducts, cisterns, and storehouses. The inhabitants do not appear to have lived within the main settlement, but in tents and caves on its outskirts. One long narrow room at Qumran, known as the Scriptorium, contained two inkwells and a series of writing benches thought to be for the use of scribes. Archaeologists believe that it was in this chamber that many of the Biblical scripts found in the caves were copied. Although no traces of manuscripts were discovered in this room, it is linked to the scroll caves by the presence of a distinctive pottery type, which was found at both sites.

Many of the Dead Seas Scrolls give an important insight into the lives and beliefs of the community that wrote them. For example, there are calendrical documents that include a sophisticated solar calendar of 364 days, as opposed to the more popular 354-day lunar calendar used at the temple in Jerusalem. Another illustrative manuscript is entitled "The War of the Sons of Light against the Sons of Darkness." The Sons of Light are probably the Dead Sea Sect, and the Sons of Darkness seems to refer to the remainder of humanity. This scroll describes an imminent cataclysmic battle, not just between these two forces, but between the cosmic forces of good and evil, and represents the way in which this community viewed Armageddon. For the Dead Sea Sect, this battle was to come perhaps sooner than they thought. During the First Jewish Revolt (A.D. 66–73) the Roman army besieged and destroyed Jerusalem and various Jewish strongholds, including Masada on the eastern edge of the Judean desert, overlooking the Dead Sea.

During the battle at Masada in A.D. 73 the Jewish defenders of the site committed mass suicide rather than fall into the hands of the Romans. Interestingly enough, among the fragments of 14 biblical, apocryphal, and sectarian scrolls found at Masada was a sectarian manuscript identical with one discovered in Qumran, and using the same 364-day solar calendar as the Dead Sea Sect. There is little evidence for what happened at Qumran when the Roman legions arrived in A.D. 70. The sect seem to have taken their scrolls to the nearby caves for safe-keeping prior to the Roman attack, though whether the inhabitants themselves perished in battle or escaped to safety is a mystery.

There are some scholars who believe that the group at Qumran were not responsible for the Dead Sea Scrolls at all. One theory is that the manuscripts were written by priests of Jerusalem's Second Hebrew Temple and then transported to Qumran and safely hidden from the Roman legions. One interpretation of this hypothesis could involve the Dead Sea Sect on one level, perhaps as those with the task of secreting the scrolls from Jerusalem and depositing them in the caves. This would mean the sect were the keepers of the scrolls rather than their authors. However, this hypothesis does not tie in well with the sect's fierce criticism of the the priesthood of the Temple. Professor Norman Golb, of the Oriental Institute of the University of Chicago, believes that the scrolls represent such a wide range of ideas that, rather than being the product of one community, they likely represent the writings of various Jewish sects and communities of ancient Israel.

The most unusual and mysterious of the ancient scrolls from the Dead Sea is without doubt the Copper Scroll.

This particular scroll was found in 1952 in Cave 3 at Qumran, and, as its name suggests, is made from copper. The scroll is written in a different form of Hebrew than the other Qumran manuscripts, and probably dates to the mid-first century A.D. Unlike the rest of the scrolls, the Copper Scroll is not a literary work, but a list of 64 underground hiding places throughout Israel. These hiding places are described as containing vast caches of gold, silver, scrolls, ritual vessels, containers of incense, and weapons. In 1960 it was estimated that the total value of this hypothetical treasure would be over $1 million. Although many have searched for these riches, nothing has ever been discovered, convincing most scholars that the actual Hebrew text of the scroll is some kind of code. The presence of groups of two or three Greek letters appended to the end of seven of the entries tends to reinforce this viewpoint. Due to the specific nature of some of the items (including ritual vessels and incense), the riches described are believed by some researchers to be the famous lost treasure from the Temple at Jerusalem, hidden away for safekeeping before the destruction of the Temple by the Roman legions in A.D. 70. One intriguing aspect of the Copper Scroll is the last entry on its list of locations, labeled as "Item 64." It reads "in a pit adjoining on the north, in a hole opening northward, and buried at its mouth: a copy of this document, with an explanation and their measurements, and an inventory of each and every thing." Does this entry mean that there is another yet undiscovered copper scroll hidden somewhere, containing more substantial information?

Although all of the manuscripts discovered in Cave 1 appeared in print between 1950 and 1956, publication of the Dead Sea Scrolls has often been a slow process. Lack of access to the Scroll material has persuaded some researchers, such as Michael Baigent and Richard Leigh in their book *The Dead Sea Scrolls Deception,* that the Vatican was behind a plot to suppress the release of the manuscripts to the public out of fear of the dangerous material related to early Christianity that the scrolls contained. Such theories have been considerably weakened by the release of more scroll material in the late 1990s and early 2000s, in particular the publication of the entire collection of Biblical scrolls. With the publication of much of the material from the caves at Qumran, the importance of the Dead Sea Scrolls can now be better appreciated. Not only do the scrolls provide fascinating religious and historical information about a poorly documented period of history, but they also shed considerable light on the sources of both Judaism and early Christianity.

An interesting parallel with the Dead Sea Scrolls material has recently been provided by the newly translated Gospel of Judas, a text which gives completely new insights into the relationship of Jesus and the infamous disciple who betrayed him.

This early Christian leather-bound papyrus manuscript includes the only known text of the Gospel of Judas, and has been dated to around A.D. 300. The manuscript was found in the 1970s in a cavern near El Minya, Egypt, and circulated among antiquities dealers in Egypt and Europe for years before it found its way to the United States where, in 2000, it was purchased by Frieda Nussberger-Tchacos, a Zurich-based antiquities dealer. Ms. Nussberger-Tchacos eventually sold the manuscript to the Maecenas Foundation in Basel, Switzerland, for restoration and translation. In April 2006, at a news conference in Washington, D.C., the National Geographic Society announced the completion of the restoration and translation of the manuscript. As with the Dead Sea Scrolls, a significant amount of the original material from the El Minya texts is missing, though some of it is believed to be in circulation among antiquities dealers or in private hands. In this light, one can only wonder what other manuscript treasures the complete library of scrolls at Qumran once included, and if, in a secluded cave somewhere around the northwestern shore of the Dead Sea, further scrolls lie buried in the sand, waiting to be discovered.

The Crystal Skull of Doom

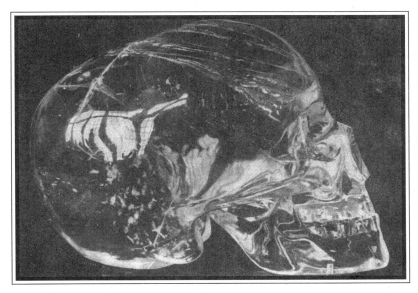

The Crystal Skull of Doom reproduced from the July 1936 issue of Man, *when the skull was the property of Sidney Burney.*

The crystal skulls are enigmatic and controversial objects. Credited by some as ancient artifacts with remarkable magical and healing properties—but dismissed by others as relatively modern forgeries—there is no agreement about their origins. Some researchers have claimed that there are 13 crystal skulls located in various places around the world, only five of which have so far been located. The objects themselves are models of human skulls carved from clear quartz crystal, and the examples so far recovered vary in size from a few inches to the size of a human head. Where the skulls originated or what they were used for is a mystery, but an origin with the pre-Columbian cultures of South America, such as the Aztecs and Maya, have been suggested. Without doubt the most fascinating and puzzling of these crystal skulls is the Mitchell-Hedges Skull, which possesses an eerie, alluring beauty, unequalled in other examples. The baffling story of the Skull of Doom, as it has become known, is almost as strange as the object itself.

The fearsome Skull of Doom is a life-size rock which weighs around 11 pounds, 7 ounces, and is beautifully carved from a single, clear, quartz crystal. The skull features a fitted detachable jaw, which would allow for movement, as if the head was speaking. Apart from small flaws in the temples and cheekbone, it is an anatomically correct model of a human skull. The origins and discovery of this enigmatic artifact are shrouded in mystery, and as a result, the Mitchell-Hedges Skull has no confirmed provenance. The story goes that in 1927 (or possibly 1924) English explorer and adventurer F.A. Mitchell-Hedges (1882–1959) was investigating the ruins of a Mayan ceremonial center at Lubaantun, Belize, as part of his search for the lost site of Atlantis. With Mitchell-Hedges on this expedition was his adopted daughter Anna Mitchell-Hedges. On Anna's 17th birthday she was wandering around the site, when she found the top part of the rock crystal skull, underneath what appeared to be an altar. Only three months later, in the same room, the jaw part of the skull was discovered. After seeing the reaction of the locals to this strange discovery, Mitchell-Hedges apparently offered this skull to them. But later, as he and his party were about to depart from the area, the local high priest gave the skull to Mitchell-Hedges as a gift, in gratitude for the food, medicine, and clothing the explorer had given to his people.

Doubts were cast on this romantic story with the discovery that Mitchell-Hedges had, in fact, bought the skull for £400 at Sotheby's, London, in 1943, from Sidney Burney, the owner of an art gallery. This would tie in with the fact that Mitchell-Hedges inexplicably makes no mention of the skull in the various newspaper articles on Atlantis which he authored in the 1930s, and the lack of photographs of the exotic artifact among those taken on his Lubaatun expedition. In fact, Mitchell-Hedges did not write anything about the skull until 1954, when he devoted only a few vague lines to it in his book *Danger My Ally*, the first time he mentions the crystal skull since its alleged discovery in 1927. Perhaps this was why Hedges wrote about the Skull of Doom "how it came to be in my possession I have reason for not revealing." Further evidence against Hedges discovering the artifact in Belize is provided in the July 1936 issue of *Man*, the journal of the Royal Anthropological Institute of Great Britain and Ireland. This issue of the journal contains an article about a study carried out of two crystal skulls, one from the British Museum, and the other called the Burney Skull. This latter artifact is none other than Hedges' Skull of Doom, obviously then the property of art dealer Sidney Burney. Nowhere in the article is there mention of its discovery at the Mayan ruins of Lubaatun, or of F.A. Mitchell-Hedges. In his book *Secrets of the Supernatural*, author Joe Nickell makes reference to a letter from Burney to the American Museum of Natural History, written in 1933. In the letter Burney states "the Rock-crystal Skull was for several years in the possession of the collector from whom I bought it and he in his turn had it from an Englishman in whose collection it had been also for several years, but beyond that I have not been able to go." Troubling evidence indeed, though it merely casts doubt on Hedges' story, not on the authenticity of the skull itself. Whatever reason Hedges had for concocting the exotic tale, it was not his first, and he seems to have had a reputation for tall stories (which included sharing a room with Leon Trotsky and fighting with Pancho Villa).

Many of the allegedly supernatural properties and sinister legends now associated with the Crystal Skull can be traced back to Mitchell-Hedges 1954 autobiography *Danger My Ally*, where the artifact first acquired its title the Skull of Doom. In this book, Hedges describes the skull as being used by a Mayan High Priest when performing magic rites involving a death curse, which invariably produced the demise of the intended victim. Such was the horrifying power of the skull that, even if left alone, it still had the ability to cause instant death. Mitchell-Hedges also stated in his book that the skull had taken an incredible 150 years to manufacture and was at least 3,600 years old. Though he provided no evidence to back up these assertions, it has become part of the folklore attached the the Skull of Doom that it must have taken hundreds of years to manufacture, the makers rubbing and polishing every day of their lives to achieve the perfect shape.

On the death of Mitchell-Hedges in 1959, the skull was passed on to his adopted daughter Anna, and it remained in her possession until 1964, when she loaned it to family friends and art conservators Frank and Mabel Dorland to make a detailed scientific study. When not being studied, the skull was kept in a bank vault for security, but on one occasion when the couple took the object home and placed it close to the fire, they noticed the amazing optical effects produced by the skull when light was shone through it. Some stories also mention poltergeist activity taking place while the skull remained in the house. In 1970, Frank Dorland took the skull to the Hewlett-Packard Laboratories at Santa Clara, California (at that time one of the world leaders in electronics, computers, and electronic quartz technology). After testing the skull, Hewlett-Packard Laboratories stated that they could find no microscopic marks on the crystal which would indicate it had been worked with metal instruments. Apparently the lab also stated that the skull had been carved against the natural grain of the crystal, and were at a loss to know why it hadn't shattered during manufacture. From this, Dorland concluded that the original quartz block must have been first chiselled into a rough shape, possibly using diamonds, before grinding and polishing with water and sand. This painstakingly slow job would, according to Dorland, have required up to 300 years to complete, doubling the already exaggerated claims for the creation of the object, and involving manufacture over several generations.

The mystery surrounding the provenance of the Skull of Doom and how it was manufactured have convinced many that a superhuman agency must have been at work. Perhaps the crystal is as much as 36,000 years old and was left behind after the destruction of lost lands such as Lemuria or Atlantis? F.A. Mitchell-Hedges thought so, and his daughter Anna herself believes the skull original came from another planet and was kept in Atlantis before being brought to the Mayan site of Luubantun. A number of people have used the skull for scrying (using a crystal or a pool of water to induce visions) and have reportedly had detailed visions of ancient civilizations. Others have noted the spontaneous appearance and disappearance of strange colors inside the crystal, or even holographic images. Weird sounds and poltergeist activity have also been associated with the skull, and a number of people have testified to its magical and healing powers. A Native American legend tells of 13 ancient crystal skulls with moveable jaws, which are able to speak or sing. According to this legend, when all 13 are found and brought together, their collective wisdom—which includes the true purpose and destiny of mankind—will be made available to the world. Many are convinced that the Skull of Doom is one of these 13 stones.

Over the years, Anna Mitchell-Hedges has toured several cities in the United States with the skull, charging an admission fee to see and touch the famous artifact. She still maintains that she and her father found the skull in Lubaatun, and claims that after the expedition F.A. Mitchell-Hedges had placed the skull with Burney as security for a loan. When her father realized that Burney was attempting to sell the crystal, he immediately bought it back.

Although to some, the Mitchell-Hedges skull appears much more lifelike than the generally stylized art of South America, it is believed by many researchers that the skull is of Aztec or Mayan origin, due to the importance of the skull in their iconography and known examples of Aztec rock crystal work. Although there is no evidence of the Mitchell-Hedges Skull, or any other crystal skull, having being found on a South American archaeological site, an Aztec origin seems at the moment to be the best hypothesis. The skull is thought to have been used as a speaking oracle, with the separate jaw attached to the head using wire and perhaps operated by a priest to give the impression that it was speaking. With the crystal reflecting the light of a fire lit behind it, this would have been an uncanny spectacle.

But the intriguing tale of the Skull of Doom does not end there. When the Mitchell-Hedges skull was first studied in 1936, another crystal skull, known simply as the British Museum Skull, was used alongside it for comparison. This crystal had been obtained in 1897 from Tiffany's, the New York jewelers, and was thought to be of Aztec origin. The study was made by anthropologist Dr. G.M. Morant, who found that the two skulls were dissimilar in one or two ways. For instance, the British Museum Skull was made in one piece, without a detachable jaw, and the Burney Skull (which is how the anthropologist refers to the Mitchell-Hedges Skull) was much more lifelike and finely detailed than the other. However, in the conclusion of his study of the two crystal skulls, Dr.G.M. Morant states "it is safe to conclude that they are representations of the same human skull, though one may have been copied from the other." He believed that, because it showed more anatomical detail, the Burney

Skull was the earlier of the two and had been modeled on a woman's skull.

In January 2005 came the sensational news that after an extensive series of tests on the British Museum Skull, using a scanning electron microscope, a team of researchers from the British Museum concluded that the artifact was in fact manufactured in the 19th century, probably in Germany. The investigations showed markings on the crystal characteristic of jeweler's equipment not developed until the 19th century, and it is now believed that the skull was created for the French collector Eugene Boban, who subsequently sold it to Tiffany's. Boban was a dealer in antiques in Mexico City between 1860 and 1880, and seems to have obtained his skulls from somewhere in Germany. In 1992 the Smithsonian Institution received a crystal skull from an unnamed person who claimed that it was Aztec and had been purchased in Mexico City in 1960. However, research at the Smithsonian revealed that the carving had been done by a wheel, or a rotary saw, tools which no pre-Columbian carvers possessed. Researcher Jane MacLaren Walsh, of the Smithsonian, discovered documents that proved Boban was the source of this skull. Not only this, but further research found that Boban had also provided several other supposedly ancient crystal skulls, some of which had ended up in various museums, including a skull formerly in Paris in the Musee de l'Homme, now in held in the Trocadero Museum in Paris. All of these skulls were actually manufactured in Germany between 1867 and 1886.

While the presence of 19th century fake crystal skulls does not necessarily affect the genuineness of the Skull of Doom, it does cast doubt on the supposed ancient origins of the number of untested crystal skulls that currently exist around the world, mostly in private collections. Many researchers wonder why Anna Mitchell-Hedges refuses to submit her crystal skull for scanning electron microscope testing, which, although it would not provide an exact date for the object (all crystal is ancient and there are no methods for dating it), it would surely prove whether this enigmatic masterpiece was of relatively recent manufacture, of possibly Mayan or Aztec origin, or something else entirely.

The Voynich Manuscript

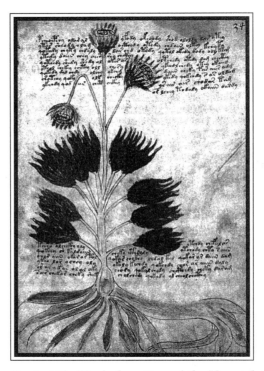

Part of the Herbal *section of the Voynich Manuscript.*

Renowned as the world's most mysterious book, the Voynich Manuscript is a 500 year-old enigma. It is written by an anonymous author in an unintelligible language and covered in unexplained symbols and strange illustrations. The book acquired its name from Wilfred M. Voynich, a Polish-American book dealer, who discovered it by chance in 1912 among a collection of ancient documents in the Jesuit College at Frascati near Rome.

What is puzzling about the Voynich Manuscript is that it is written in a unique alphabetic script whose letters do not resemble English, or any other European letter system. It has puzzled the greatest cryptographers of the 20th century and continues to do so today. After purchasing the book in 1912, Wilfred Voynich made photostats of it and distributed them to cryptographers, experts in ancient languages, astronomers, and botanists, but they could make nothing of the odd language employed in the manuscript. Dr. William Romaine Newbold of the University of Pennsylvania, a student of medieval philosophy and science (and also a cryptographer) thought he had broken the code in 1919. However, his interpretation was later disproved. During World War II, expert British and American codebreakers studied the manuscript but failed to decipher a single word.

The history of the Voynich Manuscript is fittingly mysterious and unusual. It may have originally belonged to the eccentric Emperor Rudolph II of Bohemia (1552–1612) who is said to have bought it in around 1586 for 600 gold ducats (just over $60,000 today), from an unknown seller, who some have suggested was John Dee, an English occultist and astrologer to Queen Elizabeth I. What is known for sure is that the signature of botanist, alchemist, and private physician to Rudolph, Jacobus Horcicky de Tepenecz, is on the folio. He died in 1622, after which the next identified owner of the book is an alchemist called Georgius Barschius, who called it a *sphynx*, in reference to its enigmatic contents, which he was not able to translate. At his death, some time before 1662, he left the book, along with the rest of his library, to his friend Johannes Marcus Marci, one time rector of Charles University in Prague.

The surviving manuscript has a letter dated 1666 attached to it, written in Latin by Marci to the learned German Jesuit scholar Athanasius Kircher in Rome. The letter offers the manuscript to Kircher for decoding and mentions it as once being the property of Emperor Rudolf II. Marci further adds that it was believed by some that the manuscript was written by English Franciscan friar and philosopher Roger Bacon, who lived from 1214 to 1294, though it is clear from the letter that Marci himself was not convinced of this. The manuscript became the property of Kircher's institute, the Roman Jesuit University (the Collegio Romano) where it may have been stored in its library until Victor Emmanuel II of Italy annexed the Papal States in 1870, and it was moved to the Jesuit College at the Villa Mondragone, where Voynich discovered it in 1912. After Voynich died in 1930, the manuscript was inherited by his widow, the author Ethel Lilian Voynich. After Voynich's widow died in 1960, the book was inherited by her friend, Miss Anne Nill. In 1961, New York antiquarian book dealer H.P. Kraus made headlines when he bought the manuscript from her for the sum of $24,500. The manuscript was later valued at $160,000, but Kraus was unable to sell it, and in 1969 donated it to Yale University, where it is kept today in the Beinecke Rare Book and Manuscript Library.

The manuscript itself measures about 6 by 9 inches and contains around 240 vellum pages, though it may once have had more than 270. The enciphered text was written by hand using a quill pen, which was also used for the outline of the crudely drawn figures, and later a kind of colored paint was added to these figures. The majority of the pages contain illustrations colored in red, blue, brown, yellow, and green, and these drawings indicate that the book was divided up into five parts, each dealing with different subjects. The first and longest section, filling almost half the volume, is known as the *Herbal* section. Each page in this part consists of one or sometimes two illustrations of plants accompanied by a few paragraphs of text. The plants in the drawings cannot always be identified, and some are probably fanciful inventions. The next section contains (among other things) drawings of suns, moons, and stars, and has been identified as astronomical and astrological in nature. Following this is a section called the *Biological*, as it contains some apparently anatomical figures, including small, nude women, and pipes and tubes that resemble blood vessels. The fourth is a section which has been labeled *Pharmaceutical*, as it includes pictures of plant roots, leaves, and other plant parts and labeled containers, which may be apothecary jars. The fifth and last part is the *Recipes* section, and includes a number of short paragraphs, each marked with a star in the margin; this section may have been some kind of calendar or almanac. The book ends with a page containing the *Key*.

In 1944, Hugh O'Neill, Benedictine monk and botanist at the Catholic University, identified some plants illustrated in the book as being species from the Americas, specifically an American sunflower and a red pepper. This would mean that the manuscript must date after 1493, when Columbus brought the seeds to Europe. However, the illustrations are not at all clear in the manuscript, and some have disputed O'Neill's identifications. An interesting development regarding the manuscript came in the 1970s with

Captain Prescott Currier, a U.S. military cryptology expert. Based on the statistical properties of the text, he identified two distinct styles in the manuscript, which he interpreted as two separate languages, which he dubbed *A* and *B*. His conclusion was that the manuscript had been written by at least two different people, although it is conceivable that it could have been written by a single individual at different times.

There have been many theories as to the language used in the manuscript, its origins, and its purpose. One of the names put forward most often is that of Roger Bacon, a man often persecuted for his writings and scientific discoveries when he was alive, and who mentions in his works the need to conceal certain secrets in cipher. Mainly because Bacon is mentioned as a possible author by Marci in the letter that accompanied the manuscript, Wilfred Voynich was almost sure he was the original author and undertook a great deal of historical research to try and prove it. He found out that Dr. John Dee had been a great collector of the works of Bacon and had certainly visited Rudolph at the time of the supposed first appearance of the manuscript. Evidence that page numbers on the manuscript were written by Dee has, however, been challenged by many Dee scholars. Apart from these page numbers there is no direct evidence to link Dee with the manuscript and he makes no mention of it in his detailed diaries. Nevertheless, Voynich's ideas have been a huge influence on subsequent research and attempts at decipherment. In 1943, New York lawyer Joseph Martin Feely published *Roger Bacon's*

Cipher: The Right Key Found, in which he claimed that the text was written by Bacon in a kind of highly abbreviated Medieval Latin. No one has accepted this proposal, and experts on the work of Bacon who have examined the Voynich Manuscript have denied the possibility of his authorship.

Dr. Leo Levitov, author of *Solution of the Voynich Manuscript* (1987) claims to have deciphered the manuscript and identifies it is a liturgical manual for the Cathar religion of the 12th to 14th centuries. However, his identification has been contested on the basis of its obvious disparities with the known practices of the Cathars in the south of France. In his 2004 book, *Pandora's Hope*, James Finn proposed that the language in the manuscript was visually encoded Hebrew. His ingenious theory is that the words in the cipher are the same Hebrew words repeated throughout the text in different forms, so for example, *ain*, the Hebrew word for *eye*, can be found in the text as *aiin* or *aiiin*, so it appears that different words are being employed when they are actually variations of the same word. This idea would explain why scholars and cryptographers have had so much trouble deciphering the text. On the other hand, Finn's explanation would mean that there would be a vast array of possible interpretations of the same text, and thus a great possibility that the original meaning would be lost or misinterpreted. Perhaps that is a risk the original author would not have been prepared to take.

The repeated failure to find a plausible solution to the Voynich mystery has lent it an aura of impenetrable mystery that is, perhaps, deserved.

But the indecipherability along with the manuscripts more bizarre features, such as the high rate of word repetition and its fantastical illustrations, have also led some researchers to become suspicious of its authenticity and even to suspect an elaborate hoax, perhaps perpetrated by Wilfred Voynich himself. However, the latter possibility can be discounted thanks to written evidence for its existence prior to the time it was purchased by Voynich.

A recent solution to the Voynich Manuscript pointing to a hoax was suggested in 2003 by Dr. Gordon Rugg, a senior lecturer in computer science at Keele University in England. He showed that text, with characteristics similar to the Voynich manuscript, could have been randomly generated using a device known as a Cardan Grille, invented around 1550 as a way of encrypting text. Some believe Edward Kelley, a spirit medium who worked with John Dee, perpetrated the hoax manuscript in order to sell it to Emperor Rudolf II, who was known to be interested in rare and unusual items. However, as has been mentioned earlier, there is no direct evidence linking Dee with the manuscript, and Kelley's name seems only to have been put forward because, together with Dee, he used and probably invented *Enochian*, a language allegedly revealed to Kelley by angels. However, studies of this occult language have shown that it has no relationship with the contents of the Voynich Manuscript. The difficulty with Gordon Rugg's conclusion, and any suggestion that the Voynich Manuscript is a hoax, is that statistical analysis of the book has shown patterns similar to natural languages. For instance, the text follows something known as Zipf's Law, which concerns the frequency of words in a piece of text. It is unlikely that a 16th century hoaxer could somehow produce a body of random text that followed these basic laws of language.

The manuscript then, does appear to be genuine. But that brings us no closer to identifying its puropose. The general consensus today is that it was probably written in Central Europe some time in the 15th or early 16th century. There have been suggestions that it was designed as a book of medieval herbal remedies, or an alchemical or astrological text. But known examples of such works do not resemble the Voynich Manuscript in any way. And surely no one would use such a perplexingly unbreakable code unless the information in the text was either extremely dangerous or particularly secret. If the origin of the book could be determined for sure, or if the identity of the person who brought it to the court of Rudolph II at Prague could be discovered, then perhaps we would be closer to understanding its purpose. In 2005, the whole manuscript was published in facsimile for the first time by a French editor, Jean-Claude Gawsewitch, as *Le Code Voynich*. Today, through the medium of the Internet, hundreds of scholars and enthusiastic amateurs are exchanging ideas and theories on this mysterious manuscript, and more people than ever before are working on a solution. But so far this strange book has refused to give up its secrets. Perhaps the author of the Voynich Manuscript truly invented an unbreakable cipher.

PART III

❦

Enigmatic
People

The Bog Bodies of Northern Europe

Photograph by Jan van der Crabben. (Creative Commons License. Attribution—ShareAlike 2.0)

Lütt-Witt Moor, a bog in Henstedt-Ulzburg in northern Germany.

Over the past 300 years or so, incredibly well-preserved human bodies have been discovered in the desolate peat bogs of Britain, Ireland, the Netherlands, Germany, and Denmark. The majority of these bog mummies or bog bodies date to between the first century B.C. and the fourth century A.D., though the oldest dates from the Mesolithic period (about 10,000 years ago). There are also some medieval and modern examples. The astonishing preservative powers of the bogs have prevented the decay of these ancient remains so effectively that, although the skeleton does not usually survive, we have the skin, internal organs, stomach (sometimes including the remains of the last meal), eyes, brains, and hair.

A bog consists of about 90 percent water. This water usually contains large amounts of acidic peat (decaying plant matter). Such an environment does not permit the growth of bacteria, so organic materials immersed in this bog water, such as bodies, will not be destroyed. Certain acids contained in this bog water, together with the cold temperature and the lack of oxygen, also act to preserve and tan the skin, which explains the dark brown color of most of the bodies. But how and why did these people meet their death in remote bogs thousands of years ago? One thing we do know is that a large amount of the bodies recovered show signs of extreme violence, including signs of torture and murder.

Perhaps the most famous of these bog mummies is Tollund Man, found in May 1950, near the village of Tollund in Denmark, by two brothers cutting peat. When the men first glimpsed the face staring up at them, they thought it was a recent murder victim and immediately contacted the local police. But subsequent radiocarbon dating of Tollund Man's hair showed that he had died around 350 B.C. During the operation to remove the body from his resting place, one of the helpers collapsed and died of a heart attack. Perhaps, as the late Danish archaeologist P.V. Glob suggested, this was a case of the bog claiming a life for a life. Tollund Man's body had been arranged in a fetal position at the time of death, and was naked apart from a pointed skin cap and a hide belt. His hair had been cropped extremely short and there was stubble clearly visible on his chin and upper lip. A rope consisting of two leather thongs twisted together was pulled tightly around his neck, and it is believed that he was probably hanged or garroted using this rope. Tests on the contents of his stomach reveal that Tollund Man's last meal had been a kind of vegetable and seed soup. An interesting fact about the soup is that its ingredients were a mixture of various kinds of wild and cultivated seeds, which included such an unusual quantity of knotweed that it must have been gathered especially for the purpose. One possibility is that the knotweed was an important ingredient in a ritual last meal that was somehow part of a sacred execution rite. This possibility is also suggested by the careful arrangement of the body and the fact that his eyes and mouth had been closed.

Around 500 bog bodies have been found in Denmark, although there have been no new finds there since the 1950s. Huldremose Woman, found in a bog near Ramten, Jutland, in 1879, was discovered with two skin capes, a woollen skirt, a scarf, and a hair band. Examination of the body revealed the gruesome details that her arms and legs had been repeatedly hacked, one arm being cut completely off, before she was deposited in the peat. The woman met this brutal death sometime between 160 B.C. and A.D. 340.

In 1952, near Windeby in Schleswig-Holstein, northern Germany, two bodies were found in a small bog. The first turned out to be male who had been strangled and then placed in the bog, the body held down by sharpened branches stuck firmly into the peat around him. The second body was that of a young girl of about 14 years of age, dating to the first century A.D. The girl had been blindfolded with a strip of cloth before being drowned in the bog, her body secured by a large stone and branches from a birch tree.

Location of the Yde Girl find.

A more recent find from northern Germany, from Uchte, Lower Saxony, was at first thought to be the body of a teenage murder victim. But when scientists reexamined the body in January of 2005 it was identified as a young girl aged between 16 and 20, who had been deposited in the bog in about 650 B.C. She subsequently became known as the Girl of the Uchter Moor. Even her hair had been preserved, though archaeologists weren't sure whether it was originally blonde or black, as the peat turns all hair reddish.

The earliest recorded find of a bog mummy anywhere in Europe is that of the Kibbelgaarn body in the Netherlands, unearthed in 1791. In the 19th and 20th centuries there were hundreds of discoveries made in Holland. In 1987, the Drents Museum in Assen commenced a project for the systematic research into the bog bodies in their collection, revealing fascinating and vital information about their age, sex, physique, diet, diseases, cause of death, and clothing.

In England, due to the wide variety of bog environment encountered, bodies in many different states of preservation have been discovered. The most famous of these come from Lindow Moss near Wilmslow in Chesire. The circumstances of the discovery of the first body are very curious indeed. In 1983, police in Macclesfield, Cheshire were investigating a man named Peter Reyn-Bardt for the murder of his wife, Malika, 23 years earlier. During the investigation, men working at a peat extraction site adjacent to Reyn-Bardt's garden discovered a well-preserved skull, subsequently identified as coming from a female aged between 30 and 50. Confronted with this evidence, Reyn-Bardt confessed to the crime and was convicted of murder on the strength of his confession. Prior to Reyn-Bardt's trial, the police called in the Oxford University Research Laboratory for Archaeology to examine the body. The result of their study of Lindow Woman, as she became known, was that she was between 1,660 and 1,820 years old. Reyn-Bardt has since appealed his murder conviction.

The following year, the body of a man, naked but for an arm band made of fox fur and a thin rope around his neck, was unearthed in the same area. Lindow Man had been in his 20s when he died between A.D. 50 and A.D. 100. Examination of the body revealed that he had been hit twice on the crown of his head, probably with an axe, with sufficient force to detach chips of his skull into his brain. He had also been strangled using the leather garrote still remaining around his neck, and there was a gash on the throat, which may indicate that his throat had been cut. His hair had been trimmed (using scissors) two or three days before he met his death. The contents of his stomach included burned bread and traces of pollen from mistletoe, a plant sacred to the Celts. Celtic scholar and archaeologist Dr. Anne Ross believes that the threefold death suffered by Lindow Man, along with the blackened crust in his stomach, and the traces of mistletoe, suggest that the man was the victim of a Druidic sacrifice.

More than 80 bodies have been recovered from the bogs of Ireland in the past two centuries, seven of which have been radiocarbon dated. Unlike the rest of Northern Europe, the majority of these bodies belong to the late medieval or post-medieval period, though there are some from the Iron Age. One Iron Age example, radiocarbon dated

to between 470 and 120 B.C., is Gallagh Man, found by the O'Kelly family in 1821 at Gallagh, near Castleblakeney, County Galway. After they unearthed the body, the family would, for a small fee, resurrect Gallagh Man for visitors and then re-bury him again. This happened until 1829, when the body was taken to the National Museum. Gallagh Man was naked but for a deerskin cloak tied at the throat with a band of willow rods, which may have been used as a strangling device. As with many other bog bodies that suffered violence, his hair had been cropped short. He may have been a criminal and suffered public execution, as the body had been staked to the ground with pointed wooden sticks, possibly to prevent his soul from escaping, a practice known from some Danish bog bodies.

In 1978, the body of a girl aged between 25 and 30 was discovered in Meenybradden Bog, near Ardara, County Donegal, Ireland. The girl, with short cropped hair and eyelashes and eyelids still intact, had been wrapped in a woollen cloak and carefully placed in the grave. There was no evidence of violence on the body, which was radiocarbon dated to A.D. 1570. The cause of death, and why she was buried in the bog, is still a mystery.

Two further Irish bog bodies were found in 2003. The first was discovered in Clonycavan, County Meath, north of Dublin, and the second in Croghan, County Offaly, just 25 miles away. Old Croghan Man, as he has become known, was in his mid-20s and a giant at around 6-feet 6-inches tall. He has been dated between 362 B.C. and 175 B.C. Clonycavan Man, a young male around 5-feet 2-inches tall, dates from between 392 B.C. and 201 B.C. In common with other bog bodies, they appear to have been brutally tortured before their deaths, probably as ritual sacrifices. Old Croghan Man's nipples had been cut and he had been stabbed in the ribs. A cut on his arm indicates that he had tried to defend himself during the attack. There were also holes in both his upper arms, where a hazel rope withy had been passed through to bind him. He was later decapitated and dismembered before being buried in the bog. In contrast to his violent end, Croghan Man's body revealed that he had well-manicured nails and relatively smooth hands, which indicate somebody who had probably never performed any manual work; perhaps he was a priest or a member of the aristocracy. Clonycavan Man suffered a massive wound to the head, caused by a heavy axe that shattered his skull, and also several other injuries on his body. One particularly distinctive feature was his unusual raised hairstyle, for which he had used a kind of Iron Age hair gel, actually a form of resin that had probably come from south-western France or Spain.

Ned Kelly, keeper of Irish antiquities at the National Museum of Ireland, has developed a theory to explain why 40 bodies discovered in Irish bogland were made along tribal, political, and royal boundaries. His belief is that the burials are offerings to fertility gods by kings to guarantee a successful reign. This is certainly a possible explanation for many of the Irish bog bodies, but what of the rest of Northern Europe? The variety of different ways in which many of these people were killed would suggest something more than murder, probably some kind of ritual sacrifice. Other motives can be gleaned from the Roman author Tacitus, writing in the early second century A.D. about the Germanic peoples. He mentions some interesting customs connected with crime and punishment in their culture, including how "cowards, shirkers, and those guilty of unnatural vices" (probably homosexuality and promiscuity) were forced down into the bog under a wicker hurdle. He also states that adulterous wives were stripped naked, had their heads shaved, and were turned out of the house and flogged through the village. There are certainly indications from Tacitus that suggest that many of the victims in the bogs had broken some law or taboo of the society for which they were executed.

Another interesting detail is the unusual proportion of bog bodies with physical defects of some kind. One of the bodies from Lindow Moss had six fingers, others had spinal problems or foreshortened limbs, and such people may have been chosen for sacrifice because they were seen as being physically set apart by the gods. We must also remember that bogs are treacherous places, and we cannot rule out the possibility that some of the so-called bog burials are the result of misadventure. People may simply have fallen in and drowned. Others could be the remains of paupers or women who died in childbirth and were buried in unconsecrated ground. This could be the explanation for the careful burial of the girl from Meenybradden in Ireland. Nevertheless, considering the vast array of possible scenarios, it is obvious that there can never be one single explanation for the gruesome but compelling mystery of the bog bodies.

The Mysterious Life and Death of Tutankhamun

Photograph by Michael Reeve. (GNU Free Documentation License).
The gold funerary mask of Tutankhamun, in the Egyptian Museum of Cairo.

Howard Carter's spectacular discovery in 1922 of the almost intact tomb of the boy pharaoh Tutankhamun, in the Valley of the Kings, inspired an interest in ancient Egypt that endures to this day. Indeed, the fabulous gold mask of Tutankhamun has become the popular image of Egyptian civilization. But these dazzling treasures have put the actual person behind the golden mask in the shade. The real life of the boy king of Egypt was short and somewhat mysterious; his parentage remains uncertain as does the date of his accession to the throne. Until recently, the cause of Tutankhamun's death was also completely unknown—was it a hunting accident, or did he die from a disease? Or could he have been murdered?

Tutankhamun remains a mystery despite Carter's discovery. The tomb was full of riches, more than 2000 objects in all, and the mummy of the boy pharaoh was found contained within three golden coffins. But there was practically no documentation recovered from within the tomb, which makes it very difficult to put together an accurate story of Tutankhamun's life. It is believed that his parents may have been the heretic 18th Dynasty pharaoh Akhenaten, who ruled Egypt from 1367 B.C. to 1350 B.C. (or 1350 B.C. to 1334 B.C.) and his mysterious second wife, Kiya. Akhenaten had taken the unprecedented and revolutionary step of replacing the traditional old gods of Egypt with a single sun god called the *Aten*. Thus, Tutankhamun's name at birth was actually *Tutankhaten* (Living Image of the Aten) and was only changed to *Tutankhamun* (Living Image of Amun) a year or two into his reign, when polytheism was restored to Egypt. Tutankhamun seems to have come to the throne at the age of nine, perhaps around 1334 B.C., and ruled for about 10 years. Because the new pharaoh was so young and had no living female relatives old enough, much of the considerable responsibility of his kingships (and his personal upbringing) must have been in the care of Ay, his chief minister, and Horemheb, commander-in-chief of the army.

Shortly after becoming king, Tutankhamun married his half-sister Ankhesenamun, a daughter of Akhenaten and his first wife, Nefertiti, and granddaughter of the chief advisor to the king, Ay. There is very little information about the reign of Tutankhamun, who ruled first from Akhenaten's city of Amarna, on the east bank of the Nile about 250 miles north of Luxor, before moving to his new capital at Memphis, 12 miles south of modern Cairo on the west bank of the Nile. It was Horemheb and Ay who

were probably responsible for persuading the new pharaoah to relinquish the religion of Aten, and start to return to the old ways. Preserved on his restoration stelae—at the Temple of Karnak at Thebes—are descriptions of the steps taken by Tutankhamun to bring back the old gods and traditions, which included founding a new priesthood and embarking on building and restoration programs at the temples of the ancient gods.

The pharaoh and his wife did have two known children, both stillborn girls, whose mummies were discovered in his tomb. The only other fact that is known is that when he was about 19 years old, Tutankhamun's life was mysteriously cut short. Many have viewed it as suspicious that as soon as Tutankhamun was old enough to make his own decisions and take on the role of leader of his people—rather than share it with Ay and Horemheb—he was dead. After Tutankhamun's death, his widow Ankhesenamun married Ay, her own grandfather. A signet ring bearing the names of Ay and Ankhesenamun (and seemingly representing this union) has been found. This marriage enabled Ay, who had no royal blood, to inherit the throne. Ankhesenamun disappears from the records soon after the marriage, suggesting that she was murdered, possibly at the instigation of Ay. Shortly after the death of her husband and just before she vanished forever from history, she wrote one of the most startling letters ever recovered from the ancient world.

The letter, sent by an Egyptian "royal widow" has been dated to the end of the 18th Dynasty, and was found in the archives of the Hittite capital of

Hattusa (modern Bogazkale) in Turkey. The document had been sent to King Suppiluliumas I of the Hittites, an emerging power in the Near East at the time and an obvious danger to Egypt. Part of the document states, "My husband has died and I have no son. They say about you that you have many sons. You might give me one of your sons to become my husband. Never shall I pick out a servant of mine and make him my husband! I am afraid!" The Hittite king at first expressed suspicion at the motives of Ankhesenamun, but after sending a messenger to Egypt to investigate the situation, who brought back a second letter from the Egyptian queen, he agreed to the marriage and sent his son, the Prince Zannanza, to Egypt. However, the prince only got as far as the Egyptian border before he met his death, probably murdered by an Egyptian faction who did not want a foreign king occupying the throne of Egypt. This murder ultimately led to war between the Egyptians and the Hittites, and ended in defeat for Egypt at Amqa, near Kadesh in western Syria. Some have suggested that this incredible letter was not written by Ankhesenamun at all, but by her mother Nefertiti, but this is unlikely as Nefertiti's husband Akhenaten had a successor, thus there would be no need for a letter to a foreign king.

So what possible reason could Ankhesenamun have had for instigating this treasonous correspondence, which effectively amounts to her begging an enemy king to take over her country? Tutankhamun's death (without leaving an heir) may have been at the heart of the problem. One theory is that the letters were written be-

cause the Egyptians were wary of the threat posed by the advancing Hittite Empire, and believed that an alliance with the Hittites by marriage would preserve Egypt from conquest. The queen may have planned to rule with a Hittite king supported by the military might of the Hittite Empire, but her plan was thwarted with the murder of Prince Zannanza. This brings us to the fate of Tutankhamun himself.

Ever since Tutankhamun's body was first unwrapped and examined by Howard Carter's team in the 1920s, there has been intense speculation as to how and why the king died. X-ray examinations of the skull, first in 1968 by a team from the University of Liverpool, then in 1978 by researchers from the University of Michigan, revealed a shard of bone in the skull and evidence of hemorrhage at the back of the head, possibly caused by a deliberate blow to the skull. The evidence from the x-rays, taken together with the suspicious circumstances surrounding King Tut's death, have prompted many to conclude that the boy pharaoh must have been murdered. But by whom?

The person most frequently put forward as being behind Tutankhamun's possible murder is the man who had most to gain by his death, the elderly royal servant Ay. Ay reigned for a little more than four years as pharaoh after the demise of Tutankhamun, and would seem to have had motive for murder, though there is at present no evidence that he had anything to do with the death of the king. Other researchers believe a much younger man, Horemheb, who succeeded Ay around 1321 B.C., to become the last pharaoh of ancient Egypt's 18th Dynasty, was responsible. Horemheb reigned for 27 years as pharaoh, during which time he brought about a major reorganization of the country, resulting in a much stronger and more stable Egypt than had been seen for many years. He was also determined to completely return Egypt to its traditional religious beliefs, and he therefore set about obliterating all traces of the Aten cult. It is thought that one reason why Tutankhamun was omitted from the classical king lists of Egypt is that Horemheb usurped most of the boy pharaoh's work, including monuments at Karnak and Luxor. Could either of these two shadowy figures, or perhaps both, have plotted the death of the boy pharaoh?

In January 2005, the first CAT scans (a CAT scan is an x-ray technique that produces a film representing a detailed cross section of tissue structure) ever performed on an Egyptian mummy were carried out on the 3,300 old skeleton of Tutankhamun. Surprisingly, the team of Egyptian researchers found no evidence at all of a blow to the back of the boy's head, and no other evidence of violence on the body. The report stated that the fragment of bone identified from previous skull x-rays had probably become dislodged during the embalming process. When Tutankhamun was being mummified his brain was removed and the skull filled with large amounts of resin, which has hardened over time. If the sliver of bone had been the result of an injury before death, it would not still be loose in the skull. The dark area shown at the back of the skull on earlier x-rays, thought by many to indicate some kind of trauma, was explained by the scientists as the result of the body being dismembered for

photographing after its initial discovery by Howard Carter. During this process a rod had been inserted into the back of the skull to prop it up. The general conclusion of the researchers was that Tutankhamun had been a slightly built, but relatively healthy young man standing roughly 5-feet 6-inches tall. Using high-resolution photos of the CAT scans, three teams of forensic artists from France, Egypt, and the United States constructed separate but similar models of the king's face. The result not only bears a striking resemblance to the famous gold mask which covered the mummified face of Tutankhamun, but also to a well-known image of the pharaoh as a child where he was depicted as the Sun God rising at dawn from a lotus blossom. But how did the king die?

When examining Tutankhamun's body the team found a fracture in the thighbone of his left leg, previously assumed by Howard Carter to have been sustained during the embalming process or as a result of damage to the body after mummification. On reexamination, the scientists found that this badly broken leg had occurred only days before the death of Tutankhamun and had probably led to an attack of gangrene, which swiftly brought about the king's death. At present then, the evidence does not support a murderous conspiracy by Tutankhamun's close advisors Ay and Horemheb, but more likely a broken leg, perhaps sustained during a hunting accident, and not treated quickly enough to prevent infection. The question of whether Ay or Horemheb could have actively prevented the death of the boy pharaoh from this injury is another matter.

The Real Robin Hood

Photograph by M. Rees.
Statue of Robin Hood, Nottingham.

In the popular imagination, Robin Hood is the archetypal English folk hero. His legend, so familiar to people all over the world, has remained relevant through hundreds of years of history, so that even Robin's band of outlaws (Friar Tuck, Little John, Will Scarlet, Allan a Dale, and Maid Marion) have become household names. The enduring appeal of the gallant medievel outlaw, who steals from the rich to give to the poor and fights against the injustice and tyranny of authority figures such as Prince John and the evil sheriff of Nottingham, shows no signs of waning. But where does the story originate? Was there a real Robin Hood hiding in the forests of medieval England ready to defend the rights of the poor and the oppressed?

Our earliest written refererence to the outlaw, though it amounts to a mere scrap, is in William Langland's *Piers Plowman* written in 1377, where one of the characters states "I know the rhymes of Robin Hood." The next notice, and the first where Robin is classed as an outlaw, is in Andrew de Wyntoun's *Original Chronicle of Scotland*, written around 1420. Under an entry for the year 1283, the chronicle describes Robin Hood and Little John as well-known forest outlaws in Barnsdale, Yorkshire, in the north of England. Almost 20 years later, in the *Scotichronicon*, Walter Bower mentions Robin Hood, "the famous cut-throat" and Little John, in an entry under the year 1266. Bower puts the outlaws in the context of Simon de Montfort's rebellion against Henry III, and again places them in Barnsdale Forest, north of their traditional home in Sherwood Forest, Nottinghamshire. However, at this time the forests of England covered a much wider area than they do today, and as Nottinghamshire and Yorkshire are adjacent counties, it is possible that Robin Hood's adventures spread over both forests.

The remaining early references to Robin Hood are from ballads and songs, designed to be recit or sung by wandering minstrels. The most significant early account in ballad form is *A Gest of Robin Hood*, (gest probably meaning *deeds*), of which there were a number of editions printed after 1500, following the development of the printing press in England by William Caxton. The story in the *Gest*, again set in the forest of Barnsdale, was once thought by some to date back much earlier than the printed editions, perhaps as early as 1360 or 1400, but nowadays a date of around 1450 is more widely accepted. By the time of these ballads, some of the elements of the Robin Hood story as we know it today were in place. Robin is accompanied not only by Little John, but Will Scarlet, and Much the Miller's Son. His enemies include the rich abbots of the Catholic Church (whom he robs), and the sheriff of Nottingham, and it is at this time that we first see the appearance of the archery contest set up by the sheriff to trap the outlaw. Robin sees off his enemies, he beheads both the sheriff of Nottingham and the bounty hunter Guy of Gisborne. For the murder of the sheriff, he is hunted down in Sherwood Forest by King Edward himself, but pledges his allegiance and is pardoned. Robin subsequently finds service at the court of the king, but becomes bored and restless with his position and returns to the forest where he again lives as an outlaw. Many years later he falls ill and journeys to visits his cousin, the prioress of Kirklees Abbey, for medical treatment. But unbeknownst to him, she is the lover of Robin's enemy Sir Roger of Doncaster, and lets him bleed to death. Before he dies, Robin shoots his last arrow out of the window and tells Little John to bury him where the arrow falls.

At this stage, however, there are still some popular aspects of the tale missing. The Normans are not yet portrayed as the villains, and there is no fight against an evil Prince John, or friendship with his benevolent brother, King Richard the Lionheart.

It was not until Sir Walter Scott's *Ivanhoe* in 1819 that Robin Hood as the Englishman fighting the Norman oppressor was established. Scott's novel also made the character of Friar Tuck a much more important part of the story. In contrast to later plays and stories where he is cast as a nobleman, in the early ballads Robin is seen as a yeoman (a tradesman or farmer), and there is no mention of him giving to the poor. It was not until 1598, in a play intended for an aristocratic audience, that Robin's status was elevated to become Robert, the Earl of Huntingdon. It is also in the late 16th century that the romance with Maid Marion is first established, possibly in plays written for the May Games, spring celebrations which took place in early May. But Maid Marion did not become a main character until the publication of Thomas Love Peacock's novel, *Maid Marian*, in 1822. She had, however, been connected with the tale since around 1500.

Whether there is an historical figure behind these ballads, stories, and plays, is another matter, though there are certainly many candidates for the historical Robin Hood. Unfortunately, 13th and 14th century English records contain many references to people with the surname Hood, and as Robert and its alternative form of Robin was also a fairly common Christian name at the time, finding the Robin Hood of legend is extremely difficult. There are, however, a few possibilities. At the York assizes (county court) of 1226, a Yorkshireman named Robert Hod is recorded as a fugitive, and in 1227 he appears again under the nickname Hobbehod, the meaning of which is unclear. Unfortunately nothing more is known of this Robert Hod. Another possibility is Robert Hood, son of Adam Hood, a forester who worked for John De Warenne, the Earl of Surrey. He was born in 1280 and lived in Wakefield, Yorkshire, as a tenant, with his wife Matilda. Wakefield is only 10 miles

The Major Oak, an 800- to 1,000-year-old oak tree in Sherwood Forest, Nottinghamshire, reputedly a hideout of Robin Hood.

from Barnsdale, the setting of Robin's escapades in the ballads, and in some tales Robin Hood's father was said to be a forester called Adam. The name Matilda was also Maid Marian's real name in two Elizabethan plays. In 1317, Robert Hode disappeared after failing to report for military service. Although there are certainly some similarities between this Robin of Wakefield and the Robin Hood of legend, the fact that stories surrounding the Robin Hood name were already in circulation during his lifetime would suggest he is a little too late to qualify. In fact, by this time court records show that *Robinhood* had become an epithet for an outlaw, and before 1300, there were at least eight people who either assumed the name or were given it.

This point is illustrated by the case of William de Fevre, of Enborne in Berkshire, who in 1261 is shown as an outlaw in court records from Reading. A year later at Easter, 1262, a royal document renamed him *William Robehood*. If this is not a clerical error, then it is significant in that at the early date of 1262, the Robin Hood legend appears to have been well known enough for other outlaws to be named after him. If this is the case, it would mean that any real Robin Hood cannot be dated later than 1261 or 1262. Alternatively, it might also be evidence that it was the Robin Hood nickname given to outlaws at the time that inspired the legend, so it cannot be taken as definite proof of such an early date for the existence of Robin Hood.

A fascinating theory was put forward by Tony Molyneux-Smith in a 1998 book, entitled *Robin Hood and the Lords of Wellow*, which suggests that Robin Hood was not one single man, but a pseudonym taken by descendants of Sir Robert Foliot, who held the Lordship of Wellow, close to Sherwood Forest, up until the late 14th century. This is intriguing, but further research into this family and their origins is clearly needed to positively identify the Foliot family as the origin of the famous outlaw tale.

Of course, Robin Hood was not the first or the only medieval outlaw tale. The daring escapes, rescues, and disguises of his legend have almost certainly been influenced by actual and mythical exploits of real-life outlaws. One example is the mercenary and pirate Eustace the Monk (c. 1170–1217). His deeds are related in a 13th century romance and also by contemporary historian Matthew Paris, in the *Chronica Majora (Main Chronicle)*. Another historical model for the Robin Hood legend is Hereward (the Wake). This 11th century outlaw leader led the English resistance against William the Conquerer and held the Isle of Ely, in the swampy fenland of south Lincolnshire, against the invading Normans. Hereward became a folk hero only a short time after his death, and within 100 years his exploits were being celebrated in song in taverns. The legendary Hereward was already established by the time of the *Estorie des Engles* of Geoffrey Gaimar written around 1140, and *Gesta Herewardii Saxonis (Deeds of Hereward the Saxon)* from the same period. Many aspects of the outlaw hero later associated with Robin Hood are found in the tales of Hereward. He was courageous, courteous, quick-witted, an expert at disguise, and always alert, as can be understood from his name, *the Wake*, meaning *the watchful*.

Another hero of the era was Fulk FitzWarin. A tale belonging to the start of the 12th century tells how Fulk, as a young nobleman, is sent to King John of England. Eventually, the king becomes his enemy and confiscates his family's land, so Fulk takes to the woods and lives as an outlaw. Included in the story are incidents particularly reminiscent of episodes in the Robin Hood legend. For example, Fulk tests the honesty of rich travelers he waylays, and tricks King John into the forest to be captured by his outlaw gang. There is, however, a strong element of myth (giants, dragons, epic journeys) in the tale of Fulk FitzWarin (and in all the early heroic tales from England), which we do not find in the Robin Hood legend.

A completely different interpretation of Robin Hood that has been put forward is based on his role in English folklore. Pagan themes such as the Green Man (or Robin Goodfellow) and the Wild Man of the Woods may have influenced the growth of the Robin Hood legend, and his character and story was certainly incorporated into the May Games, a celebration of nature and the coming of spring, by the 16th century. But the idea that Robin Hood is only a legend that originated from these celebrations is unlikely, especially as his story appears to have been well-known prior to any association with the May Games.

If Robin Hood existed at all, the most convincing evidence places him somewhere in the 13th century, though it is more likely that he represents a typical outlaw hero, composed in part from historical characters, but not possessing an individual historical identity. The Robin Hood tale has been built up gradually for more than 700 years, usually to meet the needs and desires of his audience. In fact, it is still developing today, as is evident from the newest myths added to the story, presented in the 1991 film *Robin Hood: Prince of Thieves*, starring Kevin Costner. Here, not only is Robin placed at the end of the 12th Century as a returning Crusader, but he is also depicted fighting fierce painted Celtic warriors in the forests, more than 1,000 years after they existed in reality. Without doubt, the tale will continue to develop and change in the future as it has done in the past; this is part of myth-history that is Robin Hood.

The Amazons: Warrior Women at the Edge of Civilization

Map of supposed Amazon homeland, produced in London, c. 1770.

For perhaps 3,000 years, the idea of a tribe of fierce warrior-women inhabiting the edge of the known world has captured our imagination. From ancient Greek and Roman writers of myth and myth-history, right up to modern television shows such as *Xena: Warrior Princess*, this war-like, women-only society has been constantly reinvented to suit the time and the place. But is there something tangible, or even historical, behind these stories and legends?

We first hear of the Amazons as a tribe of warrior women in the *Iliad*, Homer's epic tale about the Trojan War, probably written in the eighth century B.C. Here they are briefly mentioned as having attacked Priam of Troy while he was campaigning in central Turkey. Homer describes these women as "those who fight like men." After Homer, many Greek writers added more elements to the Amazon character and supposed origin. The Greek historian Herodotus, writing around the middle of the fifth century B.C., called them *Androktones* (killers of men), and has an interesting (in the light of recent archaeological discoveries) story to tell about them. After being beaten by the Greeks at the battle of Thermodon, in northern Turkey, Amazon prisoners of war were taken back to Greece by ship. During the journey, they attacked and killed their captors, but were incapable of sailing the boat, and drifted northwards across the Black Sea. They eventually landed on the shores of Scythian territory, where they stole horses and began raiding the area. Herodotus describes the Amazons reaching an agreement with the Scythians, a loose network of horse-riding nomadic steppe tribes, and subsequently intermarrying with the men. Afterwards they moved northwards and settled east of the Don, in what is now southern Russia, where they ultimately evolved into the Sauromatian culture. Another story, this time told by Roman writers, involve the Amazons fighting as allies of Priam against the Greeks in the Trojan War. Towards the end of the war, after killing many Greeks in battle, the Amazon queen Penthesilea took the field against Achilles, only to be slain in a bloody duel. A number of other Greek heroes also had life or death struggles with these formidable women.

One of the 12 labors imposed upon Hercules required him to obtain the magic girdle of the Amazon queen, Hippolyte. To fulfill this task, Hercules, in the company of another Greek hero, Theseus, journeyed to the capital city of the Amazons, Themiscyra, on the river Thermodon, on the southern shore of the Black Sea. Heracles killed Hippolyte and obtained the girdle, and Theseus carried off the princess Antiope, one of Hippolyte's sisters. In order to rescue Antiope, the Amazons invaded Greece and attacked Athens, but were defeated. In some versions of the story, Antiope is cut down fighting at the side of Theseus. The mythical battles between the Greeks and the Amazons were often commemorated in a genre of Greek art known as *amazonomachy*, one example of which, carved in marble, comes from the Parthenon, in Athens. Some biographers of Alexander the Great mention him meeting with an Amazon queen called Thalestris, and her having a child by him, though this is disputed by Greek historian and biographer Plutarch in his book, *Life of Alexander*, as well as other ancient writers.

Early Greek and Roman writers associated various strange customs with the Amazons. The very word *Amazon*, thought now to derive from the Iranian word *ha-mazan* (meaning warrior), in the Greek version means *without breast*. The Greeks probably attached this meaning to the word to explain a tradition that the Amazons had their right breast burned or cut off to facilitate the drawing of the bowstring. However, depictions of Amazons in Greek art always show them with two breasts. Another myth describes how the Amazons did not allow men to live in their territory. However, once a year, in order to sustain their race, they traveled to visit a neighboring all-male tribe called the Gargareans. Female children who resulted from this procreation were brought up by the Amazons, and trained in agriculture, hunting, and war, while males were either put to death or given back to their fathers.

Amazons were associated with a bewildering range of places, from the Black Sea coast of Turkey to southern Russia, Libya, and even Atlantis. In light of such far-fetched ideas, it is not surprising that the consensus of opinion about the Amazons is that they are a myth. But recently, thanks to archaeology, scholarly opinions have been changing. According to Herodotus, the Sauromatian people of southern Russia were descendants of the Amazons and the Scythians. Although Russian archaeologists had been finding skeletons of female warriors in the Pontic Steppe (the steppelands north of the Black Sea extending east as far as the Caspian Sea) since the mid-19th century, western scholars and archaeologists were either unaware of these finds or had not made the connection with the Amazons of Greek legend. Excavations conducted by Russian and American archaeologists and led by Jeannine Davis-Kimball (of the American-Eurasian Research Institute) have suggested that these Greek stories may have had some basis in fact. Ancient burial mounds (known as *kurgans*) found near the town of Pokrovka, near the Russian border with Kazakhstan, have produced skeletons of women buried with weapons. The burials included iron swords or daggers, bronze arrowheads, bows, quivers, and horse harnesses. The graves date from the sixth to the fourth century B.C., and indicate a culture that included warrior women of high status.

Photographer unknown.
(GNU Free Documentation License)
Amazon Preparing for Battle *by Pierre-Eugène-Emile Hébert. National Gallery of Art, Washington, D.C.*

Initially there were suggestions that the weapons served a ritual purpose, but examinations of the skeletons have revealed otherwise. Some of the skulls exhibit signs of wounds, and bowed leg bones belonging to one 13- or 14-year-old girl indicate a life on horseback. A bent arrowhead embedded in the knee of another woman suggests a battle wound. The weapons found with the women appeared to have seen frequent use in battle, and they also had smaller handles than those buried with the males, suggesting that they were made especially for women. Could these then be graves of the legendary Amazons? Probably not. In one sense, Herodotus was right—there are certainly Sauromatian women warriors. However, there is no evidence that they descended from the Amazon-Scythian intermarriage mentioned in Herodotus' *Histories*. Another factor is that Sauromatian women warriors only made up a relatively small proportion of the tribe. While 90 percent of male burials were warriors, only around 20 percent of the women were buried with weapons.

There is another reason why it is unlikely that the Sauromatians were the source of the Amazon myths. Amazons were being depicted in Greek art and literature as far back as the eighth century B.C., at least 200 years before there is any evidence of women warriors on the Eurasian steppe. The earliest Greek colonies in the Black Sea date from the seventh century B.C., though there were probably earlier trading voyages. So although it is just barely possible that female warriors existed on the steppe earlier than current archaeological evidence suggests—and that Greeks made contact with them—there is no evidence for this contact. As it stands, the women warriors of the Sauromatian culture may have influenced the Amazon myth, but they could not have been its source. Around the fourth century B.C. the Sauromatian culture evolved into the Sarmatian culture, another nomadic tribe, and women warriors are also found in early Sarmatian burials. The Sarmatians ranged much

further west than their predecessors, and came into direct contact with the Romans. In fact, Sarmatian cavalry, in the service of Rome, were active in Britain from the second to the fifth centuries A.D. Whether these Romanized cavalry included women warriors is not known, however.

There are other examples of steppe tribes that included women warriors, one of which are the Pazyryk people, another culture related to the Scythians. Though the Pazyryks were located a long way to the east of the Sarmatians, in the Altai Mountains of Siberian Russia, they had almost identical burial customs, using kurgans similar to those found in the Ukraine and southern Russia. A fifth century B.C. Pazyryk kurgan-burial found in 1993 by Russian archaeologist Natalia Polosmak has become known as the Siberian Ice Maiden, although she was not a warrior but a high-ranking priestess. Polosmak did, however, find a grave containing the skeletons of a man and a woman, each buried with arrowheads and an axe.

Perhaps it was traveler's stories of the higher social standing enjoyed by steppe women that added another, more realistic, dimension to the already existing Greek Amazon myths. In another way, the Amazons can be seen as a mythical illustration of the dangers—and perhaps the barbarism—of the unknown, which the Greeks faced when venturing into new lands, such as the Black Sea coast. It is interesting to note that for the Greeks, the Amazons always existed at the very edge of the known world, on the fringes of civilization. As the Greek world expanded, the homeland of the Amazons was pushed further away, which is probably why the actual geography associated with them shifts around so much. The earliest references begin with the Amazons to the east of Greece in Asia Minor (Turkey), supposedly founding the cities of Ephesus and Smyrna, on its eastern coast. By the time of Herodotus (fifth century B.C.) they had moved into southern Russia, and when Diodorus of Sicily was writing his *Library of World History* in the first century B.C., the Amazons were associated with western Libya.

If the Amazons myths are a memory of a factual matriarchal culture of fighting women, an important point to consider is that Homer wrote in the eighth century about them as if the audience was already familiar with the topic. Thus they must have existed earlier, probably somewhere in the Late Bronze Age/Early Iron Age period (between the dates c. 1600 B.C. and c. 900 B.C.). A location for the Amazons either in Anatolia, the Russian Steppes, or the Caucasus mountains,

seems the most likely. But for the moment at least, there is no evidence for any warrior women at this early date in these areas.

In one sense, the Amazon myth can be viewed partly as how the Greeks viewed the concept of the *other*. The characteristics given to these women in the literature and art of the time are intended to demonstrate the opposite of everything possessed by a normal society. In Greek society, women's duties were on the whole confined to the home, and they did not have any involvement in war or politics. In contrast, the Amazons made their own decisions and fought their own battles. Such reverse role myths helped to support the status quo of the Greek state by showing the unnaturalness of a society that was radically different from their own. And, of course, when barbarism comes up against culture—as in the case of the many battles between Amazons and Greeks—it loses.

The Mystery of the Ice Man

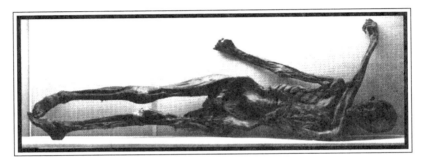

© Innsbruck Medical University, W. Platzer.
Skeleton of the Ice Man at Innsbruck Medical University.

On a clear day in September 1991, high in the desolate Ötztal Alps, close to the border between Italy and Austria, two German hikers (Helmut and Erika Simon) made what has proven to be one of the most incredible discoveries of the 20th century. Lying face down in the ice was a frozen body. Thinking they had found the remains of a mountaineer who had died in a fall, the couple informed the authorities, who arranged to visit the site the following day. Due to the melting of the glacier, it was not unusual to find the bodies of climbers who had died in accidents in the area. Three weeks earlier, the mummified remains of a man and woman who had set off hiking in 1934, never to be seen again, had been discovered. The day after Helmut and Erika Simon's discovery, the Austrian police arrived at the site and be-

gan, somewhat clumsily, to remove the body from its frozen grave. During its extraction from the ice, some of the body's clothing was shredded, a hole was punched in the hip with a jackhammer, and its left arm was snapped while attempting to force the body into a coffin.

The body was transported to the University of Innsbruck, where a careful examination revealed that it was definitely not a modern mountaineer. Radiocarbon dating showed that the remains were of a man who had died around 3200 B.C. (in the Late Neolithic period) and was thus the oldest preserved human body ever discovered. Further examinations of Ötzi, as he has become known (because he was found in the Ötztal Alps), followed, and it was determined that he was 5-feet 2-inches tall and between 40 and 50 years of age when he died, although the cause of death remained a mystery. Analysis of his stomach contents revealed the remains of two meals, the last eaten about eight hours before he died and consisting of a piece of unleavened bread made of einkorn wheat, some roots, and red deer meat. Analysis of extremely well-preserved pollen from the intestines revealed that Ötzi died in late spring or early summer.

Ötzi had a total of 57 tattoos on his body, comprising small parallel stripes and crosses, which were made with a charcoal-based pigment. As the tattoos were concentrated around the spine, lumbar region, knees, and ankles, it is believed that they may not have been decorative. Examination of the Ice Man's skeleton revealed that he had been suffering from arthritis, and the positioning of the tattoos at known acupuncture points has persuaded many researchers that Ötzi's tattoos served a therapeutic purpose.

The remains of the the Ice Man's clothing were fairly well-preserved by the ice. When he died, Ötzi was wearing shoes made from a combination of bearskin soles and a top of deer hide and tree bark, with soft grass stuffed inside for warmth. He also wore a woven grass cloak, which he probably also used as a blanket, and a leather vest and fur cap. Alongside the body, various articles, which the Ice Man had been carrying with him on his last journey, were also discovered. These items consisted of a copper axe with a yew handle, an unfinished yew longbow, a deerskin quiver with two flint-tipped arrows and 12 unfinished shafts, a flint knife and scabbord, a calfskin belt

pouch, a medicine bag containing medicinal fungus, a flint and pyrite for creating sparks, a goat-fur rucksack, and a tassel with a stone bead. All of this was invaluable material for painting a picture of the life and death of the Ice Man.

But who was this mysterious traveller, and what had prompted him to venture 1.8 miles up into the desolate Ötzal Alps? DNA analysis has shown that Ötzi was most closely related to Europeans living around the Alps. Further isotopic analysis of his teeth and bones by geochemist Wolfgang Müller, of the Australian National University, together with colleagues in the United States and Switzerland, have narrowed Ötzi's birthplace down to a site near to the Italian Tyrol village of Feldthurns, north of present-day Bolzano, about 30 miles southeast of the place where he met his death. High levels of copper and arsenic found in Ötzi's hair show that he had taken part in copper smelting, probably making his own weapons and tools.

The first widely held theory as to why the Ice Man was travelling alone up in the Ötztal Alps (and how he met his death) was that he was a shepherd who had been taking care of his flock in an upland pasture. The hypothesis was that he had been caught in an unseasonable storm and found shelter in the shallow gully where he was found. A variant on this theory, proposed by Dr. Konrad Spindler, leader of the scientific investigation into the Ice Man, was based on early x-rays of the body taken at Innsbruck. These x-rays appear to show broken ribs on the body's right side, which Spindler believed were the result of some kind of fight which Ötzi had become involved in while returning to his home village with his sheep. Although Ötzi had escaped the battle with his life, he eventually died of the injuries in the place where the hikers found him more than 5,000 years later. But new examinations of the body in 2001 by scientists at a laboratory in Bolanzo showed that the ribs had been bent out of shape *after* death, due to snow and ice pressing against the ribcage. Another theory connected the Ice Man with the various bog bodies, such as Tollund Man and Lindow Man, recovered from the peat bogs of northern Europe. Many of the first millennium B.C. examples of these bodies show that the victims had eaten a last meal similar to that of the Ice Man just before their death, and appear to have been ritually sacrificed before being thrown into the bog. Could the Ice Man have been a ritual sacrifice? Dramatic findings from the examinations at Bolanzo suggested otherwise.

A CAT scan of the body showed a foreign object located near the shoulder, in the shape of an arrow. Further examinations revealed that Ötzi had a flint arrowhead lodged in his shoulder. The Ice Man had been murdered. A small tear discovered in Ötzi's coat appears to be where the arrow entered the body. In June 2002, the same team of scientists discovered a deep wound on the Ice Man's hand, and further bruises and cuts on his wrists and chest, seemingly defensive wounds, all inflicted only hours before his death. Fascinatingly, DNA analysis shows traces of blood from four separate people on Ötzi's clothes and weapons: one sequence from his knife blade,

two different sequences from the same arrowhead, and a fourth from his goatskin coat. In light of these recent discoveries, various new theories have been put forward to explain what exactly happened to the Ice Man.

The presence of only the flint tip of the arrowhead in the body indicates that either Ötzi or a companion must have pulled the wooden shaft of the arrow out. The CAT scan revealed that the fatal arrow had been shot from below and ripped upwards through nerves and major blood vessels before it lodged in the left shoulder blade, paralyzing his left arm. The blood on his coat may indicate that Ötzi's companion was also wounded and had to be carried on his shoulder. One scenario which has been suggested is that Ötzi and one or two companions were a hunting group who took part in a battle with a rival party, perhaps over territory. The blood on Ötzi's weapons graphically illustrates that he must have killed two of the enemy party, removing his valuable arrowhead from one body and then using it again, before receiving his own fatal wound.

Not everyone, however, agrees with this version of events. According to Walter Leitner of the Institute for Ancient and Early History at the University of Innsbruck in Austria, Ötzi may have been a Shaman. Leitner believes that, because copper was a scarce material in the Late Neolithic period, only someone of great importance in the community would have owned a copper axe. Shamans are also known to commune with the spirit world in remote locations, such as high mountains. Ötzi was probably murdered, Leitner thinks, but not in an argument over territory, but rather by a rival group from the same community who wanted to assume power. By killing the Shaman and claiming he died in an accident, this end may have been achieved. A further alternative hypothesis is a sacrificial death where the victim was ritually hunted down and shot in the back with an arrow. Such ritual killings are recorded by Roman chroniclers as being practiced by the Celts, and there is archaeological evidence from a skeleton discovered in the outer ditch at Stonehenge that this kind of sacrifice took place there (see Stonehenge article).

Recently, a startling claim was made by Lorenzo Dal Ri, director of the archaeological office of the Bolzano province. Dal Ri believes that the Ice Man's death may actually have been recorded on an ancient stone stela. The decorated stone, of roughly the same age as the Ice Man, had been used to build the altar of a church in Laces, a town close to the area where the discovery of Ötzi was made. One of the many carvings on the stela shows an archer poised to fire an arrow into the back of another unarmed man who appears to be running away. Although there is no direct evidence to link the stone with the murder of the Ice Man, the resemblance between the carved image and the death of Ötzi is uncanny.

In February 2006, further light was thrown on the Ice Man when Dr. Franco Rollo (of the University of Camerino in Italy) and colleagues examined mitochondrial DNA (DNA only inherited through the mother) taken from cells in the Ice Man's intestines. The team's conclusion was that Ötzi may have been infertile. Dr. Rollo hypothesized that the social implications of his not being able to father offspring may have been a factor in the circumstances which led to his death.

Since his discovery in 1991, Ötzi has achieved such popularity that he even has his own version of the "Curse of Tutankhamun." It has to be admitted that there appears to be a high rate of mortality among the researchers connected with the discovery of the Ice Man. Apparently the latest victim was 63-year-old molecular archaeologist Tom Loy, the discoverer of the human blood on Ötzi's clothes and weapons, who died in mysterious

Photograph by Kogo. (GNU Free Documentation License).
Ötzi Memorial, Ötztal.

circumstances in Australia in October 2005. Two other well-known names connected with Ötzi who have passed away recently include Dr. Konrad Spindler, head of the Ice Man investigation team at Innsbruck University, who died in April 2005, apparently from complications arising from multiple sclerosis; and the Iceman's original discoverer, 67-year-old Helmut Simon, who plunged 300 feet to his death in the Austrian Alps, in October 2004. Incidentally Dieter Warnecke, one of the men who found Simon's frozen body, died of a heart attack shortly after Simon's funeral. However, sceptics argue that the death of five or six people associated with the Ice Man over a 14 year period is not a particularly unusual amount, they also point out that mountaineers naturally have a high rate of mortality due to the dangers of their pursuit.

There are still many unanswered questions about the life and death of Ötzi, now on display at the South Tyrol Museum of Archaeology in Bozen-Bolzano, Italy. Hopefully the answers to some of these questions will become apparent when scientists conduct the autopsy to remove the flint arrowhead from the Ice Man's shoulder. It looks like we will have to wait until then for more information on how and why Ötzi met his death in the frozen Alps, more than 5,000 years ago.

The History and Myth of the Knights Templar

The exterior of the Temple Church, London.

The Knights Templar was a powerful order of crusading warrior-monks founded in Jerusalem in A.D. 1118, ostensibly to protect Christian travelers in the Holy Land. For almost two centuries the Templars enjoyed a considerable reputation as ferocious warriors, and became the epitome of the Crusader, with their famous white mantle emblazoned with the red Templar cross. What is perhaps less known about the Templars is that their exploits in the Holy Land were financed by wealth accumulated in Europe, through the purchase and sale of land, and what was, in effect, the first banking network the world had ever seen. The violent destruction of the Templar Order, probably due to a conspiracy between the French King Philip IV and Pope Clement V, has given the Templars a mythical aura. They have been linked with almost everything mystical, from the establishment of Freemasonry to the quest for the Ark of the Covenant. What is the true story behind their foundation and demise?

Originally. the Templars were a group of nine knights led by Hughes de Payens, a nobleman from the Champagne region of northeastern France, who offered their services to King Baldwin II of Jerusalem, after the recapture of the city from the Muslims during the First Crusade in 1099. The Knights Templar were established as a strict religious-military order, committed to poverty, chastity, and obedience, and the protection of pilgrims traveling to the Holy Land after the Conquest. In A.D. 1118 King Baldwin granted one wing of the Temple Mount in Jerusalem, a palace purportedly built on the foundations of the Temple of Solomon, to the Templars to use as their living quarters. It is from this association that the Templars became known as the Poor Knights of the Temple of Solomon. The Templars received the church's official sanction at the Council of Troyes in 1128 and had their rules of conduct established by their patron abbot, the French St. Bernard of Clairvaux. Hughes de Payens, the first Grand Master of the Order, visited England in 1128 to raise money and find recruits for the Templars, and thus began the history of the English Knights Templar. In 1130 de Payens returned to Palestine at the head of 300 knights, drawn mostly from France and England; in the same year Bernard of Clairvaux wrote "In Praise of the New Knighthood" to de Payens, a letter voicing his suport for the Order. This letter was to have a profound effect on the Templars, as it quickly circulated through Europe, influencing a number of young men to join the Order, or donate land and money to their cause.

The Templar Order was organized in the same way in every country. Each had a Master of the Order for the Templars in that land. The first recorded Master in England, for example, was Richard de Hastyngs in 1160. De Hastyngs and every other Master was subject to the Grand Master, who retained that position for life, and was responsible for organizing the Order's military exploits in the Holy Land as well as their commercial dealings in Europe. The details of how one was initiated into the Order are obscure, in fact, this is one factor that worked against the Templars later in their history. It is known that apart from swearing to the vows of poverty, chastity, piety, and obedience, prospective members had to be of noble birth and willing to relinquish all material goods, signing their entire wealth over to the Order. As soldiers, the Knights Templar swore never to surrender to the enemy. A glorious death on the battlefield fighting for God (against what they saw as the forces of evil) ensured that the knight would ascend directly to heaven. This fight-to-the-death attitude, along with their rigorous training and strict discipline, made the Templars a feared enemy on the battlefield.

The Knights Templar soon gained the backing of the Holy See and the monarchies of Europe. In England, King Henry II granted the Templars land across the country, including extensive holdings in the Midlands. At the end of the 12th century, in an area between Fleet Street and the River Thames in London, the English Templars built their headquarters, the Temple Church (or the Round Church), constructed on a design based on the Church of the Holy Sepulchre in Jerusalem. There was a compound attached to the church that contained residences, military training facilities, and recreational grounds. Members of the Order were not allowed to travel into the city of London without permission from the Master of the Temple.

In the year 1200, Pope Innocent III issued a Papal Bull, which declared that all persons and goods within Knights Templar houses were immune from local laws. What this really meant was that the Templars were exempt from taxation and tithes; this was a vitally important point in the rapid accumulation of wealth the Order enjoyed. Through their massive holdings in Europe, the Templars amassed enough wealth to pay the large sums required to outfit their soldiers and support staff in the Holy Land. Numerous fortifications were erected at strategical points throughout the Holy Land, using money acquired through donations and their vast commercial enterprises in Europe (which included the buying and leasing of land and property and the lending of money). Nevertheless, in spite all these efforts, the bloody military struggles of the Templars against the numerically superior forces of Islam were to prove ultimately unsuccessful. In 1291, the remainder of the Templars were annihilated by more than 10,000 Mamluks at the city of Acre, in Western Galilee. With this defeat, the Christian hold on the Holy Land ended, and people in Europe began to doubt whether it was still God's will to send knights out to fight against Islam. With the Crusades over and the the Holy Land lost, many also began to question what purpose the Knights Templars served now that the reason for their existence was gone. The wealth and power enjoyed by the Order, with its exemption from taxes and huge landholdings throughout Europe, made them many—and often dangerous—enemies. In the end, this was to be their undoing.

In October 1307, King Philip IV (the Fair) of France had all the Templars he could find in the country simultaneously arrested and imprisoned. Philip also seized all the Templar property and possessions, accusing the entire Order of a variety of heretical crimes, including spitting and tramping on the cross, homosexuality, and the worshipping of idols. A number of the Templars were subsequently tortured by Inquisitors until the required confessions were extracted, and they were then executed. It is highly unlikely that confessions obtained under such conditions had any basis in truth. In 1314, the remaining Templar leaders, including the last Grand Master Jacques de Molay, were burned at the stake in front of Notre Dame Cathedral on the Île de la Cité, an island in the river Siene in Paris. Apparently, before becoming enveloped by the flames, de Molay is said to have prophesied that Philip IV and his co-conspirator, Pope Clement V, would be dead within the year. Whether de Molay made this prophecy or not, it is true that both men died within a year of the Grand Master's execution. With the death of de Molay, the turbulent 200 year existence of the Knights Templar ended. This, at any rate, is the conventional story.

Other European monarchs remained unconvinced of the Templars' guilt, even after Pope Clement V, under the influence of Philip, officially disbanded the Order in 1312. In England, though many Knights were arrested and tried, the majority were found not guilty. Some escaped to Scotland, at the time under the control of the excommunicated Robert the Bruce, and were therefore unaffected by the Papal Bull outlawing the Order. Many theories have been put forward to explain why Philip IV instigated this vicious attack on the Templars. Most researchers agree that the king sought to deprive the Templar's of their wealth and power, and appropriate it for himself by whatever means necessary. However, it is not clear just how much of the Templars' wealth Philip was able to lay his hands on.

The sudden end of the Knights Templar and the (apparently) complete disappearance of the Order and its assets has fueled a large amount of legend and extreme theories. While it is true that the Templars were partly absorped into other Orders (such as the Knights Hospitaller) it is not clear what became of the estimated 15,000 Templar Houses, their fleet of ships, their vast archive detailing their business holdings and financial transactions, and the Templars themselves. There were tens of thousands of Templars across Europe, only a small proportion of whom were tortured and executed. What happened to the rest? In England, the county of Hertfordshire allegedly became a sanctuary for fugitive Knights from all over Europe. The town of Baldock in Hertfordshire was founded by the

Templars being burned at the stake. Illustration from an anonymous chronicle, From the Creation of the World until 1384.

Templars, and from 1199 to 1254 it had been the Order's English headquarters. It is certainly plausible that after the official censure of the Order, the Templars continued as normal, but met in secret in hidden rooms, cellars and caves. Royston Cave in Hertfordshire, located at the crossing of two Roman roads (the Icknield Way and Ermine Street) may have been one such Templar meeting place. The cave has a number of medieval carvings on the walls, many of them Pagan, but also figures thought to be St. Catherine, St. Lawrence, and St. Christopher. Support for the theory that Royston Cave was used by the Templars comes in the form of the similar carvings at the Tour de Coudray in Chinon, France, where (in 1307) many Templars were imprisoned before their execution.

Another theory is that the Templars who escaped to Scotland after their persecution established Scotch Rite Freemasonry. Apparently John Graham of Claverhouse, the first Viscount Dundee (killed at the Battle of Killiecrankie in 1689) was found to be wearing a Templar cross beneath his armor. Some researchers believe that the Freemasons of the late 17th century were the Knights Templar under a new name.

Other legends hypothesize on the nature of the alleged treasures of the Templars. As the Order occupied the Temple Mount in Jerusalem for a long period, it has been suggested that the Knights undertook their own excavations at the site, and perhaps uncovered the Holy Grail, the Ark of the Covenant, or even fragments of the True Cross. One legend says that the Order found the Holy Grail beneath the Temple Mount and brought it with them to Scotland in the early 1300s. Apparently the Grail remains there today, buried somewhere beneath Rosslyn Chapel, a 15th Century church in the village of Roslin, Midlothian.

Some esoteric groups extant today, such as the Order of the Solar Temple, claim descent from the original Templar Order, and there are many other organizations that have attempted to revive the spirit of the original Templars. In the modern world, with its love of conspiracy theories, secret knowledge, shadowy occult groups, and long lost relics, the Knights Templar represent the archetypal secret society. However, most historians are of the belief that the real legacies of the Templars are more mundane, and revolve mainly around banking and the code of chivalry. But the Templars have such a powerful hold on the popular imagination that there will always be those who wonder if this is really all that remains of the Poor Knights of the Temple of Solomon.

The Prehistoric Puzzle of the Floresians

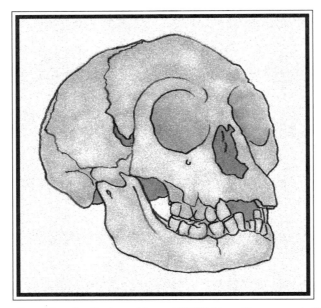

Drawing by Rainer Zenz (GNU Free Documentation License).
The skull of homo floresiensis, *drawn by Rainer Zenz.*

A strange, prehistoric world of tiny humans hunting dwarf elephants, giant rats, huge Komodo dragons, even bigger lizards. This scenario may sound similar to something out of science fiction novels, such as Arthur Conan Doyle's *Lost World*, than scientific fact, but recent discoveries on a remote Indonesian island may change all that. The Indonesian island of Flores, located between Sumatra and East Timor, has become the center of a great controversy over the last few years.

In September 2003, a joint international research team, led by R.P. Soejono from the Indonesia Center for Archaeology, and Michael Morwood from the University of New England Armidale, were digging in a large limestone cave called Liang Bua. At a depth of 20 feet they discovered the near-complete skeleton of a woman of around 30 years of age. The skeleton, which looked to them like a species of hominid, was found to be only 3 feet tall. Other scattered bones of the same species were found nearby and, to date, bones representing nine individuals have been discovered. Using radiocarbon and thermoluminescence dating, the oldest remains have been dated to about 94,000 years ago, and the most recent to 12,000 years ago.

Also found in the cave (in association with the hominid) were the remains of fish, frogs, snakes, tortoises, giant rats, birds, and bats, plus larger animals such as a dwarf species of Stegedons (an extinct pygmy elephant), Komodo dragons, and a larger lizard. The discovery of pieces of fire-cracked rock and charred bone in levels containing hominid skeletal materials suggests that the Floresians knew how to control fire. Another significant find in the cave was a relatively sophisticated stone tool assemblage, including small blades which could have been mounted on wooden shafts. Some of the stone tools were found in direct association with the Stegodon, which suggests that the Floresians were hunting them.

The team published their amazing findings in October 2004 in the science journal *Nature*. The conclusions they drew from the discoveries on Flores were incredible, to say the least. It was announced that a new species of tiny humans, which they named *Homo floresiensis*, had been discovered. The researchers also thought it possible that this species had survived on the island of Flores into historic times. The original skeleton became known as the Little Lady of Flores (or LB1) and the species nicknamed hobbits, from J.R.R. Tolkien's *Lord of the Rings* books. All the individuals were about 3-feet tall, with long arms, and grape-fruit-sized skulls. They were fully bipedal, but had an extremely small brain size (about a third of that of modern humans and slightly smaller than a chimpanzee). They made sophisticated tools, hunted miniature elephants, and were living at the same time as modern humans who were colonizing the area. The researchers concluded that the Floresians were not a pygmy form of modern humans, but a scaled down form of *Homo erectus*, the eastern relation of European Neanderthals who were wiped out by modern humans around 30,000 years ago. *Homo erectus* also disappeared from the record just before modern humans arrive in their territory.

One important question about the find is how the researchers account for the small size of *Homo floresiensis*. One theory is that the island of Flores is particularly isolated and, before modern times, was inhabited only by a limited group of animals that had managed to reach it. These animals subsequently became subject to unusual evolutionary forces that drove some toward gigantism—the giant lizard or Komodo dragon (which still survives today), and reduced the size of others—the pygmy elephant (Stegodon) for example. The team think that *Homo floresiensis* were descendents of *Homo erectus*, who may have arrived on Flores by 840,000 years ago; isolated on the island, they gradually evolved their tiny physique, undergoing the same adaptive process that reduced the size of the elephants. The small size may well have been evolved due to the shortage of resources on Flores.

The completely unexpected discovery of *Homo floresiensis* is widely considered the most important of its kind in recent history. This new member of the genus *Homo* could even change our understanding of human evolution. For example, we are inclined to believe that sophisticated tool manufacture requires a large brain. But the minute brain possessed by the Lady of Flores challenges this, and suggests that researchers need to question previously held assumptions regarding the intelligence and capabilities of our tiny-brained ancestors. One of the original discoverers, Dr. Michael Morwood, even believes that the Floresians may have had a primitive language which they used to communicate during elephant and giant lizard hunts. But others disagree, and point to the fact that chimps and even wolves can hunt cooperatively without the use of language.

The Flores discovery also challenges the conventional wisdom that humans have roamed the Earth alone since Neanderthals died out about 30,000 years ago. The Floresians managed to survive long into the modern period and, unlike the majority of the other archaic human populations, were able to coexist with modern humans. This means that two different human species, *Homo sapiens* and *Homo floresiensis,* were living parallel lives on Earth at the same time. However, although modern human remains have been found on Flores, the earliest is only 11,000 years old, so the two species need not have been around at the same time on the island.

Reactions within the scientific community and beyond were almost as extreme as the discovery. Chris Stringer, head of human origins at London's Natural History Museum, said "many researchers (myself included) doubted these claims," and added that nothing could have prepared him for the surprise of the tiny Floresians. He also speculated that the long arms possibly suggested that *Homo floresiensis* spent a lot of time in the trees. "We don't know this. But if there were Komodo dragons about you might want to be up in the trees with your babies where it's safe."

There were, and still are, many who disagree strongly with the conclusions drawn from the finds in the Liang Bua cave. Indonesia's foremost paleoanthropologist, Teuku Jacob, has claimed that LB1 was not a member of a new species at all, but belonged to the Austrolomelanesid race of modern humans, and was thus merely 1,300 to 1,800 years old. Jakob and several other prominent researchers believe that that the bones are really those of a modern human (*Homo sapiens*), most likely a pygmy with the brain defect known as microcephaly. It has even been suggested that the bones belong to ancestors of the modern day pygmy inhabitants of the Flores village of Rampasasa, close to the Liang Bua cave site. Microcephaly is a pathological condition characterised by an unusually small head and brain, and frequently associated with mental difficulties. In support of this theory, anatomist Maciej Henneberg has claimed that the LB1 skull is almost identical to that of a microcephalic example from Crete. However, Peter Brown, the main contributor to the original *Nature* article, and an associate professor at the University of New England in New South Wales, rejects this explanation. He reasons that very few humans with this condition actually reach adulthood, and that microcephalic skulls display a range of distinctive features, none of which are found in LB1. Brown also states that as there are now bones from Liang Bua representing nine individuals, all sharing the same tiny features, it is much more difficult to propose that a whole population suffered from microcephaly.

In early 2005, an independent team of international experts led by Dr. Dean Falk from Florida State University examined the skull of LB1. They published their results in the journal Science in March 2005. The team compared a three-dimensional image of the brain of LB1 with those from a number of different species: a chimpanzee, a modern human (including a modern pygmy), a microcephalic, and *Homo erectus*. There were further comparisons with primitive human-like creatures *Australopithecus africanus* and *Paranthropus aethiopicus*, and also with modern gorillas. Their conclusion was that the LB1 brain was completely unlike that of a pygmy or a microcephalic, and most like that of *Homo erectus*, and that it is "indeed a new species of human being." But these results didn't silence the critics, who claimed that Dr. Falk and her team didn't use a skull with the correct example of microcephaly. And so the controversy continues.

There is a strong possibility that the question of the true origins and identity of the Floresians might be cleared up by using DNA analysis. The comparatively recent age of the skeletal material and the fact that it is not fossilized suggest that this could indeed be done. However, as high temperatures degrade DNA, the tropical climate of Indonesia significantly diminishes the chance of success with this method. Perhaps additional finds of more complete skeletal materials from Liang Bua may allow DNA testing, though only time will tell if it can be ever be successfully extracted from LB1. Nevertheless, the fascinating possibility remains. If DNA could ever be extracted from *Homo floresiensis,* it could provide an entirely new perception of the evolution of the human lineage.

As far as the fate of the tiny island people is concerned, an eruption in the vicinity of the Liang Bua cave from one of the island's numerous volcanoes (about 12,000 years ago) appears to have wiped out the local *Homo floresiensis* population as well as much of Flores's unique wildlife. However, some of the *Homo floresiensis* population may have survived much later in other parts of the island. Interestingly, the modern inhabitants of Flores have detailed legends about the existence of little hairy people on the island, known as *Ebu Gogo,* roughly translated as *grandmother who eats anything.* Some of the features of these Ebu Gogo include a height of about 3 feet and longish arms and fingers, which are also characteristic of *Homo floresiensis.* The Ebu Gogo were also able to murmur to each other in some kind of primitive language, and could repeat what villagers said to them in a parrot-like fashion.

Apparently the Ebu Gogo were last sighted just before Dutch colonists settled in Flores in the 19th century.

There is also an interesting link between the Floresians and the island of Sumatra, where there have been reports of another 3-foot tall humanoid, known as the *Orang Pendek*. Zoologists have been cataloguing sightings of a mysterious ape in the Kerinci Seblat park area of western Sumatra for more than 150 years, and both footprints and hairs have been recovered that may belong to the creature. Researchers working on the Floresian finds have postulated that the Orang Pendek could be surviving examples of *Homo floresiensis* still living on Sumatra. Henry Gee, senior editor at *Nature* magazine, agrees, and goes even further, saying that the discovery of *Homo floresiensis* surviving until such recent times (geologically speaking) "makes it more likely that stories of other mythical, human-like creatures such as Yetis are founded on grains of truth….Now, cryptozoology, the study of such fabulous creatures, can come in from the cold."

Researchers insist that the possibility of finding a living example of *Homo floresiensis* or Ebu Gogo should not be dismissed out of hand, particularly as Southeast Asia is a relatively rich area for finds of mammals unknown to science. Examples include an antelope, *Pseudoryx nghetinhensis* (described from the Lao-Vietnamese border as recently as 1993) and the kouprey, an ox-like creature (known to Western science only since 1937). Bert Roberts and Michael Morwood are convinced that exploration of the remaining rainforest on Flores and caves associated with the Ebu Gogo stories could provide them with vital samples of hair or other material, perhaps even living specimens. They also think it probable that the skeletal remains of other, equally divergent *Homo* species, await discovery in other isolated corners of Southeast Asia. Indeed, the fact that a lost *Homo* species such as *floresiensis,* which had lived so recently, yet remained unknown until 2003, strongly suggests there are more significant gaps in our understanding of the history of humanity than we could ever have imagined.

The Magi and the Star of Bethlehem

The Three Wise Men, named Balthasar, Melchior, and Gaspar, from a late 6th century mosaic at the Basilica of San Apollinare Nuovo, Ravenna, Italy.

The Magi are familiar to most people as the Wise Men from the East in the Bible. The Gospel of Matthew describes them following the Star of Bethlehem to find the savior and offering him their gifts of gold, frankincense, and myrrh. But did these mysterious wise men bearing exotic gifts really exist outside of this biblical story? And if so, what was the Star of Bethlehem?

The word *Magi* (the plural of the term *Magus*), comes from Latin via the Greek word *Magoi*, itself borrowed from Old Persian *Maguš*. The Old English word is *Mage*, and it is from this that we get our word *magic*. One of the earliest mentions of the Magi is by the Greek historian Herodotus (c. 484 B.C.– c. 425 B.C.) who states that they were a sacred class of priests living in Media (roughly the northwestern part of Iran and the area of Kurdistan), and one of the six tribes that composed the original Medes. However, as the Persian Empire expanded into their area in the sixth century B.C., the priests of the old Median religion, which was possibly of Mesopotamian origin, found it necessary to adapt their practices to the monotheistic Zoroastrian faith, though this was a slow and painful process.

It is recorded that when Darius the Great, Persian Emperor from 521 B.C. to 486 B.C., and one of the early kings of the Achaemenid Dynasty (c. 560 B.C.–330 B.C.), discovered that the Magi at the Median court were skilled interpreters of dreams, he established them in preference to the state religion of Persia. Whatever the truth of this, by the time Herodotus was writing, the Magi had become priests in the Persian Zoroastrian religion, with a role comparable to Shamans or medicine men. Part of their duties was to serve as astrological consultants to the Persian emperors, and they soon attained a powerful religious influence and earned respect as wise men throughout the Empire.

An important source for the Magians under Darius are the Persepolis Fortification Tablets, a substantial collection of ancient Persian cuneiform administrative texts, dating from between 506 and 497 B.C. It is in these texts that the Magi are described as operating in a dual capacity, wielding both religious and political influence. This combined function of administrator and priest was a common practice in Near Eastern societies at the time. The Magi were given important religious responsibilities, as is illustrated in the description of the lan-sacrifice at the Persian capital city of Persepolis. As the tablets describe the Magi as fire kindlers, this ritual seems to have been a type of fire sacrifice to *Ahuramazda* (the wise lord), the supreme god of the ancient Persians. Together with the testimonies of ancient Greek authors, the Fortification Tablets indicate that the Magi were present at the royal court of the Persian emperors, and involved at the very highest level in Persian religious practice and administration.

With the invasion of Persia by Alexander the Great in the winter of 331 B.C. the Achaemenid Dynasty came to an abrupt end. Although ancient sources mention Magi at Alexander's court being involved in rituals of some sort, it is also clear that Alexander destroyed many Zoroastrian sanctuaries, probably because he saw their religion as a threat to his authority.

The Greek writer and geographer Strabo (c. 63 B.C.–c. A.D. 21) describes a sect of Magians in Cappadocia (central Turkey). He called them fire kindlers, who possessed fire temples containing an altar on which a fire was kept continuously burning. The Magians visited the temple daily for around an hour, where they would make incantations holding bundles of tamarisk or other branches in front of the fire and "wearing round their heads high turbans of felt, which reach down their cheeks far enough to cover their lips." It seems that some Magi also traveled west, arriving and settling in Greece and Italy. Traces of their beliefs and practices can be found in Mithraism, an ancient mystery religion based on worship of the god Mithras, which became popular among the Roman Legions around the third to fourth centuries A.D. At the time of the Roman Empire, the word *Magi* began to be used as a more general term to describe any representatives of an eastern cult, and by the time of the birth of Jesus, it had come to mean anyone involved in magic, astrology, or dream interpretation. The Magi seemed to have been accepted as part of the courts of the Roman Empire, as a number of them are mentioned as accompanying high ranking officials and governors.

The description of the Magi in the Gospel of Matthew (written between A.D. 60 and 80) visiting Jesus in Bethlehem is the only source we have for the event. The text says "there came wise men from the east to Jerusalem" and subsequently refers to the Magi's interest in stars, so it is probable the wise men he is speaking of were astrologers. This concern with the stars has suggested to some that the wise men came from Babylon, a well-known center of astrology at the time. However, to judge purely by the nature of the gifts they brought—gold, frankincense, and myrrh—Arabia would seem more appropriate, though it did not possess a Magian priesthood. Matthew never mentions how many Magi there were, but the number of gifts would indicate three. The nature of these gifts has potent symbolic power for Christians: frankincense signifying Christ's divinity; gold representing his royalty; and myrrh, which was used in anointing corpses, a symbol of the forthcoming Passion and death.

According to the Gospel of Matthew, before arriving in Bethlehem, the Magi first visited Herod, the Roman puppet king of Judea. After sighting the star in the east, they made inquiries with Herod regarding the new king. Herod, with his knowledge of Old Testament prophecy, was able to direct them to Bethlehem. He requested that the Magi return to see him when they found any news, so that he too could pay homage to the newborn savior. As they approached

Bethlehem, the star again appeared in the sky so the Magi followed it until they found the King of the Jews and presented him with their gifts. The astrologers were subsequently warned in a dream to avoid going back to Herod and traveled back to Persia by an alternative route. As a result of this trick, Herod was furious and ordered the massacre of the Holy Innocents, all the children under two years old in Bethlehem and the surrounding area. But by then Joseph had taken Mary and Jesus to safety in Egypt.

There has been a huge amount of discussion about what kind of star it could have been that brought the Magi out of the east on their long trek to Judaea. Explanations put forward for this astronomical wonder include meteors, the planet Venus, planetary conjunctions, stella novae, comets, and even UFOs. Nowadays, the two most widely accepted suggestions are that the star in the east was either the planet Jupiter, or Halley's Comet.

The Greek word *aster*, used by Matthew in his gospel to describe the Star of Bethlehem, can be interpreted to mean a comet. But is there any record of a comet at this time? In the Roman world there was a belief that the appearance of a comet often heralded catastrophic political events, even the death of an emperor, which would suggest that it could not be associated with the birth of a new messiah. But among the Magi of the Black Sea coast of Turkey, comets appear to have been good omens. The successful rule of one particular king in the area, Mithridates VI, was so much associated with comets as positive celestial portents that he even had coins minted depicting them. The appearance of Halley's Comet in 12 B.C. caused consternation throughout the Mediterranean world, especially in the skies above Rome. Because Herod is now believed to have died in 4 B.C. most scholars now place the birth of Jesus somewhere between 12 and 4 B.C., which would make Halley's Comet a possibility for the Star of Bethlehem. A problem with the comet theory however, is that Matthew mentions that Herod and the people of Jerusalem did not notice the star of Bethlehem in the night sky, which they surely would have done if it was something as obvious as Halley's Comet.

Jupiter, known as the star of Zeus, was traditionally the planet associated with kings, and astronomer Michael R. Molnar of Rutgers University in New Jersey has interpreted statements in Matthew's Gospel that the star "went before" and "stood over" as referring to to the reversal of motion and stationing of the planet Jupiter. Molnar has discovered a Roman coin issued in Antioch, the capital of Roman Syria, which dates to the time of Jesus' birth and which depicts the astrological sign of Aries the Ram turning its head to look back at a star. Molnar believes that this coin was issued to commemorate the takeover of Judaea by Roman Antioch in A.D. 6. Subsequent research revealed that in an important astrological work by Claudius Ptolemy, the *Tetrabiblos,* Aries the Ram is explained as controlling the people of "Judea, Idumea, Samaria, Palestine, and Coele Syria"—all territories ruled by King Herod. So it is possible that the star on the coin represents Judaea's destiny in the hands of Roman Antioch. This may indicate that astrologers were waiting for the birth of a great king of the Jews portended by the appearance of the Star of Bethlehem in the constellation of Aries the Ram. Molnar's research shows that the celestial events on April 17, 6 B.C., when Jupiter was in Aries and there was also a lunar eclipse of the planet, were exactly those which would indicate the birth of a divine person. Though a lot more research needs to be done on this theory, it provides the best evidence yet that the Magi from Persia were actually following a real star, in this case Jupiter, which would ultimately lead them to Bethlehem and the future King of the Jews.

The Druids

The Druids were mysterious Pagan priests in the Celtic society of Western Europe from around the second century B.C. to the first century A.D. (the end of the Iron Age). Variously given the title of Shamans, priests, teachers, and philosophers, so little is known about the Druids—who left no written record of their existence—that they have been both romanticized and demonized in equal measure. Much of what we know about the Druids comes from ancient Greek and Roman writers, and early Irish and Welsh literature. The development of neo-Druidism from the 17th century onwards has also added considerably to the image of the Druid as known today. But how much of the tales of strange secret rites in lonely forest groves or mass human sacrifice in huge wickerwork images is, in fact, based on truth?

The word *Druid* seems to derive from Indo-European roots meaning

Arch-Druid in his full Judicial Costume. An etching from Old England: A Pictorial Museum *(1845).*

oak, strong, knowledge, or *wisdom*. Our most informative source for these Pagan priests is Julius Caesar (100 B.C.– 44 B.C.), who wrote about them from first-hand experience in his *Commentaries on the Gallic War,* a history of his wars in Gaul (modern France) from 59 to 51 B.C. Unfortunately, as with most of the ancient Roman sources for the Druids, it is often hard to separate Roman propaganda from truth. Caesar mentions the Druids in his discussion of Gaulish religion and says that they were in charge of private and public sacrifice and other religious matters. Casaer's need to impress Rome with stories from his military campaign in Gaul probably accounts for the exaggerations in his statements, and nowhere is this more obvious than in his discussion of human sacrifice by these Celtic priests. He describes "huge statues of immense size, whose bodies of woven branches are filled with living men." Obviously he is describing the now famous wicker men. Caesar then goes on to say that criminals were burned alive inside these huge structures to satisfy the gods, but, he adds, if the supply of criminals fails, then the Druids think nothing of sacrificing innocent victims.

Caesar's writings indicate the existence of at least two classes among the higher echelon of Gaulic society: the nobles and the Druids. The Druids obviously held an influential and respected position in Celtic society, and Caesar mentions that large numbers of young men went to them for training. The Druids also retained power as lawgivers, acted in disputes between both individuals and tribes, and had the right to pass judgements on criminals. They were also exempt from military service and the payment of taxes. Caesar places the origin of Druidism in Britain, and mentions that serious students of the Druidic arts traveled there to study it. He also reports that a novice could continue his studies for up to 20 years, some of which included memorizing large amounts of poetry. Caesar's information on the religious doctrines of the Druids is interesting, as he states, "a lesson, which they take particular pains to inculcate, is that the soul does not perish, but after death passes from one body to another." Many ancient writers took this to mean that the Druids had been influenced by the teachings of the Greek philosopher Pythagoras on the immortality of the soul, though this seems unlikely. Caesar also mentions the Druids having knowledge of the motion of the stars and the size of the Earth, and being familiar with philosophy.

It is difficult to ascertain even roughly when the Druid priesthood originated. The earliest known reference to them is from the early first century B.C. Greek philosopher, astronomer, and geographer, Posidonius. Unfortunately his work only survives in fragments from later writers such as Greek historian and geographer Strabo (c. 63 B.C.–A.D. 24) and Posidonius' pupil, the Roman orator and statesman, Cicero (106 B.C.–3 B.C.). Cicero comments that he actually knew a Druid named Divitiacus, of a Gaulish tribe known as the Aedui, and he describes this Divitiacus as a kind of astrologer or soothsayer who was acquainted with "natural philosophy." Strabo's writings again feature the giant wicker man sacrifices referred to by Caesar, and also another type of human sacrifice supervised by the Druids. He writes: "Some men they would shoot dead with arrows and impale in the temples." While there is practically no evidence that the Celts used bows and arrows at all, intriguingly, the body of a man found in the outer ditch at Stonehenge proved to have been killed at close quarters by three arrows in his back. As the date for this possible human sacrifice at Stonehenge is between 2398 and 2144 B.C., there is obviously no direct connection between his ritual murder and the Late Iron Age Druids, unless of course the Druids practiced rituals that had been part of the traditions of the British Isles for millennia, and had been handed down to them.

In the writings of Roman author and natural philosopher Pliny the Elder (A.D. 23– A.D. 79) the Druids are called *magicians*, and he describes them venerating mistletoe and the oak tree from which it grows. Pliny mentions that the Druids never performed any of their rituals unless there was an oak branch present, and that they gathered mistletoe in a solemn ceremony on the sixth day of the moon. This ceremony involved a priest clad in white robes climbing the oak tree and cutting the mistletoe with a golden sickle; the falling mistletoe was then caught in a white cloth. The Druids afterwards sacrificed two white bulls to their gods. According to Pliny, the sixth day of the moon was the day from which the Druids began their months, their years, and their 30 year cycle. Some support for the idea that the Druids relied heavily on the phases of the moon in their calendar was provided by the discovery of the Coligny Calendar in Coligny, France, in 1897. This calendar, probably dating to the second century A.D., was engraved on a bronze tablet, and functioned as a solar/lunar ritual calendar, each month always begining with the same moon phase.

Roman geographer Pomponius Mela, writing in A.D. 43, is the first to mention that the teachings of the Druids were secret. He describes the Druids of Gaul as "masters of wisdom" who carrried out their teaching "in a cave, or in inaccessible woods." Perhaps the best known account of the Druids is that by Roman orator, lawyer, and senator, Tacitus (A.D. 56–A.D. 117). In his *Annals,* he describes an attack, in A.D. 61, by the Roman army commanded by the Governor of Britain Suetonius Paulinus, on the island of Mona (modern Angelsey), off the northwest coast of Wales. Mona (*Ynys Môn* in Welsh) was the last stronghold of the Druids

and was contributing significantly to resistence in Wales against the Roman invasion. As the Romans approached the opposite shore and looked over to the island, they saw the Britons lined up on Menai Bay, ready to defend their island. As they crossed by boat onto Mona, the soldiers noticed women (presumably Druidesses) "running through the ranks in wild disorder; their apparel funeral; their hair loose to the wind, in their hands flaming torches, and their whole appearance resembling the frantic rage of the Furies." They also saw the male Druids, standing together in a band, their hands uplifted to the sky, and their voices invoking the gods and calling down terrible curses on the Romans. At first, Suetonius Paulinus and his troops were awestruck at this weird and disturbing sight, and were unsure of what

Two druids. Roman period bas-relief, found at Autun in Burgundy, France.

to do. Eventually, according to Tacitus, the natural courage of the Romans overcame their fears, and they made a furious charge into the manic group of women and priests and mowed them down mercilessly. The Druid's sacred groves were burned to the ground and their shrines, still stained with the blood of sacrificial victims (according to Tacitus) destroyed. While Suetonius was laying waste to Mona, he received news of a revolt in the southeast of Britain, led by queen Boudica of the Iceni tribe, and returned to gain an eventual bloody victory over the rebelling Britons.

Archaeological evidence which may have a connection with this final stand of the Druids on Mona was discovered in 1943, deposited in a lake on the island known as Llyn Cerrig Bach. The remarkable cache of 150 objects included iron and bronze weapons, chariots and cauldrons, and has been dated to between the second century B.C. and the first century A.D. The items seem to have been deliberately thrown into the lake as some kind of offering. Scholars have hypothesized that this deliberate offering of precious metalwork may have been made by the surviving Druids of Mona, to propitiate their gods in response to the wholesale desecration of Druidic shrines carried out by the Romans on the island.

Following the massacre on Mona, Druidism seems to have been outlawed by Rome, which probably meant the end of an organized priesthood, although Druids certainly did not disappear completely (especially in Scotland, Ireland, and perhaps parts of Wales). In Ireland, Druids retained their prominent position in society until the coming of Christianity, where their roles were soon taken over by the clergy. Many early Welsh and Irish epics speak of the Druids, though it has to be borne in mind that almost everything that has survived has been edited by Christian scribes. In Irish literature, Druids are usually seen in the role as advisors to kings; perhaps the most famous example is Cathbad, chief Druid at the court of Conchobar, king of Ulster. Another famous example is Mug Ruith, the powerful blind druid of Munster, the southernmost province of ancient Ireland. Mug Ruith had the ability to grow to an enormous size, conjure up storms, and turn men to stone. His Shamanistic appearance included a hornless bull's hide, bird mask, and a feathered headdress. Mug Ruith's daughter, Tlachtga, was a renowned Druidess, who gave her name to a hill in County Meath and a ceremony celebrated there—the lighting of the winter fires at Samhain (November 1st), an ancient Celtic festival probably once presided over by the Druids.

It was not until the 18th century, with a revival of interest in natural religion and native traditions, that Druidism again came to the fore. Much of this interest stemmed from antiquarians such as William Stukeley, John Aubrey, and John Toland. John Aubrey (1626–1697) was the first modern writer to claim that Stonehenge, Avebury, and other prehistoric monuments in England were connected to the Druids. A follower of Aubrey's theories, Irish-born writer and radical thinker, John Toland, apparently founded the Ancient Druid Order in London around 1717; in 1726, he published his *History of the Druids.* William Stukeley (1687–1765) was a pioneering archaeologist and antiquarian, who became the Secretary of the Society of Antiquaries in 1718. His investigations, notes, and drawings of Neolithic sites, such as Stonehenge and Avebury are still of extreme value to archaeologists and historians today. However, he too was under the spell of Aubrey and attributed many prehistoric monuments to the only ancient British people then known—the Druids. He published *Stonehenge, a Temple Restored to the British Druids*, in 1740, and *Avebury, a Temple of the British Druids*, in 1743, both of which were highly influential on the modern Druid revival.

In 19th century Wales, it was believed that the Welsh poetic tradition dated back to the Druids. Welsh antiquarian Edward Williams, under the name Iolo Morganwg, founded the *Gorsedd Beirdd Ynys Prydain* (the Community of Bards of Great Britain) at Primrose Hill, London in 1792. Although the rituals were supposed to be based on ancient Druid ceremonies, many were in fact written by Williams himself. Druidism is also part of the inspiration behind the *Eisteddfod*, a Welsh festival of literature, music, and performance, dating back to at least the 12th century, though the modern-day format has been much influenced by the 18th century revival of Welsh cultural festivals. Modern Druidic orders exist, as is witnessed every year at Stonehenge on the summer solstice by the appearance of the Ancient Order of Druids. Founded in London in 1781 (along the lines of a Masonic society), this Order once boasted William Churchill as a member, who appears to have joined their Albion Lodge in Oxford in 1908.

It is difficult to say what, if anything, of original Druidic belief or ritual survives in some form today. Practically everything in modern Druidery has its roots in 18th and 19th century romanticism. Perhaps echoes of the ancient British Druids are still to be found in folkloric beliefs related to well-worship, and certain practices connected with celebrations, such as Halloween. The wearing of masks at Halloween to scare away evil spirits goes back to Celtic Samhain ceremonies, traditionally celebrated at the beginning of winter, on the 1st of November. Another major Celtic celebration was Beltaine, a festival held on April 30 or May 1 celebrating the coming of summer and the origin of May Day. On May Eve great fires were lit on hilltops and Druids drove cattle through the flames to purify them; people would also leap through the fires to secure a plentiful harvest. Perhaps even the mythical woodland folk, such as the fairies and woodwoses (hairy wildman of the woods) are the last vague survivals of the sacred traditions of the once great Druids.

The Queen of Sheba

Exotic and mysterious, the Queen of Sheba is best known from the biblical story of her celebrated meeting with King Solomon. Sheba is also celebrated in the Islamic world as a powerful queen under the name *Balqis* or *Bilqis*, and in Ethiopian tradition as *Makeda*. In the annals of ancient history, perhaps only Cleopatra has achieved more fame as a potent female ruler, yet so little is known about the the enigmatic Queen of Sheba that archaeologists and historians are not even sure whether she existed at all. However, recent archaeological discoveries are begining to throw a glimmer of light on the possible identity of history's most perplexing figure. The Queen of Sheba is referred to in the Bible in the Book of Kings simply as the "Queen of the East." No more specific details than that are given of her origin. The text describes how the

The Queen of Sheba.

queen, having heard of the renown of Solomon, travels from her homeland at the head of a caravan loaded with spices, large amounts of gold, and precious stones, to visit the great king at Jerusalem. According to the Biblical account, it is her intention to test Solomon's renowned wisdom with difficult questions. After meeting with the great king she is awed by his wisdom and the grandness of his royal court, and so bestows rich gifts on him. Solomon, in turn, offers her great treasures and "all that she desired," after which she returns to her own land. That, in essence, is the story of Solomon and Sheba.

Although this is the last we hear of the great queen in the Bible, in postbiblical times Jewish and Muslim legends elaborated on the basic Solomon and Sheba narrative and also added new—often highly fantastic—elements to it. According to Jewish historian Josephus, writing in the first century A.D., Sheba was the queen of Egypt and Ethiopia. Arabian folklore, and the Qur'an provide more imaginary stories involving the Queen of Sheba. The Qur'an narrative tells of Solomon receiving reports from a hoopoe bird of a rich kingdom ruled by a queen whose subjects worship the sun. Solomon sends a message to the queen via the bird, to the effect that she should come and pay him homage, threatening to annihilate her kingdom if she refuses. Sheba agrees to visit and is converted by Solomon to the worship of the one true God.

The question of whether there is any historical truth behind such legends has perplexed researchers for hundreds of years. The main problem is that so little is known about the Queen of Sheba. There seems to be no independent evidence for her existence outside of the Bible, and the historical record is silent on the great queen. Yet, she has become such a significant figure to so many cultures that it is difficult to imagine that her story is all fantasy. Modern archaeology has conjectured that if Sheba existed as an historical figure, then the ancient territory of Sheba which she ruled over would have been located either in the Kingdom of Axum in Abyssinia (modern day Ethiopia), or the Territory of Saba (in Yemen). Perhaps even both, as there is only a 15 miles strait of the Red Sea between them. The basis for this assumption is that when she visited Solomon, the gifts she brought with her included frankincense, which only grows in these two areas, and neighboring Oman. A date for her reign of around 950 B.C. is generally agreed upon.

But is there any evidence that Saba and Axum could have been the rich kingdom ruled over by an exotic queen as described in the Bible? There is evidence for a market for perfumes and incense in the Near East and Egypt at least as early as the third millennium B.C. The Kingdom of Saba was a prosperous trading nation, with control of the caravan routes that carried frankincence and spices across the desert to perfume the temples of the Mediterranean and beyond. The capital city of Saba was called Marib, and was built on the edge of the southern Arabian Desert in the dry delta of Wadi Adana. In this arid area, the Sabaens needed a water supply. Consequently, beginning somewhere between 750 and 600 B.C., they constructed a dam to capture the periodical monsoon rains which fall on the nearby mountains, to irrigate the parched land around the city, making it possible to grow crops.

In 2002, Los Angeles-based documentary filmmaker, photographer, and amateur archaeologist Nicholas Clapp published *Sheba: Through the Desert in Search of the Legendary Queen.* Clapp proposed that the Queen of Sheba was the renowned Yemeni Queen Bilqis, the ruler of the kingdom of Saba, probably the most influential and prosperous of the five ancient southern Arabian states. Clapp also suggested, in contrast to the Biblical description, that Sheba was actually a much more powerful ruler than Solomon, whom he sees as more of a local chieftain than a mighty king. According to Clapp, the reason for the long trek to Jerusalem by Bilqis and her retinue was to take part in important trade discussions. These talks were particularly centered on bargaining for a route through lands controlled by Solomon to facilitate long-range spice and incense trading. In effect, Sheba's embassy to Israel (as described in the Bible) could be a distorted memory of one of the first great trade missions anywhere in the world.

Bilqis is also the name given to a recently excavated temple located nine miles outside the ruins of Sabean capital Marib. The *Mahram Bilqis*, or *Temple of the Moon God*, was according to the project's field director, University of Calgary archaeology professor Dr. Bill Glanzman, a sacred site for pilgrims all over Arabia from around 1200 B.C. to A.D. 550. This huge ovoid-shaped-temple has a circumference of around 900 feet, although much of the ancient site now lies buried under the wind-blown sand. Finds from the site include bronze and alabaster statues, and large amounts of animal bones, indicating that the sanctuary was used for animal sacrifices. There is actually some written evidence in Assyrian texts of the eighth and seventh centuries B.C. that kings named *Itamru* and *Karib-ilu* were rulers of the kingdom of Saba. These kings are mentioned in connection with tributes or presents from Saba, including incense and precious stones, reminiscent of the Queen of Sheba's gifts to Solomon. However, these are references to kings and not queens; there is no specific mention of a queen of Sheba in these texts. There is also no reference to any Queen of Sheba in the many surviving Sabean inscriptions, including those from the temple site of Mahram Bilqis. Another difficulty with a Sabean origin for the 10th century B.C. biblical queen is that the kingdom of

Saba does not seem to have been fully developed by this time. While Solomon is undoubtedly an influential and noted historical ruler, we only hear of the Queen of Sheba in connection with him. Consequently, the biblical account is viewed by some researchers as an unhistorical episode written down hundreds of years after Solomon's reign, to emphasis the great king's glory and legendary wisdom.

Among the Christians of Ethiopia, located across a narrow strip of the Red Sea from Saba, there is a story (included in their epic history of kings, the *Kebra Negast*), that they are descended from Menelik I, the son of Sheba and Solomon, and the beginning of the Ethiopian royal dynasty. According to the tale, Menelik traveled to Jerusalem to see Solomon, his aging father, who begged him to stay and become king after his death. But Menelik rejected his offer and instead secretly returned home at night, taking with him the kingdom's most valuable relic, the Ark of the Covenant. Apparently Menelik brought the ark back to Aksum, in northern Ethiopia, where it remains today, in a treasury in the courtyard of the Church of Our Lady Mary of Zion. In the *Kebra Negast*, Makeda (as Sheba is known), was born in 1020 B.C. in Ophir, a port mentioned in the Bible and thought to have been somewhere in Yemen. Makeda was educated in Ethiopia, and when her father died in 1005 B.C., she became queen at the age of 15, ruling for 40 years, though other accounts have her ruling for six.

In May 1999, a team of Nigerian and British archaeologists discovered massive ramparts hidden away in

Nigeria's rain forest, which they believed could be evidence for the center of one Africa's most renowned kingdoms and the possible burial place of the Queen of Sheba. The monument at Eredo is the largest in Africa, and consists of a boundary ditch and 45 foot high rampart extending for an incredible 100 miles. Local people in the area say that *Bilikisu Sungbo*, another name for the Queen of Sheba, is supposed to have dug the vast Eredo kingdom boundary, and there is an annual pilgrimage to what is believed to be the site of her grave. Though the area has a long history of gold and ivory trade, which could be connected with Sheba's commercial activities, there is no direct archaeological or textual evidence to link Sheba with Aksum. In spite of the local legends, the monument itself seems to have been erected at least 1,000 years after the Queen of Sheba's supposed reign in the 10th century B.C.

Despite the uncertainty of the archaeological and historical evidence in support of the reality of the Queen of Sheba, the image of a woman of power combined with wisdom and beauty has continued to be an inspiration for artists, storytellers, and movie makers for hundreds of years. From the art of the Renaissance period to the glossy epics of Hollywood, Sheba's influence has been considerable. Indeed, the Queen of Sheba has been a favorite theme in the movies throughout their entire history. Some of the best known versions and variations of her story include J. Gordon Edwards' 1921 silent *The Queen of Sheba* with Betty Blythe in the title role, which tells the story of an ill-fated romance between Solomon, king of Israel, and the Queen of Sheba; *Solomon and Sheba* (1959) with Yul Brynner and Gina Lollobrigida; *The Queen of Sheba Meets the Atom Man* (1963); and *Solomon and Sheba* (1995), in which Halle Berry played the first black Sheba.

Though concrete evidence is at present lacking, it remains entirely possible that there was a historical Queen of Sheba, as portrayed in the Bible story and later legend. There were certainly powerful female rulers in ancient Arabia, and perhaps further excavation and research in the area of the ancient kingdom of Saba will one day reveal the real woman behind the Sheba story. Regardless of the archaeological and historical evidence, in parts of Africa and Arabia the story of the Queen of Sheba is still told, as it has been for perhaps 2,000 or 3,000 years.

The Mystery of the Tarim Mummies

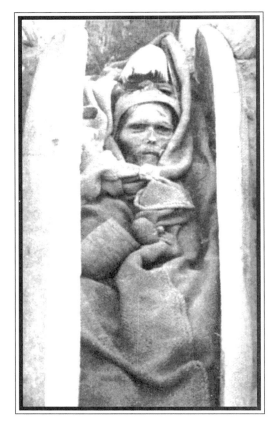

Tarim Basin mummy, photographed by Aurel Stein, c. 1910.

The Tarim Mummies constitute a baffling ancient world mystery, and one of the most remarkable archaeological finds of the 20th century. These amazingly well-preserved human remains were found in the dry salty environment of the vast Taklimakan desert, part of the Tarim Basin in western China. The bodies so far discovered have an extremely wide date range, from 1800 B.C. up until A.D. 400. But what has captured the attention of scholars all over the world is the fact that the mummies have distinctly European features, and seem to represent various Caucasian tribes who lived in this desolate area of western China up until 2,000 years ago, before mysteriously disappearing.

The mummies were first discovered in the early 1900s by Swedish explorer Sven Hedin, who was investigating the complex history of the Silk Road, an ancient series of routes which once led from China to Turkey and on into Europe. But without the necessary equipment to either preserve the bodies or transport them back to museums in Europe for study, they remained in situ and were soon forgotten. In 1978, Chinese archaeologist Wang Binghua excavated 113 of these bodies at a cemetery at Qizilchoqa, or Red Hill, in the northeast corner of the central Asian province of Xinjiang. Most of the bodies were later taken to a museum in the city of Urumqi. In the last 25 years or so, Chinese and Uyghur archaeologists have carried out sophisticated excavation and research in the area, and there are now more than 300 of these mummies known to have been discovered in western China. In 1987, Victor Mair (a professor of Chinese and Indo-Iranian literature and religion at the University of Pennsylvania) was leading a group of tourists through the museum in Urumqi when he came upon some of the mummies excavated by Wang Binghua. He found it an unnerving experience. All were dressed in dark purple woolen garments and felt boots, and their bodies were almost perfectly preserved. Fascinatingly, all the mummies had European features: brown or blonde hair; long noses and skulls; slim elongated bodies; and large, deepset eyes.

Due to the political climate in China at the time, Mair was not able to do anything about the amazing finds, but in 1993 he returned with a team of Italian geneticists who had worked on the Ice Man. The group went back to Wang Binghua's Red Hill site to examine corpses that had been reburied due to lack of storage space at Urumqi Museum. Mair and his team took DNA samples from the bodies, which proved that the mummies were Caucasoid. Mair's research also seems to show that the earliest of these European mummies represented the first settlers in the Tarim Basin.

The oldest of all the western Chinese mummies is known as the Beauty of Loulan. The perfectly preserved Loulan female body was discovered by Chinese archaeologists in 1980, near the ancient town of Loulan, situated on the northeastern edge of the Taklimakan desert. This woman, who died at the age of 40 around 4,800 years ago, was only 5-feet 2-inches tall, and had European features including a steep nose bridge, high cheekbones, and blondish-brown hair, which had been rolled up under a felt headdress. She was wearing a woolen shroud and leather boots, and buried with her in the grave was a comb and a beautiful straw basket that contained grains of wheat. Another expedition to the Loulan region in 2003, by the Xinjiang Archaeological Institute, revealed some remarkable finds. Excavations were undertaken at a cemetery consisting of a sand mound measuring 25 feet in height, located 110 miles from the ancient town of Loulan. A particularly interesting find at the grave site was made close to the center of the mound, and proved to be another impressive mummy. Contained in a boat-shaped coffin, the female mummy had been wrapped in a woolen blanket and was wearing a felt hat and leather shoes. She had been buried with a red-painted face mask, a bracelet containing a jade stone, a leather pouch, a woolen loincloth, and ephedra sticks. Ephedra is a medicinal shrub that was used in the Zoroastrian religious rituals of Iran, so there was perhaps some connection between these two areas.

A further group of mummies found in the Tarim Basin region consisted of one man, three women, and a baby, and have become known as the Cherchen Mummies. The four adult bodies, thought to date to around 1000 B.C., were dressed in the same color, with red and blue cords wrapped around their hands, perhaps indicating a close kinship. Chercean Man, the male mummy, was more than 6-feet tall and died at the age of 50. He had long, light brown, braided hair; a thin beard; and multiple tattoos on his face. The man was buried with no less than 10 different styled hats and was dressed in a purple and red two-piece suit. Similar to Cherchen Man, the main female burial had numerous tattoos on her face, and was almost 6-feet tall. She was wearing a red dress and white deer skin boots, and had her light brown hair gathered in two long plaits. There was also a three-month-old baby buried with the adults, who was wearing a blue felt bonnet, and had blue stones covering its eyes. Buried beside the infant were a cow-horn cup and a nursing bottle made from a sheep's udder. The family is thought to have died in some sort of epidemic.

What has fascinated archaeologists most about these discoveries is the amazing preservation of the brightly-colored and patterned European-looking clothing the people were wearing. Dr. Elizabeth Barber, professor of linguistics and archaeology at Occidental College in Los Angeles, has made a detailed study of the textiles recovered from the Tarim Basin and found striking similarities to Celtic tartans from northwest Europe. She has also proposed that the tartan from the Tarim mummies and that from Europe share a common origin in the Caucasus mountains of southern Russia, where the earliest evidence for such fabrics dates back at least 5,000 years. The rich array of textile finds from western Chinese mummy burials includes robes, caps, shirts, cloaks, tartan-weave trousers, and striped woolen stockings. At Subeshi on the northern route of the Silk Road, three female mummies, dating from around 500 to 400 B.C., were found with enormously tall, pointed hats, and have since become known as the Witches of Subeshi.

But who were these apparently European peoples and what were they doing in western China? The mummies are scattered over such a wide geographical area and date range that there can be no question that they are a single tribe. They seem to represent several eastward migrations from different areas over a thousand or more years. There are some ancient sources referring to groups inhabiting the areas of the Tarim basin, where mummies have been found, which may give a clue to the origins of at least some of the mummy people. First millennium B.C. Chinese sources mention a group of "white people with long hair" known as the *Bai* people. The Bai lived on the northwestern border of China, and the Chinese apparently bought jade from them. Another group on the northwestern borders of China were the *Yuezhi*, mentioned in 645 B.C. by the Chinese author Guan Zhong. The Yuezhi also supplied the Chinese with jade, which they got from the nearby mountains of Yuzhi at Gansu. After being defeated by the nomadic Xiongnu people, the majority of the Yuezhi migrated to Transoxiana (part of southern Asia equivalent to modern Uzbekistan and southwest Kazakhstan) and later to northern India, where they founded the Kushan Empire. Depictions of Yuezhi kings on coinage have suggested to some that this group may have been a Caucasoid people.

The final group who inhabited this area were the Tocharians, who represent the easternmost speakers of an Indo-European language (a language group comprising most of the languages of Europe, India, and Iran). Some scholars argue that the Tocharians and the Yuezhi were in fact the same people under different names, though there is no proof of this at present. The areas of western China where European-type mummies have been found, in the northeastern part of the Tarim basin, and further east in the area around Lopnur, correspond well to the later distribution of the Tocharian language. Chinese writings mention that the Tocharians had blond or red hair, and blue eyes. Frescoes from Buddhist caves in the Tarim Basin dating to the ninth century A.D. show a people with distinctly European features. The Tocharians remained in the Tarim basin and later adopted Buddhism from northern India, their culture surviving at least until the eighth century A.D., when they seem to have been assimilated by the Uighur Turks of the eastern Asian steppes.

Although no Tocharian texts have ever been found together with mummies in the Tarim basin, the almost identical geographical location of both, as well as depictions of Tocharians showing European features, strongly suggests that at least some of the mummy people of the area were the ancestors of the Tocharians. But did these people trek all the way across Europe and half of Asia to find their homeland in the arid deserts of western China? Judging by the textile evidence for the origin of tartan in the Caucasus mountains of south Russia, and the linguistic evidence placing the beginnings of the Indo-European language in the same area, it seems that perhaps there was migration from the Caucasus at a very early date. Dr. Elizabeth Barber hypothesizes that there may have been two migrations from the possible Indo-European homeland northwest of the Black Sea—one to the west, resulting in Celtic and other European civilizations; and the other migration, the ancestors of the Tocharians, moving east, and eventually finding their way into the Tarim basin of central Asia. In light of the finds of the Tarim mummies, the theory that east and west developed their civilizations in complete isolation from each other may have to be abandoned.

The Strange Tale of the Green Children

© *Scott Brown*
Thetford Forest, Norfolk, where the Green Children are
said to have roamed.

During the troubled reign of king Stephen of England (1135–1154), there was a strange occurrence in the village of Woolpit, near Bury St. Edmunds, in Suffolk. At harvest time, while the reapers were working in the fields, two young children emerged from deep ditches excavated to trap wolves, known as wolf pits (hence the name of the village). The children, a boy and a girl, had skin tinged with a green hue, and wore clothes of a strange color, made from unfamiliar materials. They wandered around bewildered for a few minutes, before being taken by the reapers to the village, where the locals gathered round to stare at them. No one could understand the language the children spoke, so they were taken to the house of local landowner Sir Richard de Calne, at Wikes. Here they broke into tears and for some days refused to eat the bread and other food that was brought to them. But when recently harvested beans, with their stalks still attached, were brought in, the starving children made signs that they desperately wanted to eat them. However, when the children took the beans they opened the stalks rather than the pods, and finding nothing inside, began weeping again. After they had been shown how to obtain the beans, the children survived on this food for many months until they acquired a taste for bread.

As time passed, the boy, who appeared to be the younger of the two, became depressed; he sickened and died. But the girl adjusted to her new life, and was baptized. Her skin gradually lost its original green color and she became a healthy young woman. She learned the English language and afterward married a man at King's Lynn, in the neighboring county of Norfolk, apparently becoming "rather loose and wanton in her conduct." Some sources claim that she took the name Agnes Barre, and the man she married was a senior ambassador of Henry II. It is also said that the current Earl Ferrers is descended from her through intermarriage. What evidence this is based on is unclear, as the only traceable senior ambassador with this name at the time is Richard Barre, chancellor to Henry II, archdeacon of

Ely and a royal justice in the late 12th century. After 1202, Richard retired to become an Austin canon at Leicester, so it is seems unlikely that he was the husband of Agnes.

When questioned about her past, the girl was only able to relate vague details about where the children had come from and how they arrived at Woolpit. She stated that she and the boy were brother and sister, and had come from "the land of Saint Martin" where it was perpetual twilight, and all the inhabitants were green in color, as they had been. She was not sure exactly where her homeland was located, but another "luminous" land could be seen across a "considerable river" separating it from theirs. She remembered that one day they were looking after their father's herds in the fields and had followed them into a cavern, where they heard the loud sound of bells. Entranced, they wandered through the darkness for a long time until they arrived at the mouth of the cave (presumably the wolfpits), where they were immediately blinded by the glaring sunlight. They lay down in a daze for a long time, before the noise of the reapers terrified them and they rose and tried to escape, but were unable to locate the entrance of the cavern before being caught.

Is there any truth behind this extraordinary story, or should it be listed among the many fantastical marvels listed by chroniclers of medieval England? The two original sources are both from the 12th century. The first is William of Newburgh (1136–1198), an English historian and monk, from Yorkshire. His main work, *Historia rerum Anglicarum* (*History of English*

Affairs), is a history of England from 1066 to 1198, in which he includes the story of the Green Children. The other source is Ralph of Coggeshall (died c. 1228), who was the sixth abbot of Coggeshall Abbey in Essex from 1207 to 1218. His account of the Green Children is included in the *Chronicon Anglicanum* (English Chronicle) to which he contributed between 1187 and 1224. As can be seen from the dates, both authors recorded the incident many years after it was supposed to have taken place. The fact that there is no mention of the Green Children in the *Anglo-Saxon Chronicles*, which deals with English history up until the death of King Stephen in 1154, and includes many of the wonders popular at the time, could indicate a date for the incident early in the reign of Henry II, rather than in the reign of King Stephen.

Ralph of Coggeshall, living in Essex, the neighboring county to Suffolk, certainly would have had direct access to the people involved in the case. In fact, he states in his *Chronicle* that he had frequently heard the story from Richard de Calne himself, for whom Agnes worked as a servant. In contrast, William of Newburgh, living in a remote Yorkshire monastery, would not have had such first-hand knowledge of events, though he did use contemporary historical sources, as is indicated when he says, "I was so overwhelmed by the weight of so many and such competent witnesses." The story of the Green Children remained in the popular imagination throughout subsequent history, as testified by references to it in Robert Burton's *The Anatomy of Melancholy*, written in

1621, and a description based on the 12th century sources in Thomas Keightley's *The Fairy Mythology* (1828). There was even a supposed second sighting of Green Children in a place called *Banjos* in Spain, in August 1887. However, the details of this event are almost exactly the same as in the Woolpit case and the story seems to originate with John Macklin in his book *Strange Destinies* (1965). There is nowhere called Banjos in Spain, and the account is merely a retelling of the 12th century English story.

Various explanations have been put forward for the enigma of the Green Children of Woolpit. The most extreme include that the children originated from a hidden world inside the earth, that they had somehow stepped through a door from a parallel dimension, or they were aliens accidentally arrived on Earth. One supporter of the latter theory is the Scottish astronomer Duncan Lunan, who suggests that the children were aliens transported to Earth from another planet in error by a malfunctioning matter transmitter. A local legend links the Green Children with the Babes in the Wood folktale first published in Norwich in 1595, and probably set in Wayland Wood, close to Thetford Forest on the Norfolk-Suffolk border. The story concerns a medieval Norfolk earl who was the uncle and guardian of two young children, a boy (age three) and a younger girl. In order to inherit their money, the uncle hires two men to take them into the woods and murder them, but they are unable to perform the deed and abandon them in Wayland Wood, where they eventually die of starvation and exposure. The Woolpit variation moves the story to Woolpit Wood, just outside the village, and has the children surviving an attempted arsenic poisoning only to emerge onto Woolpit Heath where they were found by the reapers. Arsenic has been put forward by some as the reason for the their green skin. The possibility that they were the real-life 12th century babes in the wood who inspired the folktale cannot entirely be discounted.

The most widely accepted explanation at present was put forward by Paul Harris in *Fortean Studies* (1998). His theory is roughly as follows: First of all, the date for the incident is moved forward to 1173, into the reign of King Stephen's successor Henry II. There had been a continued immigration of Flemish (north Belgian) weavers and merchants into England from the 11th century onwards, and Harris states that after Henry II became king these immigrants were persecuted, culminating in a battle at Fornham in Suffolk in 1173, where thousands were slaughtered. He theorizes that the children were Flemish, and had probably lived in or near to the village of Fornham St. Martin, hence the St. Martin references in their story. This village, a few miles from Woolpit, is separated from it by the River Lark, probably the "very considerable river" mentioned by the girl in account. After their parents had been killed in the conflict, the two children escaped into the dense, dark woodland of Thetford Forest.

Harris proposes that if the children remained there in hiding for a period of time without enough food, they could have developed chlorosis due to malnutrition—hence the greenish tinge to the skin. He believes that they later followed the sound of the church bells of Bury St. Edmunds, and wandered into one of the many underground mine passages which were part of Grimes Graves, flint mines dating back more than 4,000 years to the Neolithic period. By following mine passageways they eventually emerged at Woolpit, and here the bewildered children in their undernourished state, with their strange clothes, and speaking the Flemish language, would have seemed alien to villagers who hadn't had any contact with Flemish people.

Harris's ingenious hypothesis certainly suggests plausible answers to many of the riddles of the Woolpit mystery. But the theory of displaced Flemish orphans accounting for the Green Children does not stand up in many respects. When Henry II came to power and decided to expel the Flemish mercenaries previously employed by King Stephen from the country, Flemish weavers and merchants who had lived in the country for generations would have been largely unaffected. In the civil war battle of Fornham in 1173, it was Flemish mercenaries, employed to fight against the armies of King Henry II, who were slaughtered, along with the rebel knights they had been fighting alongside. These mercenaries would hardly have brought their families with them. After their defeat, the remaining Flemish soldiers scattered throughout the countryside, and many were attacked and killed by the local people. Surely a landowner such as Richard de Calne, or one of his household or visitors, would have been educated enough to recognize that the language the children spoke was Flemish. After all, it must have been fairly widespread in eastern England at that time.

Harris's theory of the children hiding out in Thetford forest, hearing the bells of Bury St. Edmunds, and thus being led through underground passages to Woolpit also has problems of geography. First of all, Bury St. Edmunds is 25 miles from Thetford forest; the children could not have heard church bells over such a distance. In addition, the flint mines are confined to the area of Thetford forest; there are no underground passages leading to Woolpit, and if there were, it is almost 32 miles from the forest to Woolpit, surely too far to walk for two starving children. Even if the Green Children originated from Fornham St. Martin, it is still a 10 mile walk to Woolpit, and as to the "considerable river" mentioned by the girl—the River Lark is far too narrow to qualify for this.

There are many aspects of the Woolpit tale that are found in English folk beliefs, and some see the Green Children as personifications of nature, related to the Green Man or Jack-in-the-Green of English folklore, or even the Green Knight of Arthurian myth. Perhaps the children are related to the elves and fairies which, until a century or two ago, were believed in by many country folk. If the Green Children story is a fairytale, then it has the unusual twist of the girl never returning to her otherworldly home, but remaining married and living as a mortal. Perhaps Ralph of Coggeshall's slightly enigmatic comment that the girl was "rather loose and wanton in her conduct" is a suggestion that she had retained some of her fairy wildness. The color green has always been associated with the otherworld and the supernatural. The children's fondness for green beans does suggest another link with the otherworld, as beans were said to be the food of the dead. In Roman religion, the *Lemuria* was an annual festival in which people used offerings of beans to exorcise the evil ghosts of the dead (the Lemures) from their homes. In ancient Greece, Rome, and Egypt, as well as in medieval England, beans were believed to contain the souls of the dead.

Though the Woolpit story is included in two 12th century sources, it must be born in mind that the chronicles of the time, though describing political and religious events, also listed many signs, wonders, and miracles that would not be accepted today, but were widely believed at the time, even by educated men and women. Perhaps then, the strange apparition of the Green Children was a symbol of disturbed and changing times intermingled with local mythology and folk beliefs of fairies and the afterlife. Whatever the truth of the matter, unless descendents of Agnes Barre can be traced, as some have suggested, or further contemporary documentary evidence unearthed, the story of the Green Children will remain one of England's most puzzling mysteries.

Apollonius of Tyana: Ancient Wonder Worker

Apollonius of Tyana *by Jean-Jacques Boissard,*
probably late 16th century.

Apollonius of Tyana was a first century neo-Pythagorean, a charismatic philosopher, teacher, vegetarian, and miracle worker. He was perhaps the most famous philosopher of the Greco-Roman world and a contemporary of Jesus, with whom he has frequently been compared. Apollonius traveled extensively for his time; he visited Syria, Egypt, and India, among other places, and was credited with many wonders and much wisdom. During his lifetime and afterward, he achieved almost mythical fame, and his teachings have been an influence on both scientific and spiritual thought for more than 2,000 years.

During his life, Apollonius wrote numerous books and treatises on various subjects, including philosophy, science, and medicine, but unfortunately none of these survived. There are brief mentions of him in ancient works by Christian authors such as St. Jerome and St. Augustine, but the main source for Apollonius is the *Life of Apollonius* written by the Athenian author Flavius Philostratus (c. A.D. 170–A.D. 245). Composed in Greek in A.D. 216, this work consists of eight books and is the only surviving biography of the great sage. It is apparently based on a journal kept by Apollonius's companion, Damis, and was commissioned by Julia Domna of Syria, second wife of the Emperor Septimius Severus, and Caracalla's mother. One reason that has been suggested for Julia requesting such a work was to counter the influence of Christianity on Roman civilization. Indeed, some have even seen it as an attempt to construct a miracle-working rival to Jesus Christ. The work itself is an odd mixture of historical truth and outright romantic fiction, which is one of the reasons why so little is known about Apollonius. In fact, there are so many miraculous occurrences in the book that many people believed Apollonius of Tyana to be a completely fictitious character. Even today, there are a few people of this opinion.

Apollonius was born around A.D. 2 in Tyana (modern day Bor in southern Turkey), in the Roman province of Cappadocia. He was born into a wealthy and respected Cappadocian Greek family, and received the best education, studying grammar and rhetoric in Tarsus, learning medicine at the temple of Aesculapius at Aegae, and philosophy at the school of Pythagoras. At the age of 16 he adopted the discipline of the Pythagorean School and pursued its austere lifestyle. He allowed his hair to grow long; abstained from marriage, wine, and animal flesh; wore only linen clothing; never shaved; and slept on the bare earth. Before long, Apollonius became well-known for his habits and also for his severe criticism of the Pagan practice of sacrificing animals to the gods. He later gave most of his family inheritance to his elder brother, and the remaining to his poor relations, retaining only enough to meet his basic needs. He then began a five year period of complete silence. This silence seems to have enhanced the deeply spiritual aura already surrounding him and increased his reputation as a knowledgeable seer. Philostratus describes Apollonius as a superhuman, who possessed knowledge of all languages without studying, could read people's minds, understood the language of birds and animals, and had the ability to predict the future.

Fascinated by the secret doctrines of the religions of the world, and devoted to the purification of the numerous cults throughout the Roman Empire, Apollonius embarked on a quest to discover, understand, reform, and teach his own unique brand of neo-Pythagorean philosophy wherever he could. He visited Nineveh and Babylon and traversed much of Asia Minor (modern day Turkey), Persia, India, and Egypt, where he visited the cataracts of the Nile. It was on these travels that he came into contact with and learned from the oriental mysticism of Magi, Brahmans, and gymnosophists, and also met his scribe and main disciple, Damis, whose records of the events in the life of the philosopher supposedly influenced Philostratus's biography.

For a time the great sage and his disciple were based at the ancient city of Ephesus (in modern Turkey), where he became well-known for condemning the idleness and materialistic lifestyle of the population. During his stay at Ephesus, Apollonius sought entry into the mysteries of the Ephesian goddess, but was violently rejected by the priests there. Before leaving the city he prophesized that a dreadful plague would infest it and that the priests would soon be begging for his help. At first they ignored this seemingly baseless warning, but soon afterward, when the deadly disease arrived, the priests had no choice but to send for the great magician. When he came, he identified the cause of the problem as an old, filthy beggar, who he instructed the crowd to stone to death immediately. Naturally, they were unwilling to perform such a cruel act, but Apollonius persisted in his accusations, and the poor man was pelted with a volley of stones. When the people removed the pile of stones to extract the body, they found the corpse of a huge black dog lying underneath. Apollonius identified this as the cause of the pestilence, which stopped at that moment. After this performance, a second request for admission into the Ephesian mysteries was immediately granted. Apparently, Apollonius was also allowed entrance into the Mysteries of the Temple of Apollo at Antioch in Syria, and became an initiate of the Eleusinian Mysteries at Eleusina, west of Athens.

An odd tale told about Apollonius involves the wedding of a former student of his, a young man called Menippus, who lived in Corinth. Menippus was about to marry a beautiful rich woman, whom he had first glimpsed in a vision. Apollonius was one of the guests at the feast and noticed that something about the bride was not right. After watching her carefully for a while, he proclaimed that she was in fact a *Lamia* (a kind of vampire), and used his powers to make all the luxuries of the banquet—including the guests—disappear, thus showing them to be hallucinations constructed by the girl. After this, the disguise faded and the real Lamia was revealed. This bizarre tail was used as the basis for John Keats's 1819 poem "Lamia" and has the flavor of an allegorical story, illustrating Apollonius's philosophy regarding the dangers of an overly materialistic society.

During the reign of the infamous emperor Nero (A.D. 54–A.D. 68), Apollonius and eight of his disciples were living in Rome, despite the fact that Nero was known for persecuting philosophers. It seems that Nero's consul, Telesimus, was impressed with the group, who were even allowed to assist in modifying existing temple practices. Whether it was this that incited the fury of Nero is not known, but the group was soon in danger of losing their lives. In the end, they somehow managed to escape, probably due to Tigellinus's fear of Apollonius. During his stay in Alexandria, in Egypt, the sage became friends with Vespasian, who had recently put down the Great Jewish Revolt in Jerusalem, and was to be emperor of Rome from A.D. 69 to A.D. 79. Through Vespasian's son Titus, ruler of the Roman Empire from A.D. 79 to A.D. 81, Apollonius became acquainted with many important Roman officials and seems to have been in favor of a well-run and democratic Empire. Unfortunately, Titus's successor as Roman emperor was the paranoid and reckless Titus Flavius Domitianus, who banished all philosophers from Rome, and had a host of spies and informers at work throughout the Empire. These spies soon heard of Apollonius's condemnation of Domitian's methods, and Apollonius was accused of treason. Apollonius forestalled prosecution by arriving in Rome voluntarily and was immediately arrested and flung into prison. Domitian sent for the famous philosopher with the intention of interviewing him privately and then putting him on public trial. But the imposing yet reverent steadfastness shown by Apollonius somehow won over the emperor. Either that, or he was extremely intimidated by him, and Apollonius was allowed to go free.

On one occasion, Apollonius was delivering a speech in Ephesus when his voice suddenly dropped and he seemed to be losing concentration. He then fell silent, glanced at the ground then suddenly shouted "Smite the tyrant, smite him." The huge crowd of spectators were struck dumb in bewilderment. The sage paused for a moment, and then said: "Take heart, gentlemen, for the tyrant has been slain this day." It was revealed afterward that at the very moment Apollonius had spoken his prophetic words, Emperor Domitian had been murdered in Rome.

Apollonius subsequently set up a school at Ephesus and apparently it was in this city, during the reign of Emperor Nerva, from A.D. 96 to 98, that he died at an extremely advanced age. However, no one knows exactly where and when he died, though a shrine was built to honor him in his native town of Tyana, and it remained an object of veneration for many years. Such was his fame as a philosopher that there were also statues of him set up in many other temples throughout the Empire. The mystery of the philosopher's death encouraged much mythology and hearsay at the time. It was said that he had ascended bodily to heaven, and appeared after his death to certain people who doubted the existence of the afterlife. Philostratus perpetuated the mystery by saying, "Concerning the manner of his death, if he did die, the accounts are various." Apollonius enjoyed a reputation of considerable awe in the centuries following his death. Near the end of the third century, during the final stages of the hostile struggle between Christianity and Paganism, some anti-Christians attempted to establish Apollonius as a rival to Jesus of Nazareth. They were helped in this by the many existing temples and shrines erected to the sage in Ephesus and other parts of Asia Minor, and also by stories of the miracles he had performed, especially in connection with his renowned influence over evil spirits, such as the Lamia. Philostratus's *Life* was used by a provincial governor in Diocletian's empire (named Hierocles) as anti-Christian ammunition, and thus began a hostile debate between Pagans and Christians. The Christian historian Eusebius wrote a discourse in answer to Hierocles, claiming that Apollonius was a charlatan, and that if he possessed any powers at all they must have been achieved with the help of evil spirits.

More recently, Apollonius of Tyana became an important influence in the occult revival of the 19th century. French occultist Eliphas Levi (1810–1875) even tried to conjure up the spirit of the great sage. Apparently when visiting London in 1854, Levi was asked by a mysterious lady in black to attempt to raise Apollonius's phantom, as there were some vital questions she wished to learn the answers to. Levi's preparations for the ritual included two weeks without eating meat and a week of fasting and meditation on the subject of Apollonius. The ritual was to take part in a chamber in the lady's house, with four concave mirrors on the walls, and a marble table on which were placed two metal dishes. After the necessary preparations, Levi, wearing a white robe and carrying a sword, lit fires in the dishes and began to invoke the sage. His incantations continued for hours, until the room began to shake beneath him and a vague shape of a man appeared in the smoke, only to quickly dissolve again. He repeated his incantations, and this time the shape turned into an apparition of a beardless man wrapped from head to foot in a gray shroud. As the shape advanced toward him, Levi turned cold and was unable to speak. The phantom brushed against his ritual sword, and Levi's arm suddenly went numb and he lost consciousness. In his book *Transcendental Magic* (1865), where he describes this incident in detail, Levi relates that his arm was painful for days afterward. He does not claim that he actually invoked the shade of

Engraving of Apollonius from the book Antiquity Unveiled *by Jonathan M. Roberts (1892).*

Apollonius, but he does mention that he received answers to the lady's questions telepathically, though he never discloses the questions.

Apollonius of Tyana continues to fascinate people in the 21st century. Current theories, which are really restatements of old ideas, include that he was actually the apostle Paul, or even Jesus of Nazareth, and that the image on the Turin Shroud is actually that of Apollonius. But Apollonius of Tyana should not be remembered merely as a magician or a miracle-worker. He had a single-minded devotedness to a high and pure ideal, and it was this sense of purpose that gave him the courage to sit face-to-face with the most powerful and dangerous leaders in the world, and not waver an inch from his true beliefs.

King Arthur and the Knights of the Round Table

A bronze King Arthur in plate armor, early 16th century,
from The Book of Knowledge, *the Grolier Society (1911).*

There is a grave for March, a grave for Gwythur,
a grave for Gwgawn Red-sword;
the world's wonder a grave for Arthur.
Englynion y Beddau (The Stanzas of the Graves)

The national hero of Britain, a figure who seemingly straddles both myth and history with equal ease, King Arthur is the archetypal warrior king. For many people, he is the one point of light in a bleak British Dark Age. The very mention of the name *King Arthur* conjures up images of knightly duels, beautiful damsels, mysterious wizards, and treacherous deeds performed in tumbling castles. But what lies behind these essentially medieval romantic ideas? There is certainly a literary Arthur; there is, in fact, a whole cycle of stories known as the Arthurian Romance. A mythological Arthur-like character can also be traced in Celtic literature, but what of the historical Arthur? Is there any evidence that the stories of a great British king who led his countrymen in ferocious battles against the invading Saxons might have a basis in fact?

Briefly, the outline of the main Arthur myth is this: Arthur was the first born son of King Uther Pendragon, born in Britain during extremely troubled and chaotic times. The wise magician Merlin advised that the child Arthur should be brought up in a secret place and that no one should know his true identity. With the death of Uther Pendragon, Britain was without a king. Merlin had magically set a sword in a stone, on the sword were words written in gold, saying that whoever managed to pull the sword from the stone would be the next rightful king of Britain. Many attempted the feat, but none succeeded, until Arthur withdrew the sword and Merlin had him crowned. After breaking this sword in a fight with King Pellinore, Merlin took Arthur to a lake

and a mysterious hand rose out of the waters and gave him the famed Excalibur. With this sword (given to him by the Lady of the Lake), Arthur was invincible in battle.

After marrying Guinevere, whose father (in some versions of the tale) gave him the Round Table, Arthur gathered an impressive group of Knights around him, and he established his court at his castle of Camelot. The Knights of the Round Table, as they became known, defended the people of Britain against dragons, giants, and black knights. They also searched for a lost treasure: the cup used by Christ at the Last Supper, also known as the Holy Grail. After numerous hard-fought battles against the invading Saxons, Arthur led the Britons in a great victory at Mount Badon, where the Saxon advance was finally halted. However, all was not well at home, as the heroic knight Lancelot had fallen in love with Arthur's queen, Guinevere. The couples' intrigues eventually came to light, and Guinevere was sentenced to death, while Lancelot was banished. However, Lancelot returned to rescue the queen and took her away to his castle in France. Arthur then undertook a military expedition to find Lancelot. While he was away, Mordred (Arthur's son by his half-sister, the witch Morguase, with whom he had slept as a youth without realizing who she was) attempted to seize power in Britain. When Arthur returned, father and son went into battle on opposite sides at Camlann, where Arthur killed Mordred but received a mortal wound himself. The body of Arthur was placed on a mysterious barge and floated down river to the isle of Avalon where his wounds were healed by three strange queens dressed in black. Soon after hearing of the death of Arthur, Lancelot and Guinevere died of grief. However, Arthur's body was never found, and many say that he lies sleeping under a hill in company with all his knights—waiting to ride forth once more to save Britain.

The sources for the tale of King Arthur and the Knights of the Round Table come from many different ages. The first reliable reference comes in *Historia Britonum (The History of the Britons)*, attributed to a shadowy Welsh monk known as Nennius, and written around A.D. 825. In this work, Arthur is described as a military commander, and Nennius lists 12 battles in which he overcame the Saxons, culminating in his victory at Mount Badon. Unfortunately, the place-names used by Nennius for the battles have long since ceased to exist, and none of the sites can now be identified with certainty. According to the 10th century *Annales Cambriae (The Annals of Wales)*, Arthur and his son Mordred were both killed at the Battle of Camlann in A.D. 537. Again, the site of this battle has not been identified, though two possibilities that have been put forward are Queen Camel in Somerset (which is close to South Cadbury hillfort, identified by some as Camelot), or much further north near the Roman fort of Birdoswald (or that at Castlesteads, on Hadrian's Wall).

One of the major sources for Arthur is the *History of the Kings of Britain*, written by Welsh clergyman Geoffrey of Monmouth around 1136. It is in Geoffrey's narrative that we first

glimpse the chivalry that was later to be associated with King Arthur and his knights. It is here also that the rivalry with Mordred first appears, as well as the sword Excalibur, Merlin the magical advisor to the king, and the final departure to the isle of Avalon. However, Sir Lancelot, the Holy Grail, and the Round Table are not mentioned in the *History*. The works of Geoffrey of Monmouth (he also published two books on the prophecies of Merlin) were criticized by his contemporaries as being nothing more than elaborate fiction, and modern scholars are, in general, of the same opinion. Nevertheless, as in the case of the ancient Greek historian Herodotus, modern archaeological findings are beginning to bear out some of what Geoffrey wrote. One example is the British king, Tenvantius, whose only source until recently was Geoffrey's *History*. However, modern archaeological discoveries of Iron Age coins bearing the name *Tasciovantus*, who seems to be the same person as the Tenvantius mentioned by Geoffrey, indicates that Geoffrey's works need to be reevaluated. Perhaps other elements of the Arthur story as related in the *History of the Kings of Britain*, will one day prove to have a basis in fact.

With Sir Thomas Malory's *Le Morte D'Arthur,* first published in 1485, the story of King Arthur and the Knights of the Round Table reaches the form in which it is recognized today. In his work, Malory, a native of Warwickshire, drew on earlier French sources, such as the 12th century French poets Maistre Wace and Chretien de Troyes, who in turn drew partly on Celtic mythology, as well as on the work of Geoffrey of Monmouth.

However, the problem with these literary sources is that they are written at least three centuries after the supposed existence of Arthur, which is put somewhere around A.D. 500. How do we bridge this huge gap in time to give Arthur the possibility of a historical basis? There are tantalizing glimpses of an Arthur figure dating back probably before the sixth century A.D., in early Celtic literature, especially Welsh poems. The oldest of the Welsh poems is probably *The Gododdin* (c. A.D. 594) attributed to the Welsh poet Aneirin, who states "he fed black ravens on the ramparts, although he was no Arthur." The *Black Book of Carmarthen* contains "The Stanzas of the Graves," which includes the lines, "There is a grave for March, a grave for Gwythur, a grave for Gwgawn Redsword; the world's wonder a grave for Arthur." These lines imply that although the graves of other Arthurian heroes are known, the grave of Arthur himself cannot be found, probably because he was rumored to be still living.

In "The Spoils of Annwn" from *The Book of Taliesin*, Arthur is portrayed as leading a band of warriors on a raid into the Welsh otherworld (Annwn) searching for a magical cauldron "kindled by the breath of nine maidens." The cauldron was not only a magical object but a potent symbol in Celtic religion, as is indicated in myths of the chief god of Ireland, Dagda, who possessed a magic cauldron that could bring the dead back to life. Arthur's quest for the cauldron in the Celtic otherworld was a disaster from which only seven of his warriors returned. The parallels between Arthur's mythical quest in Celtic literature and the

quest for the Holy Grail are obvious. However, the mythical Arthur is obviously a separate character from the warrior who halted the advance of the Saxons in A.D. 517.

Perhaps archaeological evidence can point us in the direction of the historical Arthur. The places most associated with King Arthur in the literature are all in the English West Country—Tintagel, the king's birthplace; Camelot, the site of the meetings at the Round Table; and the alleged site of his burial at Glastonbury. The supposed discovery of the graves of King Arthur and Queen Guinevere by the monks at Glastonbury Abbey in A.D. 1190 is now thought to have been an elaborate hoax, contrived by the monks in order to raise money for the Abbey, which had recently been desecrated by fire. However, some researchers believe that Glastonbury itself had connections with Arthur, suggesting that the region around Glastonbury Tor (a hill just outside the modern town) may well have been the isle of Avalon, where Arthur was taken after receiving his fatal wounds at the Battle of Camlann. Cadbury Castle, lying only 12 miles away from Glastonbury, is an Iron Age hillfort which was reoccupied in the Dark Ages, and is the site most often identified with Camelot. In the sixth century A.D. the fort was converted into a vast citadel, with huge defensive ramparts, and it is apparent from the finds at the site, which include wine jars imported from the Mediterranean, that this was the seat of an important and influential Dark Age ruler. Could this have been the base of Arthur's power?

An alternative site, alleged to have been Arthur's birthplace, is Tintagel Castle in Cornwall, a county rich in Arthur place-names. Although the main structure at Tintagel is medieval, archaeological work at the site has revealed that it was an important Dark Age stronghold and commercial center, with finds including massive amounts of wine and oil jars from Asia Minor, North Africa, and the Aegean Sea. In 1998, a small piece of slate was found at the site inscribed in Latin: "Artognou, father of a descendant of Coll, has had (this) constructed." *Artognov* is the Latin form of the Celtic name *Arthnou*, or *Arthur*. But is it the King Arthur of legend? Unfortunately, there is no way of knowing. As with Cadbury Castle, we have an important fortress and commercial center, obviously the home of a powerful British chieftain living in the sixth century A.D., at the time of the Arthur of legend. We have the background to the legends but, on present evidence, that is as far as we can go.

There has been much speculation as to whom Arthur could have been if he was a historical person. One theory is that Arthur was a Romano-British leader named Ambrosius Aurelianus, who fought against the Saxons, not in the sixth but at the end of the fifth century, a few decades after the Roman legions left Britain. Other researchers, including noted Arthurian scholar Geoffrey Ashe, identify Arthur as Riothamus, a military leader active around the fifth century A.D., and called the "King of the Brittones" in one source. Fighting alongside the Romans with a huge army at his side he took part in their campaign against Euric, king of the Visigoths in Gaul (France), but subsequently disappeared somewhere in Burgandy in A.D. 470. The name *Riothamus* seems to be a Latinization of *highest leader* or *supreme king*, and was thus a title rather than a personal name, which would account for its dissimilarity to the name Arthur. A fascinating detail which appears to lend support to the theory of Riothamus as Arthur, is that the armies of this British King were apparently betrayed to the Goths by a letter sent by one Arvandus, who was subsequently executed for treason. In one medieval chronicle the name *Arvandus* is rendered *Morvandus*, which sounds similar to a Latinized version of *Mordred*, the treacherous son of the legendary Arthur. Unfortunately, outside of his activities in Gaul, nothing is known about Riothamus, so it is not possible to say if he was the seed from which the legend of King Arthur and the Round Table grew.

From the archaeological and textual evidence, the most likely theory is that Arthur is a composite of one or more of these British chieftains defending Britain against the marauding Saxons, merged with elements from Celtic mythology and medieval romance, to form the legendary Arthur we know today. In essence then, there was a historical basis for the Arthur traditions. For the legend to survive so long testifies that the character of Arthur touches a nerve in human consciousness and answers some deep-seated need to identify not with just a hero, but with a king who symbolizes the spirit of the land of Britain itself.

PART IV

Some Further Mysteries to Ponder

The collection of the world's ancient mysteries contained in *Hidden History* is, of course, far from exhaustive; there are thousands of other enigmas to consider. As new discoveries in archaeology and history are made almost daily, there will always be a constant supply of riddles from our ancient past to raise fascinating questions about the lifestyle, religion, technology, and origins of our ancestors. What follows is a selection of 40 additional mysteries from antiquity, separated into the same categories as *Hidden History*, with a brief description of the site, artifact, or people.

Mysterious Places

The Hill of Tara—With a history going back to 2500 B.C., this was the seat of the ancient high kings of Ireland, sacred dwelling place of the gods, and entrance to the Celtic otherworld. As a center for the ancient religion of the Pagans, Tara was allegedly visited by St. Patrick in his attempt to bring Christianity to Ireland.

The Ohio Serpent Mound—This enigmatic Native American structure is the largest effigy earthwork in the world, and one of a number of enigmatic ancient mounds in North America. When was this huge structure built and what was its purpose?

Avebury—A huge stone circle and henge monument at the heart of a prehistoric landscape in southern England, Avebury is older than Stonehenge and is one of the most important megalithic sites in the world.

Rennes-le-Château—A village in southern France which has become the center of speculation regarding the hidden treasure of the Knights Templar. Apparently the village also has connections with sacred geometry, the Priory of Sion, and the Holy Grail.

The Tower of Babel—Known from the Book of Genesis as a tower built by man to reach the heavens, could the story have its origin in a historical structure in the ancient city of Babylon?

The Legends of Lake Titicaca—Legends of lost cities and Inca gold surround this lake, the highest in the world navigable to large vessels. Could recent archaeological discoveries provide solid evidence for these stories?

Glastonbury—Supposedly the birthplace of Christianity in Britain and the location of a possible ancient zodiac in the lanscape, this small town in Somerset, England, is associated with legends concerning Joseph of Arimathea, the Holy Grail, and King Arthur.

The Eleusinian Mysteries—In ancient Greece, mysterious initiation ceremonies based on the cult of Demeter and Persephone were performed at Eleusis, a small town west of Athens. What did these strange rites involve and who were the initiates?

Carnac—Located on the south coast of Brittany, northeast France, the village of Carnac is famous as the site of more than 3,000 prehistoric standing stones, which legend describes as a Roman legion turned to stone by the British wizard Merlin. Why are there so many of these megaliths in this small area, and who erected them?

Chaco Canyon—An amazing Native American urban ceremonial center located deep in the remote deserts of New Mexico. What was the purpose of the mysterious lines radiating out from the Chaco complex for as much 32 miles into the wilderness?

Mohenjo-daro—A sophisticated city of 35,000 inhabitants, with baths, an elaborate drainage system, and two-story buildings, dating back more than 5,000 years to the Indus Valley Civilization of modern-day Pakistan and northern India.

Tenochtitlan—The capital of the Aztec empire, built on an island in Lake Texcoco in what is now central Mexico. Under the Aztecs, the island was artificially enlarged to become the largest and most powerful city in Meso-America.

Chartres Cathedral—Located southwest of Paris in the town of Chartres, this Gothic cathedral was allegedly built on the site of a sacred grove of the Druids, and has been connected with sacred geometry, the mysterious Black Madonna, and the Knights Templar.

Lyonesse—Legendary sunken land believed by some to lie off the Isles of Scilly, to the southwest of Cornwall, England. This mysterious kingdom has sometimes been associated with King Arthur's Avalon, as well as various locations mentioned in Celtic and fairy mythology. Could the Lyonesse legends preserve a folk memory of the flooding of the Isles of Scilly and part of Cornwall?

King Solomon's Temple—According to the Bible, this was the first Jewish Temple in Jerusalem, and allegedly the resting place of the Ark of the Covenant and a fabulous treasure. Did the temple exist, and if so, do its remains still lie beneath modern Jerusalem?

Nabta Playa—By the fifth millennium B.C. the peoples in Nabta Playa—once a large lake in the Nubian Desert 500 miles south of modern day Cairo—had constructed the world's earliest known astronomical device. Who were these mysterious people and how advanced was their astronomical knowledge?

Unexplained Artifacts

The Ark of the Covenant—The ark was described in the Bible as a sacred container holding the stone tablets on which were inscribed the Ten Commandments. Did this miraculous artifact ever exist, and if so, is it the mysterious object that now lies in a church in Axum, Ethiopia?

Minoan Linear A—A script of the Late Bronze Age culture of the Minoans on Crete. Examples have been found etched on jars and tablets found on some Aegean islands and on the Greek mainland, but so far the language remains undeciphered, and is considered to be one of the holy grails of ancient scripts.

The Ashoka Pillar—Located near Delhi, India, this pillar—apparently made almost entirely of iron—is completely uncorroded, despite exposure to the elements for more than 1,000 years. Who erected it and what was its purpose?

The Origins of the Zodiac—Were the Egyptians, the Babylonians, or the Greeks the first to develop the 12 Zodiacal constellations, or is there a prehistoric origin for the mysterious Zodiac?

The Philosopher's Stone—In the mystical process of alchemy, the philosopher's stone was a substance that could turn any metal into gold, and also create an elixir that would make humans younger. What lies behind these mysterious notions, and has anyone ever discovered the philosopher's stone?

The Oxyrhynchus Papyri—The site of Oxyrhynchus in Egypt has yielded a vast collection of ancient papyrus texts from the Greek and Roman periods of Egyptian history. Among these are poems by Sappho, Hebrew Gospels, and specimens of Greek documents relating to magic and astrology.

Ancient Cave Art—Dating as far back as 40,000 years ago, European prehistoric rock art represents the oldest known painting in the world. What were our ancestors trying to communicate when they painted on cave walls, and how did they achieve such high levels of skill?

The Spear of Destiny—Known in Christian mythology as the Holy Lance, this was the spear used to pierce the body of Jesus. The relic was apparently once kept in Jerusalem before being moved to Constantinople, where its history becomes confused. Does this sacred lance still exist, and if so, where is it kept?

The Wands of Horus—Also known as the Rods of Ancient Egypt, these short cylindrical objects are usually depicted clutched in the fists of statues of ancient Egyptian kings or pharaohs. Do these wands represent rolls of folded cloth, sacred symbols, or healing rods?

The Holy Grail—In Christian religion, this was the dish, plate, or cup used by Jesus at the Last Supper. Should the Grail be understood as a metaphor for spiritual fulfillment, or does a physical Grail exist? If so, where is it?

The Dendera Reliefs—Do strange carvings in the Temple of Hathor at Dendera, Egypt, represent an ancient knowledge of electricity, or are they to be interpreted as depicting mythological religious scenes?

Stone of Destiny—More popularly known as the Stone of Scone or the Coronation Stone, this block of sandstone was used for centuries in the coronation of the monarchs of Scotland and England. What are the origins of this enigmatic stone? Why is it associated with royalty?

The Ogham Script—Ogham was an alphabet used by the ancient Irish, Welsh, and Scots, mainly to represent the Gaelic languages. Thought to be named after the Irish god Ogma, what were the origins of this mysterious script, and why did it die out?

The Bosnian Pyramid—Located in the Bosnia-Herzegovina town of Visoko, northwest of Sarajavo, Visocica Hill gained world-wide attention in October 2005 when Bosnian-American businessman/explorer Semir Osmanagic sensationally announced that the mound was in fact a huge man-made pyramid, perhaps dating back some 12,000 years to the last ice age. Osmanagic claimed that the hill, once the site of a medieval walled town, possessed four perfectly symmetrical slopes facing toward the cardinal points, a flat top, and an entrance.

During excavations at the site, Osmanagic and his team discovered large stone blocks, believed by him to come from the outer layer of the pyramid; tunnels, interpreted by the excavators as ventilation shafts for the structure; and cut and polished stone slabs, possibly once part of the pyramid's sloping sides. Osmanagic is convinced that the hill, one-third taller than Egypt's Great Pyramid of Giza, is man-made and has labelled the enormous structure the Pyramid

of the Sun, due to its similarity to the Pyramid of the Sun at the pre-Columbian city of Teotihuacán, Mexico. Satellite photographs and thermal imaging of the area revealed two further pyramid-like hills in the Visoko Valley. In fact, Osmanagic maintains that there is a whole complex of ancient structures on the site, including the Bosnian Pyramid of the Moon, the Bosnian Pyramid of the Dragon, the Bosnian Pyramid of the Love, and the Temple of the Earth.

A booming tourist industry has grown up around the astounding discoveries in the area of Visocica Hill, with souvenir models of the pyramid already available. Further marketing products, such as tourist facilities and an archaeological park, are in the pipeline.

However, there is growing unease among archaeologists throughout the world about the genuineness of the discovery. Many archaeologists believe that Osmanagic's findings are actually the remains of Roman and medieval structures on the hill. Professor Anthony Harding, president of the European Association of Archaeologists, who visited the site, believes the hill to be a natural formation. Harding has expressed his disbelief at the idea that the Upper Palaeolithic hunter-gatherers who roamed the area at the end of the last ice age would have had the time, resources, or inclination to construct such a vast edifice.

Some of Osmanagic's claims certainly demonstrate a lack of knowledge of European prehistory. For example, his statement that Visocica

Hill "is actually Europe's first pyramid in the heart of Bosnia" is untrue. There are at least 16 examples of pyramids in Greece, the oldest being the pyramid of Hellinikon, located southwest of Athens in the Argolid. Although this pyramid has been dated to 2720 B.C., some archaeologists dispute these results, and believe a date at the end of the fourth century B.C. more likely. In appearance, the Greek pyramids resemble those at Giza in Egypt, though they are much smaller in size.

Osmanagic's excavations are ongoing at the site of Visocica Hill, while the world waits for convincing evidence (in the form of securely dated structures or artifacts) to back up his claim of ice age pyramids in Bosnia. Hopefully, when excavation has uncovered the supposed structures, they will be able to speak for themselves.

Enigmatic People

Who Murdered Hypatia?—Female philosopher, mathematician, and teacher who lived in the ancient Egyptian city of Alexandria, and was brutally murdered by a mob in the early fifth century A.D.

Merlin the Magician—The origins of this powerful wizard and prophet of Arthurian legends go back to Celtic myth—and perhaps even further to a magical ancestral figure in prehistoric times—who allegedly erected the megalithic monument of Stonehenge.

The Phoenicians—An ancient seafaring and trading culture active over a wide area of the ancient world. They are known to have inhabited the coastal plains of what are now Lebanon and Syria, the origins of this extraordinary maritime culture are shrouded in mystery to this day.

Heinrich Cornelius Agrippa—A massively influential German magician and occult writer, astrologer, and alchemist of the 15th and 16th centuries.

The Rosicrucians—A legendary secretive Order dating from the 15th or 17th century, but with supposed origins much earlier, whose esoteric rites were based on a mixture of early Christianity and Egyptian mysteries. Branches of the Rosicrucian Order still exist today, but what are their real origins, and how have they influenced modern Freemasonry?

The Neanderthals—The Neanderthal was a species of the *homo* genus that inhabited Europe and parts of western Asia from about 230,000 to 29,000 years ago, before they apparently disappeared with the arrival of modern humans. What happened to the Neanderthals? Why did they die out?

Queen Boudicca—Queen of the Celtic Iceni tribe of eastern Britain, who led a devastating revolt against the Roman invaders in A.D. 61. Boudicca and her 250,000 British burned the newly built London to the ground before being finally defeated in battle at a location which has never been discovered. Where was this battle, and what happened to Boudicca afterwards?

The Dorians—Supposedly an ancient Greek tribe who either invaded or migrated southwards into southern Greece with the collapse of the Late Bronze Age palace civilizations, centered on fortified citadels such as Mycenae. Are the Dorians just a myth, or is there evidence for the existence of these enigmatic people?

The Boxgrove People—Around 500,000 years ago a group of *Homo heidelbergensis* (an extinct species of the genus *homo)* inhabited an area near the modern village of Boxgrove in Sussex, England. What was life like for these remote ancestors of modern humans and what happened to them?

The Fairy Folk of Britain and Ireland—Although fairies in the form of spirits or supernatural beings are found in the legends, folklore, and mythology of many different cultures, they are especially prevalent in Britain and Ireland. What lies behind the myths and tales of these legendary beings?

Further Information

The Lost Land of Atlantis

Castleden, R. *Atlantis Destroyed*. New York: Routledge, 2001.

Fagan, B. (ed) *The Seventy Great Mysteries of the Ancient World*. London: Thames & Hudson, 2001.

James, P. *The Sunken Kingdom: the Atlantis Mystery Solved*. London: Pimlico, 1996.

Joseph, F. *The Atlantis Encyclopedia*. Franklin Lakes, N.J.: New Page Books, 2005.

Spence, L. *The History of Atlantis*. New York: Dover Publications, 2003.

"Echoes of Plato's Atlantis" by Dr. Iain Stewart. *www.bbc.co.uk / history / ancient / greeks / atlantis_01.shtml*.

"Satellite images show Atlantis." *http:/ / news.bbc.co.uk / 2 / hi / science / nature / 3766863.stm*.

America's Stonehenge: The Puzzle of Mystery Hill

Feder, K.L. *Frauds, Myths, and Mysteries: Science and Pseudoscience in Archaeology*. Columbus, OH: McGraw-Hill Publishing Co., 2005.

Fell, Dr. Barry. *America B.C.* New York: Pocket Books, 1976.

Williams, S. *Fantastic Archaeology: The Wild Side of North American History*. Philadelphia: University of Pennsylvania Press, 1991.

"The Persistence of Memory: Cultural Amnesia at the Millennium" by Angela Labrador. *http:/ / www.simons-rock.edu / ~alabra / writing / thesis.html*.

America's Stonehenge homepage. *www.stonehengeusa.com*.

Petra: The Mysterious City of Rock

Giulia Amadasi Guzzo, Maria, et al. *Petra*. Chicago: University Of Chicago Press, 2002.

Taylor, J. *Petra and the Lost Kingdom of the Nabataeans*. Boston: Harvard University Press, 2005.

Westwood, J. (ed) *The Atlas of Mysterious Places*. London: Guild Publishing, 1987.

Jordan Ministry of Tourism and Antiquities. *www.tourism.jo / PastandPresent / PetraII.asp*.

The Silbury Hill Enigma

James, P. & N. Thorpe, *Ancient Mysteries*. New York: Ballantine Books, 1999.

Pitts, M. *Hengeworld*. London: Arrow Books, 2001

Pollard, J. & A. Reynolds *Avebury: Biography of a Landscape*. Stroud, Gloucestershire, U.K.: Tempus Publishing, 2002.

Article in the magazine *British Archaeology. www.britarch.ac.uk / ba / ba80 / feat1.shtml*.

English Heritage page on Silbury Hill. *www.english-heritage.org.uk / server / show / conProperty.310.*

Where Was Troy?

Fagan, B. (ed) *The Seventy Great Mysteries of the Ancient World.* London: Thames & Hudson, 2001.

James, P. & N. Thorpe. *Ancient Mysteries.* New York: Ballantine Books, 1999.

Woods, M. *In Search of the Trojan War.* London: BBC Books, 2005.

"Was there a Trojan War?" Article by Manfred Korfmann on *Archaeology* magazine website. *www.archaeology. org / 0405 / etc / troy.html.*

Website of the new excavations at Troy. *www.uni-tuebingen.de / troia / eng / index.html.*

Chichén Itzá: City of the Maya

Coe, M. D. *The Maya.*(7th edition) London: Thames & Hudson, 2005.

Sharer, R.J. & Morley, S. G. *The Ancient Maya.* (6th edition) Palo Alto, Cali: Stanford University Press. 2005.

Mysterious Places. *www.mysteriousplaces.com / mayan / TourEntrance.html.* Tour of Chichén Itzá.

The Sphinx: An Archetypal Riddle

Bauval, R. & G. Hancock. *Keeper of Genesis: A Quest for the Hidden Legacy of Mankind.* London: Arrow, 2001.

Fagan, B. M. (ed). *The Seventy Great Mysteries of the Ancient World.* London: Thames & Hudson, 2001.

James, P. & N. Thorpe. *Ancient Mysteries.* New York: Ballantine Books, 1999.

Jordan, P. & J. Ross. *Riddles of the Sphinx.* New York: New York University Press, 1998.

"Guardian's Sphinx—Guardian of the Horizon." *http:/ / guardians.net / egypt / sphinx.*

"The Great Sphinx of Giza—An Introduction" by Allen Winston. *www.touregypt.net / featurestories / sphinx1.htm.*

The Knossos Labyrinth and the Myth of the Minotaur

Cadogan, G. *Palaces of Minoan Crete.* London: Routledge, 1991.

Dickinson, O. *The Aegean Bronze Age.* Cambridge, U.K.: Cambridge University Press, 1994.

James, P., & N. Thorpe. *Ancient Mysteries.* New York: Ballantine Books, 1999.

The British School at Athens Knossos page. *www.bsa.gla.ac.uk / knosos / index.htm.*

Hellenic Ministry of Culture Knossos page. *www.culture.gr / 2 / 21 / 211 / 21123a / e211wa03.html.*

The Stone Sentinels of Easter Island

Fischer, S.R. *Island at the End of the World: The Turbulent History of Easter Island.* London: Reaktion Books Ltd., 2006.

Flenley, J. & P. Bahn. *The Enigmas of Easter Island.* Oxford, U.K., Oxford University Press, 2003.

Pelta, K. *Rediscovering Easter Island.* Minneapolis, MN: Lerner Publications, 2001.

Unofficial Easter Island hompage *www.netaxs.com / ~trance / rapanui.html.*

The Lost Lands of Mu and Lemuria

Churchward, J. *The Lost Continent of Mu.* C.W. Waldon, U.K.: Daniel Co. Ltd., 1994 (1931).

Ramaswamy, Sumathi. *The Lost Land of Lemuria: Fabulous Geographies, Catastrophic Histories*. Berkeley, Calif.: University of California Press, 2005.

Account of the Yonaguni structures. *www.lauralee.com/japan.htm*.

"Drowned Indian city could be world's oldest." *www.newscientist.com/article.ns?id=dn1808*.

Stonehenge: Cult Center of the Ancestors

Atkinson, R.J.C. *Stonehenge: Archaeology and Interpretation*. London: Penguin Books, 1990.

Chippendale, C. *Stonehenge Complete*. London: Thames and Hudson, 2004.

Pitts, M. *Hengeworld*. London: Arrow, 2001.

Pryor, F. *Britain B.C.* London: Harper Perennial, 2004.

The Amesbury Archer burial. *www.wessexarch.co.uk/projects/amesbury/introduction.html*.

The Boscombe Bowmen burial. *www.wessexarch.co.uk/projects/wiltshire/boscombe/bowmen/index.html*.

El Dorado: The Search for the Lost City of Gold

Nicholl, C. *The Creature in the Map*. New York: William Morrow & Co., 1995.

Hemmings, J. *The Search for El Dorado*. New York: E.P. Dutton, 1978.

Westwood, J. (ed) *The Atlas of Mysterious Places*. London: Guild Publishers, 1987.

http://news.bB.C.co.uk/1/hi/world/americas/776952.stm—"Explorer finds lost city."

The Lost City of Helike

"Echoes of Plato's Atlantis" by Dr. Iain Stewart. *www.bbc.co.uk/history ancient/greeks/atlantis_01.shtml*.

Homepage of the Helike Foundation. *www.helike.org/index.shtml*.

"The Road to Ancient Helike." *www.naturalhistorymag.com/features/1100_feature.html*.

Egyptian Treasure From the Grand Canyon

Christensen, S. *Frommer's Grand Canyon National Park*. Frommers. 2004.

Kaiser, J. *Grand Canyon: The Complete Guide : Grand Canyon National Park*. Hoboken, N.J.: Destination Press, 2006.

Powell, J.L. *Grand Canyon: Solving Earth's Grandest Puzzle*. Upper Saddle River, N.J.: Pi Press, 2005.

Pyne, S.J. *How the Canyon Became Grand: A Short History*. Upper Saddle River, N.J.: Pi Press, 1999.

"Lost City of the Dead in the Grand Canyon." *www.bibliotecapleyades. net/esp_orionzone_8.htm*.

"Canyonitis: Seeing evidence of ancient Egypt in the Grand Canyon." *www.philipcoppens.com/egyptiancanyon.html*.

Newgrange: Observatory, Temple, or Tomb?

O'Callaghan, C. *Newgrange—Temple to Life*. Cork, Ireland: Mercier Press, 2004.

O'Kelly, M. & C. O'Kelly. *Newgrange: Archaeology, Art and Legend*. London: Thames & Hudson, 1988.

Pryor, F. *Britain B.C.* np. HarperPerennial, 2004.

Stout, G. *Newgrange and the Bend of the Boyne*. Cork, Ireland: Cork University Press, 2002.

Information about Newgrange and other Irish monuments. *www.knowth.com / newgrange.htm*.

Machu Picchu: Lost City of the Incas

Burger, R.L. & L.C. Salazar. (eds) *Machu Picchu: Unveiling the Mystery of the Incas*. New Haven, Conn: Yale University Press, 2004.

D'Altroy, T.N. *The Incas*. Oxford, U.K.: Blackwell Publishers, 2003.

Machu Picchu on the National Geographic website *www.nationalgeographic.com / traveler / machu.html*.

What Happened to the Library of Alexandria?

Canfora, L. (trans. Martin Ryle). *The Vanished Library. A Wonder of the Ancient World*. Berkeley, Calif.: University of California Press, 1989.

El-Abbadi, Mostafa. *Life and fate of the ancient Library of Alexandria*. Paris: UNESCO, 2nd edition.1992.

MacLeod, R. (ed) The Library of *Alexandria: Centre of Learning in the Ancient World*. London: I.B. Tauris, 2004.

"The Foundation and Loss of the Royal Serapeum Libraries of Alexandria" An article by James Hannam. *www.bede.org.uk / Library2.htm*.

Website of the new Library of Alexandria. *www.bibalex.org / English / index.aspx*.

BBC news article about the possible discovery of the site of the Library of Alexandria. *http:// news.bbc.co.uk / 1 / hi / sci / tech / 3707641.stm*.

The Great Pyramid: An Enigma in the Desert

Bauval, R. & A. Gilbert. *The Orion Mystery : Unlocking the Secrets of the Pyramids*. London: Arrow, 1994.

Edwards, I.E.S. *The Pyramids of Egypt*. London: Penguin Books, 1993.

James, P. & Thorpe, N. *Ancient Mysteries*. New York: Ballantine Books, 1999.

Lehner, M. *The Complete Pyramids*. London: Thames & Hudson, 1997.

Mendelssohn, K. *The Riddle of the Pyramids*. London: Thames & Hudson, 1986.

www.guardians.net / egypt / pyramids.htm.

"This Side up, Rolling Stones, & Building the Great Pyramid. A New Hypothesis." Roumen V. Mladjov, S.E. and Ian S. R. Mladjov, B.A. *www-personal.umich.edu / ~imladjov / pyramids.doc*.

The Nazca Lines

Aveni, A. F. Between *the Lines: The Mystery of the Giant Ground Drawings of Ancient Nazca, Peru*. University of Texas Press, 2000.

Hadingham, E. *Lines to the Mountain God: Nazca and the Mysteries of Peru*. London: Harrap Ltd., 1987.

James, P. & Thorpe, N. *Ancient Mysteries*. New York: Ballantine Books, 1999.

Article about the Nazca lines. *www.crystalinks.com / nazca.html*.

"The Nazca Lines Revisited: Creation of a Full-Sized Duplicate." *www.onagocag.com / nazca.html*.

The Piri Reis Map

McIntosh, G. C. & N.J.W. Thrower. *The Piri Reis Map of 1513*. University of Georgia Press, 2000.

Soucek, S. *Piri Reis and Turkish Mapmaking After Colombus: The Khali Portolan Atlas*. London: Khalili Collections, 2004.

"The Mysteries of the Piri Reis Map" by Diego Cuoghi. *http://xoomer.virgilio.it/dicuoghi/Piri_Reis/PiriReis_eng.htm*.

The Piri Reis Map at The Internet Sacred Text Archive. *www.sacred-texts.com/piri/index.htm*.

The Unsolved Puzzle of the Phaistos Disc

Butler, A. Knight, C. & R. Lomas. *The Bronze Age Computer Disc*. Berkshire, U.K.: Foulsham, 1997.

Fagan, B.M. (ed). *The Seventy Great Mysteries of the Ancient World*. London: Thames & Hudson, 2001.

Hagen, O. *The Phaistos Disc Alias the Minoan Calendar*. Bloomington, Ind.: AuthorHouse, 2001.

Article about the Phaistos Disc on the Interkriti Website. *www.interkriti.org/culture/festos/phaist2.htm*.

The Shroud of Turin

Fagan, B. (ed) *The Seventy Great Mysteries of the Ancient World*. London: Thames & Hudson, 2001.

Knight, C. & R. Lomas. *The Second Messiah*. London: Arrow Books, 1998.

Picknett, L & C. Prince. *Turin Shroud: How Leonardo Da Vinci Fooled History*. London: Time Warner Paperbacks, 2006.

Schwortz, B. & I. Wilson. *The Turin Shroud: The Illustrated Evidence*. London: Michael O'Mara Books Ltd., 2000.

"Turin Shroud 'shows second face.'" BBC World News article. *news.bbc.co.uk/1/hi/world/europe/3621931.stm*.

"Turin Shroud 'older than thought.'" BBC News article. *news.bbc.co.uk/2/hi/science/nature/4210369.stm*.

Unofficial Shroud of Turin Website edited by Barrie Schwortz. *www.shroud.com*.

The Stone Spheres of Costa Rica

Lothrop, S.K. *Archaeology of the Diquís Delta, Costa Rica*. New York: Kraus Reprint, 1978.

Stone, D. *Introduction to the archaeology of Costa Rica*. Museo Nacional. 1966.

Zapp, I. & G. Erikson. *Atlantis in America: Navigators of the Ancient World*. Kempton, Ill.: Adventures Unlimited Press, 1998.

Stone Balls of Costa Rica. *www.ku.edu/~hoopes/balls*.

Landmarks Foundation Project Diquis. *www.landmarksfoundation.org/projects_diquis.shtml*.

Talos: An Ancient Greek Robot?

Apollodorus. *The Library of Greek Mythology* (trans. Robin Hard). Oxford, U.K.: Oxford Paperbacks, 1998.

Apollonius of Rhodes. *The Voyage of Argo* (trans. E.V. Rieu). London: Penguin Books Ltd., 1975.

Graves, R. *The Greek Myths*. London: Penguin Books Ltd., 1992.

University of Connecticut—"da Vinci Project." *www.engr.uconn.edu/davinci*.

Timeline of Robotics. *www.thocp.net/reference/robotics/robotics.html*.

The Baghdad Battery

Welfare, S. & J. Fairley. *Arthur C. Clarke's Mysterious World*. London: Book Club Associates, 1981.

"Experiments with homemade batteries"
by Mike Bullivant and Jonathan
Hare *www.creative-science.org.uk/
sea1.html*.

"Riddle of Baghdad's batteries."
*news.bbc.co.uk/1/hi/sci/tech/
2804257.stm*.

Museum of Ancient Inventions.
*www.smith.edu/hsc/museum/
ancient_inventions/battery2.html*.

The Ancient Hill Figures of England

Castledon, R. *Ancient Hill Figures of
Britain*. Sussex, U.K.: SB
Publications, 1999.

Newman, P. *The Lost Gods of Albion:
The Chalk Hill-Figures of Britain*.
Stroud, Gloucestershire, U.K.: Sutton
Publishing Ltd., 1997.

James, P & N. Thorpe. *Ancient
Mysteries*. New York: Ballantine
Books, 1999.

Westwood, J. (ed) *The Atlas of
Mysterious Places*. London: Guild
Publishing, 1987.

The Coso Artifact

Steiger, B. *Mysteries of Time and Space*.
New Jersey: Prentice-Hall, 1974.

"The Coso Artifact. Mystery from the
Depths of Time" by Pierre Stromberg
and Paul V. Heinrich.
www.talkorigins.org/faqs/coso.html

"Archaeology from the dark side" *http://
dir.salon.com/story/news/feature/
2005/08/31/archaeology/index.html*.

The Nebra Sky Disc

The Nebra Disc on the Official
Landesmuseum Website.
www.archlsa.de/sterne.

BBC Horizon documentary of the Disc.
*www.bbc.co.uk/science/horizon/
2004/stardisctrans.shtml*.

"Bronze Age Sky Disc Deciphered."
*www.dw-world.de/dw/article/
0,2144,1915398,00.html*.

Noah's Ark and the Great Flood

Best, R.M. *Noah's Ark and the Ziusudra
Epic: Sumerian Origins of the Flood
Myth*. Winona Lake, Ill.:
Eisenbrauns, 1999.

Cohn, N. *Noah's Flood: The Genesis
Story in Western Thought*. New
Haven, Conn.: Yale University Press,
1996.

Fagan, B.M. (ed) *The Seventy Great
Mysteries of the Ancient World*.
London: Thames & Hudson, 2001.

Foster, B. R. (ed) *The Epic of Gilgamesh*.
London: W.W. Norton & Co., 2001.

Ryan, W. & W. Pitman. *Noah's Flood:
The New Scientific Discoveries About
the Event That Changed History*. Old
Tappan, N.J.: Touchstone, 2000.

The Mayan Calendar

Aveni, A.F. *Skywatchers of Ancient
Mexico*, Austin: University of Texas
Press, 1980.

James, P. & N. Thorpe. *Ancient
Mysteries*. New York: Ballantine
Books, 1999.

Sharer, R.J. & S.G. Morley. *The Ancient
Maya*. (5th edition) Palo Alto, Calif.:
Stanford University Press, 1994.

The Antikythera Mechanism:
An Ancient Computer?

De Solla Price, D. *Gears from the Greeks:
The Antikythera Mechanism—A
Calendar Computer from ca. 80 B.C.*
New York: Science History
Publications, 1975.

James, P. & N. Thorpe. *Ancient
Inventions*. London: Michael O'Mara
Books Ltd., 1994.

Russo, L. *The Forgotten Revolution:
How Science Was Born in 300 BC and
Why it Had to Be Reborn*. Berlin:
Springer, 2004.

"The Antikythera Mechanism—The Clockwork Computer" *www.economist.com / displaystory. cfm?story_id=1337165.*

Ancient Aircraft?

James, P. & N. Thorpe. *Ancient Inventions.* London: Michael O'Mara Books Ltd., 1994.

"Top Ten Out-Of-Place-Artifacts" by Joseph Robert Jochmans, Lit. D. *www.atlantisrising.com / issue5 / ar5topten.html.*

"Model Airplane?" *www.catchpenny.org / model.html.*

"The Abydos Mystery" *www.enigmas.org / aef / lib / archeo / abydosm.shtml.*

"Prehistoric "plane" flies!" *www.philipcoppens.com / bbl_plane.html.*

The Dead Sea Scrolls

Baigant, M. & R. Leigh. *The Dead Sea Scrolls Deception.* New York: Pocket Books, 1993.

Cross, Frank Moore, Jr. and Mary A. Tolbert. (ed) and Segovia, Fernando F. (ed). *The Ancient Library of Qumran.* (3rd Edition) Sheffield, U.K.: Sheffield Academic Press/ Fortress Press, 1995.

Fagan, B. (ed) *The Seventy Great Mysteries of the Ancient World.* London: Thames & Hudson, 2001.

Golb, N. *Who Wrote the Dead Sea Scrolls? The Search for the Secret of Qumran,* New York: Scribner, 1995.

Scrolls from the Dead Sea—The Ancient Library of Qumran and Modern Scholarship. An Exhibit at the Library of Congress, Washington, D.C. *www.ibiblio.org / expo / deadsea.scrolls.exhibit / intro.html.*

National Geographic article on the lost Gospel of Judas. *www9.nationalgeographic.com / lostgospel.*

The Crystal Skull of Doom

Morant, G.M. "A Morphological Comparison of Two Crystal Skulls." *Man* 36 (July 1936): 105–107.

Morton, C. & C.L. Thomas. *The Mystery of the Crystal Skulls.* London: Thorsons, 1997.

Nickell, J. & J.F. Fischer. *Secrets of the Supernatural: Investigating the World's Occult Mysteries.* Buffalo, N.Y.: Prometheus Books, 1991.

Article about British Museum crystal skull *www.sgallery.net / news / 01_2005 / 09.php.*

The Voynich Manuscript

Kennedy, G & R. Churchill. *The Voynich Manuscript.* London: Orion, 2004.

Goldstone, L & N. Goldstone. *The Friar and the Cipher: Roger Bacon and the Unsolved Mystery of the Most Unusual Manuscript in the World.* London: Doubleday, 2005.

René Zandbergen's site. *www.voynich.nu / index.html.*

The Bog Bodies of Northern Europe

Fagan, B. (ed) *The Seventy Great Mysteries of the Ancient World.* London: Thames & Hudson, 2001.

Glob, P.V. *The Bog People.* London: Paladin Books, 1971.

Parker Pearson, M. & A.T. Chamberlain. *Earthly Remains: The History and Science of Preserved Human Bodies.* Oxford University Press, 2002.

Bodies of the Bogs. *www.archaeology.org / online / features / bog.*

"Iron Age 'bog bodies' unveiled." *news.bbc.co.uk/2/hi/science/nature/4589638.stm*.

The Mysterious Life and Death of Tutankhamun

David, R. *Religion and Magic in Ancient Egypt*. London: Penguin Books, 2002.

Brier, B. *The Murder of Tutankhamen: A True Story* np: New York: Berkley Trade, 2005.

Fagan, B. (ed) *The Seventy Great Mysteries of the Ancient World*. London: Thames & Hudson, 2001.

Reeves, N. *The Complete Tutankhamun: The King, the Tomb, the Royal Treasure*. London: Thames & Hudson, 1990.

"King Tut died from broken leg." BBC News article. *http://news.bbc.co.uk/1/hi/sci/tech/4328903.stm*.

The Real Robin Hood

Holt, J.C. *Robin Hood*. London: Thames & Hudson, 1989.

Keen, M. *The Outlaws of Medieval Legend*. London: Routledge, 2000.

Pollard, A.J. *Imagining Robin Hood: The Late Medieval Stories in Historical Context*. London: Routledge, 2004.

Molyneux-Smith, T. *Robin Hood and the Lords of Wellow*. Nottinghamshire County Library, 1998.

"Robin Hood and his Historical Context" by Dr Mike Ibeji *www.bbc.co.uk/history/state/monarchs_leaders/robin_01.shtml*.

"Robin Hood Outlaw Legend of Loxley." *myweb.ecomplanet.com/kirk6479/default.htm*.

The Amazons: Warrior Women at the Edge of Civilization

Behan, M. & J. Davis-Kimball. *Warrior Women: An Archaeologist's Search for History's Hidden Heroines*. New York: Warner Books, 2003.

Herodotus. *The Histories*. (trans. Aubrey de Selincourt). London: Penguin Books Ltd., 2003.

James, P. & N. Thorpe. *Ancient Mysteries*. New York: Ballantine Books. 1999.

Rolle, R. *The World of the Scythians*. New York: B.T. Batsford Ltd., 1989.

Rothery, G.C. *The Amazons*. (Reprint of original published by Francis Griffiths, 1910). Senate. 1995.

Salmonson, J.A. *The Encyclopedia of Amazons: Women Warriors from Antiquity to the Modern Era*. New York: Anchor Books, 1992.

Tyrell, W.B. *Amazons: A Study in Athenian Mythmaking*. Baltimore, M.D.: John Hopkins University Press, 1984.

The Mystery of the Ice Man

Fagan, B. (ed) *The Seventy Great Mysteries of the Ancient World*. London: Thames & Hudson, 2001.

Fowler, B. *Iceman: Uncovering the Life and Times of a Prehistoric Man Found in an Alpine Glacier*. New York: Random House, 2000.

James, P. & N. Thorpe. *Ancient Mysteries*. New York: Ballantine Books, 1999.

Spindler, K. *The Man in the Ice*. London: Weidenfeld & Nicolson, 1994.

South Tyrol Museum of Archaeology webpage about the Iceman. *www.archaeologiemuseum.it/f01_ice_uk.html*.

The History and Myth of the Knights Templar

Baigent, M. & R. Leigh. *The Temple and the Lodge*. New York: Arcade, 1991.

Barber, M. *The New Knighthood: A History of the Order of the Temple.* Cambridge University Press, 1994.

Lord, E. *Knights Templar in Britain*, White Plains, N.Y.: Longman, 2004.

Martin, S. *The Knights Templar: The History and Myths of the Legendary Military Order*. New York: Thunder's Mouth Press, 2005.

The Prehistoric Puzzle of the Floresians

"Critics silenced by scans of hobbit skull." *www.bioedonline.org / news / news.cfm?art=1615.*

"Flores Man Special" in *Nature* magazine. *www.nature.com / news / specials / flores / index.html.*

"New 'Hobbit' disease link claim." *news.bbc.co.uk / 2 / hi / science / nature / 4268122.stm.*

New Scientist article. *www.newscientist.com / article.ns?id=dn6588.*

The Magi and the Star of Bethlehem

Gilbert, A. *Magi: Uncovering the Secret Society that Read the Birth of Jesus in the Stars*. Montpeler, VT: Invisible Cities Press, 2002.

Molnar, M.R. *The Star of Bethlehem: The Legacy of the Magi*. New Brunswick, N.J.: Rutgers University Press, 1999.

Vincent, K.R. *The Magi: From Zoroaster to the "Three Wise Men."* Richland Hills, Tex: D. & F. Scott Publishing, 1999.

The Druids

Berresford Ellis, P. *A Brief History of the Druids*. London: Constable & Robinson, 2002.

James, P. & N. Thorpe. *Ancient Mysteries*. New York: Ballantine Books, 1999.

Piggott, S. *The Druids*. London: Thames & Hudson Ltd., 1985.

Ross, A. *Pagan Celtic Britain*. London: Routledge & Kegan Paul Ltd., 1967.

The Queen of Sheba

Clapp, Nicholas. *Sheba: Through the Desert in Search of the Legendary Queen*. Wilmington, Mass.: Mariner Books, 2002.

Schippmann, K. *Ancient South Arabia: From the Queen of Sheba to the Advent of Islam*. Princeton, N.J.: Markus Wiener Publishers, 2002.

A complete guide to the Queen of Sheba, edited by Tim Spalding. *www.isidore-of-seville.com / sheba / index.html.*

The Mystery of the Tarim Mummies

Fagan, B. M. (ed) *The Seventy Great Mysteries of the Ancient World*. London: Thames & Hudson, 2001.

Mallory, J.P. & V.H. Mair. *The Tarim Mummies: Ancient China and the Mystery of the Earliest Peoples from the West*. London: Thames & Hudson, 2000.

Wayland Barber, E. *The Mummies of Urumchi*. New York: W.W. Norton & Company, 2000.

The Strange Tale of the Green Children

Appleby, J.T. *The Troubled Reign of King Stephen*. London: G. Bell & Sons Ltd., 1969.

Briggs, K.M. *A Dictionary of Fairies*. London: Penguin Books Ltd., 1977.

Moore, S. (ed). *Fortean Studies: No. 4*. London: John Brown Publishing, 1998.

Shuker, K. *The Unexplained: An Illustrated Guide to the World's Natural and Paranormal Mysteries*. London: Carlton Books Ltd., 2003.

Homepage of the village of Woolpit. *www.woolpit.org/home.htm*.

Apollonius of Tyana: Ancient Wonder Worker

Levi, E. *Transcendental Magic: Its Doctrine and Ritual*. London: Rider & Co., 1984 (originally published: 1854).

Mead, G.R.S. *Apollonius of Tyana: the philosopher-reformer of the First Century AD*. London: Theosophical Publishing Society, 1901.

Philostratus, Bowerstock, G.W. *Life of Apollonius of Tyana*. London: Penguin, 1971.

Shirley, R. *Occultists & Mystics of all Ages*. New York: University Books, 1972.

King Arthur and the Knights of the Round Table

Alcock, L. *Arthur's Britain: History and Archaeology A.D. 367–634*. London: Penguin Books Ltd., 2002.

Ashe, G. *The Discovery of King Arthur*. Gloucestershire, U.K.: Sutton Publishing, 2005.

Barber, R. *King Arthur in Legend and History*, Suffolk, U.K.: Boydell Press, 2004.

Cavendish, R. *King Arthur and the Grail: The Arthurian Legends and Their Meaning*. New York: Taplinger Pub. Co., 1984.

James, P & N. Thorpe. *Ancient Mysteries*. New York: Ballantine Books, 1999.

Malory, Sir Thomas. *Le Morte D'Arthur*. New York: University Books, 1961.

Morris, J. *The Age of Arthur: A History of the British Isles*. London: Weidenfeld & Nicholson, 2001.

Index

About the Author

BRIAN HAUGHTON was born in Birmingham, England, in 1964, of Irish-Welsh parents. He studied archaeology at Nottingham and Birmingham Universities, and has worked on archaeological projects in England and Greece. He has written on the subject of unusual people in history for various print and Internet publications, and has also authored a book, *Coaching Days in the Midlands* (Quercus 1997), about stage coaches and highwaymen in the English midlands. His particular interests include the sacred landscapes of prehistory, the modern mysteries and traditional folklore surrounding ancient sites, historical human enigmas, and the occult in the 19th and early 20th centuries. At present he lives in Patra, Greece, where he teaches English and writes for his *Mysterious People* Website. He long ago fell for the lure of ancient mysteries and the supernatural, initially inspired by television programs such as *Arthur C. Clarke's Mysterious World* and Leonard Nimoy's *In Search of...* series, and later by visits to the ancient sites of Greece, Crete, Britain, and Ireland.